Feeding Your Poodle Wisely

Giving your Poodle a bite of your bologna and white bread sandwich isn't the best food choice, but the occasional splurge won't hurt. Rich sauces and gravies, however, although not poisonous, can upset your Poodle's tummy. And certain foods can seriously affect your Poodle's health. See Chapter 7 for full details on feeding your Poodle.

Healthy goodies

Don't overdo treats, but if you want to add a little something tasty to your Poodle's food bowl, opt for one of these healthy choices:

- Apples
- Canned pumpkin
- Carrots
- Cooked broccoli
- Cooked eggs
- Cooked green beans
- Cooked sweet potatoes
- Cottage cheese
- Plain yogurt, especially with live cultures
- Small amounts of cheese
- Small bits of lean chicken or turkey
- Strawberries and blueberries

Hazardous foods

Some foods can cause more problems than just an upset tummy. Avoid the following hazardous foods:

- Alcohol
- Chocolate
- Coffee and tea
- Egg whites
- Grapes and raisins
- Macadamia nuts
- Nicotine
- Onions
- Xylitol

Poisonous products

A major task you should undertake before bringing a Poodle home is dog-proofing your living area (see Chapter 5). Keep the following potentially dangerous (and fatal) items out of reach:

- Antifreeze
- Cleaning products
- Fertilizers
- Herbicides, insecticides, pesticides, and rodenticides
- Medicines
- Mothballs
- Mushrooms

For Dummies: Bestselling Book Series for Beginners

Poodles For Dummies®

Cheat Sheet

Keeping Emergency Numbers Handy

Keep emergency numbers where you can get to them quickly. I list mine in the back of my phone book, and I also have my veterinarian's number, a poison hotline number, and the local emergency clinic number on my refrigerator. Your "best spot" may be in your cell phone directory or in a computer file. If you travel, keep a set of numbers in your tack box or your glove box, too.

Veterinarian's phone number: _____

Emergency clinic's phone number: _____

Pet Poison Helpline: 800-213-6680

ASPCA Animal Poison Control Center: 888-426-4435

Kansas State University College of Veterinary Medicine's 24-hour poison control hotline: 785-532-5679

Stocking a Basic First-Aid Kit

You may want to add other items to your Poodle's first-aid kit, but these basics are a good start (see Chapter 16 for more details on first-aid kits):

- ✔ Activated charcoal
- ✔ Adhesive tape and vet wrap
- ✔ Antibiotic ointment
- ✔ Artificial tears
- ✔ Benadryl
- ✔ Betadine
- ✔ Children's aspirin
- ✔ Cotton balls
- ✔ Gauze (both a roll and pads)
- ✔ Hydrocortisone ointment
- ✔ Hydrogen peroxide
- ✔ Kaopectate
- ✔ Petroleum jelly
- ✔ Rubber gloves
- ✔ Scissors
- ✔ Syringes
- ✔ Syrup of ipecac
- ✔ Thermometer
- ✔ Tweezers or hemostats
- ✔ Veterinary first-aid handbook and your veterinarian's phone number (as well as other important emergency numbers)

For Dummies: Bestselling Book Series for Beginners

Poodles
FOR
DUMMIES®

by Susan M. Ewing

Wiley Publishing, Inc.

Poodles For Dummies®

Published by
Wiley Publishing, Inc.
111 River St.
Hoboken, NJ 07030-5774
www.wiley.com

Copyright © 2007 by Wiley Publishing, Inc., Indianapolis, Indiana

Published simultaneously in Canada

For general information on our other products and services, please contact our Customer Care Department within the U.S. at 800-762-2974, outside the U.S. at 317-572-3993, or fax 317-572-4002.

For technical support, please visit www.wiley.com/techsupport.

Wiley also publishes its books in a variety of electronic formats. Some content that appears in print may not be available in electronic books.

Library of Congress Control Number: 2006939522

ISBN: 978-0-470-06730-7

Manufactured in the United States of America

10 9 8 7 6 5 4 3 2 1

1B/RW/QR/QX/IN

WILEY

About the Author

Susan M. Ewing has been "in dogs" since 1977 and enjoys showing and trying various performance events, with an emphasis on "trying."

She holds a master's degree in Television/Radio from Syracuse University in New York and has attended canine seminars at Cornell University. She's a member of the Dog Writers Association of America, as well as the Cat Writers' Association, and is listed in the 2005 edition of *Who's Who in America*.

Ewing has been writing professionally since she was 16 and is the author of several books: *The Pembroke Welsh Corgi: Family Friend and Farmhand* (Howell); *A New Owner's Guide to Pembroke Welsh Corgis, The Pug, The Dachshund,* and *German Shepherd Dogs* (all TFH Publications); and *Bulldogs For Dummies* (Wiley). Her column, "The Pet Pen," appears in *The Post-Journal* (Jamestown, New York) every Saturday. One of her essays is a part of the book *Cats Do It Better Than People*.

Other articles of Ewing's have appeared in *AKC Gazette, Family Dog, Bloodlines, German Shepherd Dog Review, Good Dog!, Pet Odyssey, Dog Fancy, Dog World, Puppies USA,* the national Schipperke Club newsletter, ASPCA's *Animal Watch, Bird Talk, Kittens USA, Cats USA,* and *Cats Magazine*.

She has also worked as a radio copywriter, owned and operated a boarding kennel, and served as the director of the Lucy-Desi Museum in Jamestown, New York.

Ewing currently lives in Mesa, Arizona, with her husband, Jim, and her two dogs, Griffin and Rhiannon.

Dedication

For the usual suspects: Jim, who is the "purple bead"; my mother, Joyce Morris; and my brother, Gregory Morris.

Also, for John Monroe-Cassel. Iechyd da, dear friend.

To the memory of my father, Robert Morris; my grandmother, Gladys Taylor; and Walton Strahl.

Author's Acknowledgments

Every book I write makes me realize how many people are involved in the writing process. Sure, I sit at the keyboard, but if that was all that went on, there'd never be a book.

Huge, enormous, and very large thanks to everyone at Wiley, especially Acquisitions Editor Stacy Kennedy, Project Editor Georgette Beatty, and Copy Editors Josh Dials and Sarah Westfall. Also, thanks to Caroline Hair for her incredible technical advice.

Thank you, thank you, thank you to Janine Adams, Darlene Arden, Debbi Baker, Alice Bixler, Grace Blair, Tom Carneal, Anne Rogers Clark, Suzi Cope, Carol Pernika, Gail Roberson, Peggy Singletary, Stephanie Smith, Betsy Stowe, and Cathi Winkles.

Thanks to Amy Munion, DVM, and the staff at Pet Haven Animal Hospital.

Thanks to the groomers at Annety's Pet Grooming Salon in Mesa, Arizona.

Thanks always to the members of the Dog Writers Association of America. DWAA is my network and my safety net.

Thanks to all the breeders, judges, handlers, and exhibitors over the years who have generously shared what they know.

Publisher's Acknowledgments

We're proud of this book; please send us your comments through our Dummies online registration form located at www.dummies.com/register/.

Some of the people who helped bring this book to market include the following:

Acquisitions, Editorial, and Media Development

Project Editor: Georgette Beatty

Acquisitions Editor: Stacy Kennedy

Copy Editor: Josh Dials

Technical Editor: Caroline Hair

Editorial Manager: Michelle Hacker

Editorial Assistants: Erin Calligan, David Lutton

Cover Photo: ©ULRIKE SCHANZ / Animals Animals - Earth Scenes — All rights reserved.

Cartoons: Rich Tennant (www.the5thwave.com)

Composition Services

Project Coordinator: Jennifer Theriot

Layout and Graphics: Lavonne Cook, Stephanie D. Jumper, Erin Zeltner

Special Art: © Barbara Frake

Anniversary Logo Design: Richard Pacifico

Proofreaders: Melanie Hoffman, Christy Pingleton,Techbooks

Indexer: Techbooks

Special Help Sarah Westfall

Publishing and Editorial for Consumer Dummies

Diane Graves Steele, Vice President and Publisher, Consumer Dummies

Joyce Pepple, Acquisitions Director, Consumer Dummies

Kristin A. Cocks, Product Development Director, Consumer Dummies

Michael Spring, Vice President and Publisher, Travel

Kelly Regan, Editorial Director, Travel

Publishing for Technology Dummies

Andy Cummings, Vice President and Publisher, Dummies Technology/General User

Composition Services

Gerry Fahey, Vice President of Production Services

Debbie Stailey, Director of Composition Services

Contents at a Glance

Table of Contents

Introduction

*A*t first, I thought I could get through this introduction to *Poodles For Dummies* by following the good ol' five Ws of journalism — who, what, where, when, and why — but the system broke down because I don't have a *where* or a *when*. Still, I can follow the three remaining Ws to entice you to enter this world of Poodles.

The *who* question is, "Who is the book for?" The answer is that this book is for anyone who may be interested in Poodles. I include enough information to satisfy the curiosity of beginners and to enlighten people who've owned Poodles for years.

What is this book about? Well, that's easy! It's about Poodles. I haven't written a step-by-step training manual; I don't give you a list of the top ten kennels or the most famous Poodles; and I don't give you the locations of the top producing sire and dam in the country. What I give you is an overview of the Poodle — how the breed developed and what you can expect when living with and caring for a Poodle.

Why write the book? Because we live in a throwaway society in which dogs are becoming fashion accessories. If you're considering buying a Poodle, and you read this book first, I want you to realize either that the Poodle is the perfect breed for you or that buying a Poodle would be a huge mistake. Either way, I hope this book helps both you and Poodles.

Another why is because I have fond memories of two very special Poodles: a silver Miniature named Pierre, who belonged to my cousins when I was growing up, and a black Standard named Tiki, who was my dog's playmate when my family lived in Vermont. They were both a complete joy, and they live forever in my heart.

About This Book

This book is 288 pages long. The end. (Sorry, I couldn't resist.) Seriously, folks, this book is about Poodles. It may not tell you everything that you ever wanted to know about Poodles, but I hope it comes close. I explain the history of the breed, and I include information about all three varieties: Toy, Miniature, and Standard. I give you tips on how to add a Poodle to your family and how to feed and care for your Poodle. You can find information on health and training. Although this isn't written to be a training manual, I do include some tips on how to start training and where you can go for more training.

The book also includes advice on activities you and your Poodle can do together and how you should travel with your Poodle (or when you should leave her safely behind).

If you're thinking about getting a Poodle, this book is here to help you choose your perfect puppy, and if you already have a Poodle, this book can help you and your Poodle live happily ever after.

You can read this book from cover to cover if you like, but you don't have to. Feel free to dip into and out of any chapter you want at any time.

Conventions Used in This Book

The _For Dummies_ people worked hard to make the text you find here as clear and as easy to read as possible. Here's how:

- **Boldfaced** words highlight the key words in bulleted and numbered lists.
- _Italics_ indicate emphasis and mark key terms.
- Monofont is the font of choice for Web addresses.

  Here's another point about Web addresses: During the printing of this book, some Web addresses may have extended to two lines of text. If you spot one of these wrapping addresses, rest assured that I added no extra characters, such as a hyphen or a space, to indicate the break. If you use one of these addresses, just type the address exactly as you see it, pretending that the line break doesn't exist. Besides, you don't get the chance to pretend nearly often enough!

The _For Dummies_ people don't run the whole show, though. I've inserted some of my own conventions, too:

- I alternate gender by chapter. In odd-numbered chapters, the dog I discuss is a male; in even-numbered chapters, I discuss a female. I hate using "it" to refer to animals, so I give each gender equal time. Along those same lines, when I refer to a Poodle as "she," I refer to a vet or trainer as "he," and vice versa.
- I spell out organization names that are commonly abbreviated the first time I use them in a chapter.
- When I talk about a Poodle's ears, I say "flap," because I think most readers will know what I mean; however, the correct term among dog people is _leather_.

✔ I use the term "lead" for the thin strap that connects a Poodle to her person. In the show world, you often hear the word "lead." You can still say "leash" if you show your Poodle, but no one says "show leash." You lead your Poodle with a show lead.

✔ I waffle when faced with the dilemma of what to call dog wastes. I tend to say "urine sample" or "stool sample" when talking about waste you need to take to your vet's office. I say "excrement" here and there, but I also call it "poop"! (Hey, I'm better at picking it up than I am at naming it.) As you read, feel free to substitute whatever word you're comfortable with.

✔ Speaking of comfort levels, unless you're around plenty of dog people most of the time, you may not be comfortable using the term "bitch," so I often use "male" and "female" when talking about the sexes. You can say "bitch" rather than "female" if you want to be technically correct.

What You're Not to Read

This isn't a textbook, and I won't quiz you at the end of the final chapter, so don't read anything that doesn't interest you. Specifically, though, you can skip all the paragraphs that I mark with the Technical Stuff icon. Most of the information isn't that technical, and much of it is interesting, but you can skip it without missing anything essential to your Poodle's well-being. You also can skip all the Anecdote paragraphs I use to describe personal experiences. It's fine, really. I can handle rejection.

Sidebars (those shaded gray boxes throughout the book) are there for your reading pleasure, but you don't have to read them. They offer information that isn't essential to your understanding of the text. I enjoy sidebars, but again, it's your call.

And if you're a total couch potato, you may want to skip Chapter 13, which discusses Poodle competitions and activities. However, you may enjoy finding out about all the things a Poodle can do, even if you and your Poodle never join in the fun.

What I *do* hope you read are the acknowledgments at the front of the book. Without the people I mention there, this book wouldn't exist.

Foolish Assumptions

I make assumptions throughout this book, which may indeed be foolish, but that's the only way I could write it. First, of course, I assume that if you're reading this book, you have an interest in Poodles. That may be more than an assumption; that may be a sure thing.

Beyond that, I don't know if you're new to dogs or if you've had Poodles for years. You may be thinking about getting a Poodle, or perhaps you've just gotten a Poodle and want to have a successful relationship with your new companion.

So, in each chapter, I need to make a lot of assumptions. For instance, to discuss the history of the breed, I need to assume that you know absolutely nothing. To discuss the process of choosing a puppy, I need to assume that you've never done it before. I need to assume that you have other pets and children, so I can write about what you need to know, including tips on feeding, training, and healthcare. Also, I need to assume that you don't already have a veterinarian.

One thing, however, isn't an assumption: I've tried, by making assumptions, to cover the topic of Poodles as thoroughly as possible.

How This Book Is Organized

Poodles For Dummies has five parts. Each part stands alone, so you don't need to read the chapters in order, and you can quickly find the part that you need at any given time.

Part I: Picking the Poodle of Your Dreams

The first part covers the history of the breed, the three different varieties of Poodle, and the breed standard. I cover the typical temperament and personality of the Poodle, and I help you decide if a Poodle is the right dog for you. After you decide to get a Poodle, I talk about puppies versus older dogs (among other characteristics), and I let you know how to choose a source for your dog.

Part II: Living Happily with Your Poodle

This part covers the basics you need to know for everyday living. I include a shopping list of the items you'll need before your Poodle joins your household. I present some safety tips, and I provide information on how to introduce your Poodle to children and other pets.

You'll find a chapter on food to help you decide between commercial, homemade, and raw-food diets. Dog nutrition has come a long way from table scraps and the occasional bone from the butcher.

Finally, you need to know that grooming is a huge part of owning a Poodle. Rescue organizations estimate that almost 50 percent of all Poodles who appear in their shelters are given up because of grooming issues. This part helps you understand the importance of grooming.

Part III: Training and Having Fun with Your Poodle Pal

Poodles are intelligent, active dogs, and they need training and exercise in order to be happy (and if your Poodle isn't happy, you won't be either). This part covers socialization, housetraining, basic commands, and all the wonderful activities you can participate in with your Poodle. For instance, you can visit hospitals and nursing homes; you can compete in obedience and agility competitions; and you can take to the field for a day of hunting. This part also features information on traveling with your Poodle.

Part IV: Maintaining Your Poodle's Health

We all want our dogs to live forever; however, because that isn't possible, I include this part to help you make sure that your Poodle has the longest, healthiest life you can give her. I provide tips for how to choose a veterinarian, information on common vaccines, and information on nontraditional ways to treat health issues (such as acupuncture).

You'll find a chapter on common Poodle health problems and one on first aid, which may help you in an emergency. You also find a chapter on senior Poodle care. Seniors are so precious, and you should take the time to give yours some extra attention.

Part V: The Part of Tens

The Part of Tens is the final part in every *For Dummies* book. In this Part of Tens, you find fantastic Poodle resources, and you discover ten ways to help your Poodle in case disaster strikes.

Icons Used in This Book

Icons are the cute little illustrations you find in the left margins of *For Dummies* books. They sit next to paragraphs that contain interesting information you should take with you long after you put this book down. Well, all the paragraphs are interesting, but these little nuggets are especially fascinating!

 Do your best to remember the information highlighted by this icon. The stuff you discover here will help keep your Poodle happy and healthy.

 This icon comes with text that gives you a shortcut or tells you an easier way to do something with or for your Poodle.

 If you're stubborn and refuse to read anything else, please read these paragraphs. Your Poodle's health and safety are at stake.

 You can skip paragraphs marked with this icon if you want to. I always find this information interesting, but it isn't essential. You can raise a happy, healthy Poodle without knowing the technical stuff.

These paragraphs contain stories from my experiences with dogs. I use them to illustrate points I make.

Where to Go from Here

When reading a *For Dummies* book, you can go anywhere you like. It doesn't matter where you start or end.

You can, of course, start with Part I, Chapter 1 and read straight through. Or you can skip around. Heck, you can read from back to front if that suits you. However, allow me to give you some tips if you're open to suggestion. If you've just gotten a puppy, Chapter 9 on housetraining may be more important to you now than reading about Poodle history in Chapter 2. If you're leaving on vacation next month, head to Chapter 12, which discusses traveling with your Poodle. My point is that where you start depends on your situation.

Here's my method: I like to look at all the color photos in the color section and then read all the cartoons. Next, I like to flip through and read "Tips," "Warnings," and "Remembers." At that point, I check out the Part of Tens, and *then* I start reading the rest of the book.

Whatever method you choose, I hope you enjoy reading this book as much as I enjoyed writing it.

Part I
Picking the Poodle of Your Dreams

"I think we're most interested in a Toy Poodle."

In this part . . .

Picking the perfect Poodle takes time, thought, and effort. Adding a dog of any breed to your family shouldn't be an impulse decision. Part I helps you understand the Poodle's history and the breed standards set by a couple of the world's largest organizations. I also ask you to consider the costs that come with owning a Poodle, as well as whether your lifestyle will work with an active, intelligent dog for the next 14 to 16 years.

If, after reading this part, you're convinced that a Poodle is the dog for you, you can find suggestions here on how to choose your special puppy or adult Poodle, including which variety best suits you: Toy, Miniature, or Standard.

Chapter 1

Making a Match with a Poodle

*W*elcome to the world of Poodles! This chapter helps you decide whether the Poodle is the breed for you. If it is, I'll help you find that perfect Poodle and give you information on training, health, and more.

No matter what type of Poodle you choose, and no matter what kind of activities you want to share with your pet, when you buy a Poodle, you add a new member to your family. Your new companion will be with you for years and will always give you his best; you should be prepared to give him your best as well.

Understanding the Poodle Breed

The following sections give you background information on Poodles and on the different varieties: Standard, Miniature, and Toy. Chapter 2 has full details on the Poodle breed if you want to know more.

Strolling through a brief history

Many people look at Poodles and think "froufrou." It must be the hairdo, I guess, and the fact that sometimes the hairdo includes bows. A Poodle may even wear nail polish, which does make it hard for him to look "macho." Or maybe the Poodle get its feminine label because people used to, or still, refer to Poodles as French Poodles, with the connotation that a French dog is dainty and above everyday doggy pursuits such as chasing a ball or chewing a stick.

In reality, the Poodle was bred as a working farm dog — ready, willing, and able to kill rats, herd livestock, and retrieve fallen game. Although the exact origin of the breed is unknown, the Poodle likely originated in Germany, not France. Early breeders designed the froufrou hairdo as a way to lighten the weight of a waterlogged coat while providing warmth and protection for vital organs and joints. Can you say the same for your designer cut? And as for the bows? Well, maybe they're used to attract affection.

Reviewing sizes and personality traits

When researching a Poodle to add to your family, one of the most important decisions you make is whether to go small, medium, or large (sorry, no supersizing). The following list breaks down the three Poodle varieties:

- A Standard Poodle, according to the breed standard (see the following section and Chapter 2), measures over 15 inches tall at the *withers* (the highest part of the back, between the shoulder blades). Most Standards are between 23 to 25 inches, and you may see some that are 27 to 28 inches. Females weigh between 40 and 45 pounds, and males weigh between 50 and 55.

- Miniature Poodles stand between 10 and 15 inches at the withers and weigh between 12 and 15 pounds.

- Toy Poodles measure less than 10 inches at the withers and weigh between 5 and 10 pounds.

As dogs go, a Poodle has a relatively long life span, living anywhere from 14 to 18 years. Standards usually come in at the lower end, and Toys commonly have the longest lives.

All Poodles should be lively, friendly dogs who get along well with other dogs and with people, and every dog has his own unique personality. The following list presents the different personality traits that the different varieties may exhibit. Remember that you're dealing with a living creature, so there are no hard and fast rules:

- Standard Poodles are a bit more reserved and self-contained than Minis and Toys, and they appreciate having jobs to do. Yes, they enjoy work! They also may be a bit calmer. I'm not saying that Standards are mellow and laid-back; they have tons of energy and enough bounce for any family.

- A Miniature Poodle wants to be active all the time, whether that activity involves playing with a ball, taking a walk, chasing a Frisbee, or going for a swim. Because Minis are small but still sturdier than Toys, they often are an excellent choice for families that have children but aren't able to meet the space and exercise needs of a Standard.

✔ A Toy Poodle is happy to cuddle, though he's active when he needs to be. Many professional breeders and handlers consider the Toy to be a natural in the show ring, with personality plus to charm judges.

All Poodles, no matter the size or type, have a sense of humor. They like to have fun, and they want to make you laugh!

Considering breed standards

A breed standard is the "blueprint" for a given breed. It describes what makes the Poodle a Poodle and not, say, a Basset Hound. Conscientious breeders follow the standard and try to produce the ideal dog. For instance, the Poodle standard calls for a "square dog"; a long, low Poodle wouldn't be used in a breeding program.

The following list breaks down how two governing bodies of Poodle standards separate the varieties (see Chapter 2 for more info):

✔ **The American Kennel Club (AKC)** places the Standard and Miniature Poodles in the non-sporting group and the Toy in the toy group.

✔ **The United Kennel Club (UKC)** puts the Standard Poodle in the gun dog group and the Miniature and Toy in the companion dog group.

To Poodle or Not to Poodle: Is One the Best Dog for You?

So, you've read and heard some information about Poodles, and you're wondering whether a Poodle is the right dog for you. Before you run to a breeder or a shelter and stock up on pretty bows, you should ask yourself a few questions:

✔ Will a Poodle fit in with your lifestyle? Poodles like people and require quality time with their owners.

✔ Do you have room in your home for a Poodle? A Poodle needs an adequate amount of room to be comfortable.

✔ Can a Poodle handle living with your children or other pets? You need to take care when introducing a Poodle to kids and other animals.

You also need to consider the costs of Poodle ownership. Not only do you need to factor in financial costs — such as the price of buying a Poodle, healthcare costs, and grooming fees — but also time issues. Do you have enough time to train, groom, feed, and exercise your Poodle?

Chapter 3 has information on everything you need to think about to determine whether a Poodle is the best dog for you.

Selecting the Perfect Poodle for You

Have you done your research to determine whether a Poodle is the right dog for you? Are you ready to go out and get your Poodle? Have you scoured the Internet for cute doggie merchandise? Not so fast! First, you should pick out the traits you would like:

- ✔ Puppy or adult?
- ✔ Toy, Miniature, or Standard?
- ✔ Male or female?
- ✔ Which color?

You can go to a breeder to buy a Poodle, or you can check out shelters and rescue groups in your area. However, you should stay away from pet shops. Among other pitfalls, you don't get to see the mother's temperament, you don't receive a health guarantee, and the price is sky high.

Registering your dog with a reputable organization, such as the American Kennel Club or the United Kennel Club, gives you proof that your dog is a purebred Poodle. This proof is important if you plan to breed your Poodle. Even if you have no plans for breeding, your Poodle will need to be registered if you want to show in conformation. If you just want a pet and have no plans for breeding or competing, then you don't need to register your dog.

Head to Chapter 4 for additional advice on choosing a specific Poodle and on registration.

Adjusting to Life with a Poodle

Life with a Poodle is wonderful, but there are adjustments to make when you add a new member to your family. You need bowls, beds, toys, and a collar and lead, for starters. See Chapter 5 for more information about all the gear you need.

You also need to consider where in your home your Poodle will spend his days and nights, and you need to introduce him to other family members, both two- and four-legged. Check out Chapter 6 for complete details on welcoming home your Poodle.

Whether you decide to feed your Poodle commercial dog food, make home-cooked meals, or opt for raw food, make sure you provide your Poodle with a balanced diet that includes the proper proportions of nutrients. Always watch your dog's weight; extra pounds can lead to arthritis, heart problems, and diabetes. Head to Chapter 7 for the dish on feeding.

Grooming should also be near the top of your list in terms of Poodle care. Your first task is to create a grooming schedule for your Poodle. With a schedule in place, you can decide whether to groom your Poodle yourself or take him to a professional. Important grooming tasks, no matter who's holding the clippers, include

- Brushing
- Bathing
- Clipping
- Checking your Poodle's nails, eyes, ears, and teeth

You can get the full grooming scoop in Chapter 8.

Training and Enjoying Your Poodle

At the top of your "to do" list will be housetraining, and Poodles quickly learn this important lesson. Be consistent, and give your Poodle plenty of opportunities to do the right thing, in the right place. See Chapter 9 for more information on housetraining.

The same intelligence that makes Poodles easy to housetrain also means that without proper training, they'll try to run their homes themselves. This attitude leads to all kinds of trouble. A yappy, ill-mannered dog, no matter his size, isn't cute. Train your Poodle, whether he's a Standard, Miniature, or Toy; I give you guidance on training in Chapter 10.

I don't mean to sound like a puppy drill sergeant. Just because you're training doesn't mean you can't have fun. In fact, training means you can have more fun! The better trained your dog is, the more places you can go and the more activities you can try. For instance, you'll have an easier time socializing your Poodle, as you find out in Chapter 11, or you can travel with your Poodle, which Chapter 12 discusses.

For even more fun, you can consider competing with your Poodle. Chapter 13 outlines many of the exciting options available to you and your Poodle. Some of these include conformation showing, rally, obedience, agility, hunting, and tracking.

Keeping Your Poodle Healthy

Poodles don't need designer clothes or the latest in video games (although some do get the clothes). Your dog won't ever ask for a car, and you won't need to finance his college education (maybe just his obedience education). You won't spend your time carpooling your dog and his friends (I assume). And you certainly won't go into debt to pay for his wedding (I hope!).

I'm not trying to say that Poodles don't need care and maintenance. They do. They also cost their owners money, but compared to what a child costs, you'll spend way less, and you'll probably worry less, too!

According to the American Society for the Prevention of Cruelty to Animals (ASPCA), the annual cost of owning a dog — not including illness or spaying or neutering — is between $420 and $780. If you settle on $600 a year, over a span of 14 years, you'll spend about $8,400 caring for your Poodle over his lifetime. That covers only half of your child's sweet 16 car or a year of college tuition!

Here are a few important health-maintenance tasks to add to your to-do list after you get a Poodle (I cover these in Chapter 14):

- ✔ Schedule regular visits with your veterinarian. Keep your dog up-to-date with needed vaccinations.

- ✔ Spay or neuter your Poodle.

- ✔ Exercise and examine your Poodle at home on a regular basis.

Any dog can have the occasional upset stomach, cut, or bump. You don't need to panic, but you do need to be aware and react properly. In addition, there are also breed-specific problems, such as patellar luxation in Toys and Miniatures See Chapter 15 for more information on common Poodle health conditions.

In an emergency, quick action on your part can help stabilize your Poodle before you make that trip to the vet's. Head to Chapter 16 for details on handling emergencies and first aid.

Senior dogs, just like senior humans, may need a different routine and a different diet to remain happy and healthy. Check out Chapter 17 for the full scoop.

Chapter 2

Unwrapping the Whole Poodle Package

*Y*ou can just own a Poodle, period, or you can add to your enjoyment by understanding where Poodles came from, what makes a good Poodle, and maybe a little bit about why Poodles act the way they do. In this chapter, you find a bit of general canine history, discover the different sizes of Poodles, examine the anatomy of a Poodle, and get the standard: what makes a Poodle a Poodle. I also give you the scoop on a Poodle's temperament and personality.

Walking through the History of the Breed

In the following sections, I take you on a tour of the history of the Poodle breed, from its beginnings to modern times.

In the beginning, there was dog . . .

All dogs are descended from the wolf, which may explain why they howl at sirens and the like. The original dog was domesticated between 13,000 and 17,000 years ago. From those early beginnings, man has created over 300 breeds, from tiny Chihuahuas and Yorkshire Terriers to giant Great Danes, Irish Wolfhounds, and shaggy Newfoundlands. Each breed was developed with a specific purpose in mind, from sitting in a person's lap and being a companion, to guarding livestock and property, to retrieving fallen game.

As time went by, people began expecting dogs to be able to do more than their primary tasks, because it's easier and cheaper to have one dog do many jobs than to have a separate dog for each task. The Poodle, for example, was bred to hunt and retrieve game and to have an instinct to herd livestock.

Just when and where the Poodle emerged as a separate breed is hard to say. Romans carved Poodle-like dogs on tombs as early as 30 A.D., and they were pictured on Greek and Roman coins, but experts don't know if those dogs died out or if they further evolved into the modern Poodle.

Poodles are sometimes called "French Poodles," but the breed is generally considered German even though its actual country of origin is unclear. Dogs from Russia and France contributed to the modern Poodle, and one theory states that the Poodle's ancestors came from Portugal or Spain.

The FCI, the European organization that sponsors pan-European dog shows, regards France as the official "country of origin" of the Poodle and uses the French breed standard as the standard of judging in FCI shows. The ancestors of poodles actually originated in a number of places in Europe.

The following list gives you a sampling of the beginnings of the Poodle in Europe:

- ✔ Fifteenth-century writings and art from France, Holland, and Italy refer to Poodles. Many paintings show the Poodle in trims similar to today's show trims (Chapter 8 has more about trims).

- ✔ German writings from the 1500s describe the "Pudel" as a large, black water retriever. *Pudel* or *pudelin* means to splash in the water. In Belgium and France, the dog was called the "Poedel." The English name, Poodle, came from these original titles.

- ✔ In France, where the dog was popular, people also called the Poedel the *Caniche,* meaning duck dog. Early writings described the dog as intelligent and sturdy, with curly hair.

- ✔ The German Poodle, or Pudel, was thickset and had a wooly coat texture. Early German artwork shows the dog with both a curly and a corded coat.

All these varieties of Poodles are famous for working in the water. So much so, in fact, that the Poodle's coat was trimmed to facilitate swimming, yet keep the chest and joints warm.

The appearance of Poodle varieties

Authorities agree that the Standard Poodle is the oldest of the three varieties, but the Toy and the Miniature Poodles weren't far behind. (See the section "Measuring up sizes," later in this chapter, for info on Standards, Toys, and Miniatures.) Fifteenth-century paintings feature Toy Poodles, including drawings by German artist Albrecht Durer. Paintings created by Goya in the late 18th century show the Toy Poodle as one of the main pets in Spain.

People most likely developed Toy and Miniature Poodles by crossing small Standards with Maltese and Havanese, and possibly Toy Spaniels. Experts also concede the possibility of dash of Terrier.

Both Toy and Miniature Poodles were popular with the French court during the reigns of Louis XIV, Louis XV, and Louis XVI, during the 17th and 18th centuries, and these smaller dogs were also popular as circus performers in the 18th and 19th centuries. Their intelligence made them easy to train as entertainers.

The Poodle's modern rise in popularity

Most of Europe embraced the Poodle from the beginning, but it wasn't until the end of the 19th century that the breed became popular in Britain. In 1887 in the United States, the American Kennel Club (AKC) registered its first Poodle, a dog named Czar, but the breed didn't become popular until after World War II. Standard Poodles imported mainly from Britain attracted the most interest in those early years. The majority of the dogs were black, white, or brown.

The United Kennel Club (UKC), based in the U.S., recognized the Poodle as a breed in 1914, and in 1999, it divided the Poodle into two separate breeds (I cover both the AKC and the UKC later in this chapter):

- ✔ The Standard Poodle, in the gun dog group
- ✔ The Poodle, with Miniature and Toy varieties, in the companion dog group

In 1930, the AKC had registered only 34 Poodles. In the spring of 1931, though, Helene Whitehouse Walker imported three Standard Poodles from England and established Carillon Kennels. Shortly thereafter, she and nine others formed the Poodle Club of America. Her father, Henry J. Whitehouse, served as the first president of the club, and Mrs. Walker was secretary/treasurer. And from 1939 through 1945, she was president of the club.

Look both ways when Poodle crossing

Poodle crosses, such as Labradoodles and Cockapoos, are becoming very popular because it has become trendy to own a "designer breed." People also believe that these mixed breeds will have the advantage of non-shedding, hypoallergenic coats, and that they may be easy to train because of the intelligence of the Poodle half of the mix. There's no guarantee of any of this, though. The only sure thing is that these dogs aren't purebreds (that is, they don't "breed true"). Breed a Poodle with another Poodle and all the puppies will be Poodles, with Poodle coats and Poodle temperaments, instincts, and size. With a purebred, you know what you're getting.

If you breed a Poodle-Labrador cross with another Poodle-Labrador cross, some of the puppies may look more like Poodles and some may look more like Labradors. You have no way of knowing how many puppies will have the coat of a Poodle and how many will sport the coat of a Labrador. You won't know what size the puppies will grow to as adults, nor what health issues they may face. And don't kid yourself: You will have to deal with health issues. Mixed breeds aren't necessarily healthier than pure-breds. In spite of claims to the contrary, crossbred dogs don't inherit the "best of both breeds." In fact, they often have the least desirable traits of their two parents' breeds.

"Designer dogs" sell for just as much, if not more than, purebred puppies. If you want a mixed breed, check out your local shelter; chances are, you'll find just what you're looking for and spend a lot less money. If you want all the positive aspects of a Poodle, get a Poodle.

By the 1960s, the Poodle had become the most popular breed in the United States, and it stayed at the top for 23 years. In 1994, the Poodle dropped to fifth in AKC registrations, and in 2006, it still stood in the top ten, ranking eighth.

Because the AKC considers all three sizes of Poodle as varieties of one breed, it publishes no separate registration figures.

Today's Poodle is as versatile as the first Pudel that roamed a German farm, which may explain its great popularity. All three sizes make wonderful pets, and the Poodle can still herd, retrieve game, and protect. In competitive events, you'd be hard pressed to find a contest the Poodle can't conquer, from the glamour of conformation showing to the fast-paced agility ring, to a pond of cold water in a hunt test (see Chapter 13 for more about these types of events).

Picturing a Poodle's Physical Traits and Personality

The Poodle is considered one breed, with three "varieties" within the breed. That means that, except for the size difference, each variety is identical to the rest. No matter what the size, a Poodle is an intelligent, friendly companion. In the following sections, I describe the size, anatomy, and temperament of the Poodle breed.

Measuring up sizes

The Poodle comes in three sizes; each size is essentially the same dog, save the difference in height. The sizes, from largest to smallest, are

- ✔ Standard
- ✔ Miniature
- ✔ Toy

You can see the three different sizes in Figure 2-1.

Figure 2-1: The Poodle breed comes in Standard, Miniature, and Toy sizes.

Scoping out a Poodle's anatomy

Figure 2-2 shows a side view of the Poodle. Note that the Poodle is essentially square, measuring the same from withers (the highest part of the back) to ground as from the point of the chest to the point of the rump.

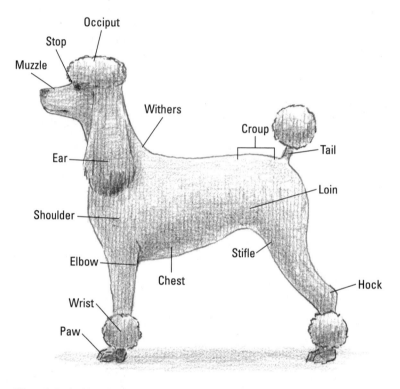

Figure 2-2: A side view of the Poodle.

Figure 2-3 shows a Poodle's front and back. The Poodle's front paws face front, and the legs are straight and parallel. The same is true of the hind legs.

Check out the top view of a Poodle in Figure 2-4. Note that there is a slight indentation behind the ribs, giving the Poodle a "waist."

Figure 2-3: The front and back of a Poodle.

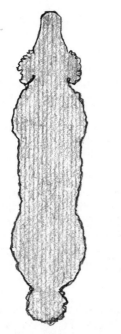

Figure 2-4: The top view of the Poodle.

Taking a look at temperament

All three types of Poodles are intelligent and have a definite sense of humor, and all three should conform to breed standards (see the following section), but you should be aware of general differences in temperament between the three varieties:

- ✔ A Standard tends to be more aloof and self-contained.

- ✔ A Miniature picks her person and wants to always be with that person. A Mini never lets up; she always wants to do something — anything — with her person.

- ✔ A Toy is happy to curl up on your lap and cuddle.

I'm not saying that a Toy can't excel in agility or doesn't enjoy obedience training or that a Standard isn't a loving companion, but, in general, the three types of Poodles do exhibit different personalities.

No matter what size you prefer, you're going to get a dog willing to participate in family activities. Poodles also are intelligent, which means that if you don't give them something to do, they'll invent something, which may not meet with your approval. Their intelligence means they're the perfect partners for performance event competition, but you don't have to compete (see Chapter 13 for more information if you *do* want to compete). Teach your Poodle tricks. Have her pick up dirty laundry and put it in a basket. She can do the same with her toys when company's coming.

All three sizes are friendly and greet invited guests with a wagging tail. That doesn't mean that they won't sound the alarm if a stranger's at the door, and Standards can be effective guard dogs. Poodles shouldn't be shy or fearful of new people or events.

Surveying Breed Standards

A *registered* dog is affiliated with an organization created solely for the purpose of registering dogs. The label of "registered" doesn't guarantee quality, proper temperament, or good health; if your dog is registered with the American Kennel Club (AKC) or the United Kennel Club (UKC), which are the two largest registries in the United States, it just means that the dog is a purebred. Many people register their dogs in more than one registry to take advantage of more competitive events.

I explain the standards for the Poodle breed set by the AKC and the UKC in the following sections. Refer to Figure 2-2 to find the different parts of the Poodle mentioned in the breed standards.

The American Kennel Club

The AKC, founded in 1884, is the world's largest purebred dog registry. Besides its dedication to being a registry, the AKC promotes purebred dogs as companions, works to promote responsible dog ownership, and invests in research to help keep dogs healthy. You can visit www.akc.org to get more information about the group and to find the exact Poodle breed standard.

The AKC places the Standard and Miniature varieties in the nonsporting group and the Toy in the toy group (pretty tough gig at the AKC!). Except for size, the standards for the three varieties are identical. In the following sections, I summarize the important traits and the major faults set by the AKC breed standard. (A *major fault* is a distinct deviation from the standard's desired characteristics.)

Throughout the standard, some aspects of temperament or structure are major faults. If you're showing your Poodle, a major fault will likely get you eliminated. If your Poodle is a pet and won't be shown, some major faults aren't that major. For instance, a nose that is part black and part pink is a major fault in conformation, but it won't affect your pet's ability to be a loving companion.

General appearance and size

What makes a Poodle a Poodle? Leaving aside specifics, most people know a Poodle when they see one. The breed standard wants to make sure that fact is always true.

- ✔ **General appearance:** A Poodle is active, smart, dignified, and elegant. It should be squarely built and well proportioned, and should move soundly and carry itself proudly.

- ✔ **Size:** Size separates the three Poodle varieties in the AKC. Otherwise, the standard for each variety is identical:

  - A Standard Poodle is over 15 inches at the shoulders' highest point.

  - A Miniature Poodle is 15 inches or less at the shoulders' highest point but measures at least 10 inches.

  - A Toy Poodle stands 10 inches or less at the shoulders' highest point.

- ✔ **Proportion:** Poodles are a square breed. The length of a Poodle's body from the breastbone to the point of the rump should about equal the height from the highest point of the shoulders to the ground.

✔ **Substance:** The Poodle is no lightweight. The forelegs' and hind legs' bone and muscle should be in proportion to the Poodle's size. A Poodle doesn't have thin, spindly legs and weak feet. These dogs were developed to work.

The head and neck

The standard discusses the proper Poodle in sections, starting at the front with the head and neck:

✔ **Eyes:** Your Poodle's eyes should be very dark, oval, and set far enough apart so that your Poodle has an alert, intelligent expression. Round, protruding, large, or very light eyes are considered a major fault.

✔ **Ears:** A Poodle's ears should hang close to the head and be set at or slightly below eye level. The flap should be long, wide, and thickly feathered, but the fringe shouldn't be too long.

✔ **Skull:** A Poodle's skull should be moderately rounded and have a slight but definite stop (the area between the muzzle and the head). The length between the occiput and the stop should be about the same as the length of the muzzle.

✔ **Muzzle:** Look for a long, straight muzzle with a little chiseling under the eyes. A major fault here is a lack of chin.

✔ **Teeth:** A Poodle's teeth should be white and strong, and they have a scissors bite. Major faults include having an undershot, overshot, or wry mouth.

✔ **Neck:** A Poodle's neck should be well proportioned, strong, and long. The skin at the throat should be snug, and the neck should rise from strong, smoothly muscled shoulders. The major fault here is *ewe neck,* which means that the top of the neck is concave rather than convex.

✔ **Topline:** The *topline,* or back, should be level, and it shouldn't slope or be convex from the shoulder blade's highest point to the tail's base. However, there should be a slight hollow just behind the shoulder.

The body

Next, the breed standard describes a Poodle's square body in detail:

✔ **Body:** A Poodle's chest should be deep and moderately wide. The loin should be short, broad, and muscular, and the tail should be straight, set on high, carried up, and cut to a proper length so that the Poodle's outline is balanced. A tail set low, curled, or carried over the back is considered a major fault.

✔ **Forequarters:** A Poodle needs strong, smoothly muscled shoulders. A steep shoulder, which shortens a dog's gait and makes the way it moves less efficient, is a major fault.

✔ **Forelegs:** A Poodle's forelegs are straight and parallel from the front. From the side, the elbows should be directly below the shoulders' highest points.

✔ **Feet:** The feet should be small and oval, have well-arched toes, and be cushioned on thick, firm pads. The nails should be short but not too short, and the feet are turned neither in nor out. A major fault here is a paper or splay foot. A *paper foot* is a very thin, flat foot. A dog with a thin, flat foot or splayed toes will tire easily, and she may even injure herself because the foot isn't providing the proper support.

✔ **Hindquarters:** A Poodle's hind legs should be muscular, straight, and parallel from the rear. When the Poodle stands, the rear toes should be only slightly behind the point of the rump. Cow-hocks are a major fault. *Cow-hocks* are when the hock joints turn in and the feet point out. The hock joint corresponds to the heel of a person, although in a dog, it doesn't touch the ground as a human heel does.

The coat, clips, and color

The descriptions of the clips listed in the standard must be followed if you're showing your dog in conformation. If your dog is a pet or competing in performance events, however, the choice of clip is yours. Just make sure that your choice includes keeping your dog clean and brushed. See Chapter 8 for more information on coat care and for detailed descriptions of different clips.

✔ **Coat:** A Poodle's coat is curly; it has a naturally harsh, dense texture. Corded hair should hang in tight, even cords of varying length. It should be longer on the mane or body coat, head, and ears and shorter on puffs, bracelets, and pompons.

✔ **Clip:** A Poodle under 12 months may be shown in the *puppy* clip. In all regular classes, Poodles 12 months and over must be shown in the *English saddle* or *continental* clip. In the Stud Dog and Brood Bitch classes and in a non-competitive Parade of Champions (see Chapter 13 for details), Poodles may be shown in the *sporting* clip. A Poodle shown in any other type of clip doesn't meet AKC standards. Chapter 8 has full descriptions of these clips.

In all types of clips, you can leave the hair of the topknot (on the skull, from the stop to the occiput) free or hold it in place with elastic bands. The topknot is the only area where you may use elastic bands.

✔ **Color:** The coat's color should be even and solid at the skin. In blues, grays, silvers, browns, cafe-au-laits, apricots, and creams (see Chapter 4 for more about colors), the coat may show varying shades of the same color. Natural color variation isn't considered a fault.

Brown and cafe-au-lait Poodles have liver-colored noses, eye rims, and lips; dark toenails; and dark amber eyes. Black, blue, gray, silver, cream, and white Poodles have black noses, eye rims, and lips; black or self-colored toenails; and very dark eyes. The AKC prefers the foregoing coloring in apricots, but liver-colored noses, eye rims, and lips and amber eyes are allowed.

A major fault is an incomplete color of the nose, lips and eye rims, or a wrong color for the color of the Poodle. A Poodle's nose should be a solid color, either black or liver. If either of these colors is mixed with a lighter color, it's a fault.

Parti-colored dogs, whose coats have two or more colors at the skin — are disqualified by AKC standards.

Gait and temperament

Wrapping up the AKC breed standard are notes on the Poodle's gait and temperament:

- **Gait:** A Poodle should trot lightly and have a strong drive from the hindquarters. It should carry its head and tail up and move soundly and effortlessly.

- **Temperament:** Poodles are very active and intelligent, and they have a dignified air. The standard considers shyness or sharpness to be a major fault. Responsible breeders work hard to eliminate these types of faults.

The United Kennel Club

The UKC, founded in 1898, is the world's largest performance dog registry and the second oldest all-breed registry in the United States. The UKC supports the "total dog" philosophy. It also offers a wide variety of performance and conformation events. You can visit www.ukcdogs.com to find out more about the group and to find the exact Poodle breed standard.

The UKC places the Standard Poodle in the gun dog group and the Miniature and Toy varieties in the companion dog group. Except for references to work in the field and height, the standards for all three varieties are identical.

In the following sections, I summarize the UKC breed standard. The Poodle standard for both the AKC and the UKC are similar, but some differences exist, especially in colors allowed. Both registries call for steady temperaments and the ability to move well.

General appearance and characteristics

The UKC standard first gives an overview of the Poodle and then discusses individual features to give more detail to the "blueprint":

- ✔ **General appearance:** The Poodle is dignified, proud, medium sized, and squarely built, and it has a harsh, curly coat that may be clipped traditionally or corded. The ears should be long, drop, and be densely feathered. The tail is normally cut to a proper length, set high, and carried erect. The length of body (from the sternum to the point of the buttocks) is equal to the height (from the withers to the ground).

- ✔ **Characteristics:** The Poodle is most easily identified by its harsh, dense coat, which can be presented in various traditional trims or corded (which happens less frequently). The Poodle also is noted for its high intelligence and trainability. Although Poodles are suspicious of strangers, they need human companionship and don't do well without regular, close interaction with family. They're also affectionate with children.

The gait and temperament noted for the Poodle in the UKC standard is similar to those listed in the AKC standard.

The head and neck

The UKC standard starts at the front of the Poodle and works back, describing the perfect Poodle.

The head should be in proportion to the Poodle's size. From the side, the skull and muzzle should be roughly parallel to each other and joined by a slight but definite stop. The skull should be long and moderately rounded on top, with clean, flat cheeks.

In profile, the muzzle should be straight and roughly equal in length to the skull. The lips should be tight with black or liver pigment appropriate to the coat color. Serious faults here include incomplete lip pigment, wrong color for the color of the coat, and a weak underjaw.

Standards for a Poodle's teeth, nose, eyes, ears, and neck are similar to those of the AKC standard.

The body

The UKC and the AKC agree on the overall build of a Poodle, including its forequarters, hindquarters, feet, and tail, although the official wording may differ in some places.

The UKC adds to its description of a Poodle's body that the loin appears short, broad, and muscular. The ribs extend well back and are well sprung from the spine, curving down and in. The brisket (or chest) extends to the elbow.

The coat, clips, and color

The UKC standard also lists the qualities of coat, color, and proper clips for a Poodle:

- ✔ **Coat:** A Poodle has a harsh, dense, curly coat. If you're interested in conformation shows (see Chapter 13 for details), you may present the coat naturally, corded, or in a traditional clip.

- ✔ **Clips:** Like the AKC, the UKC recognizes several different clips for the conformation ring: puppy, English saddle, continental, and sporting. See Chapter 8 for full details about these clips.

- ✔ **Color:** Both the UKC and the AKC recognize solid colors (apricot, black, blue, cream, gray, silver, white, and different shades of brown, such as café-au-lait), but the UKC also approves parti-colored Poodles, phantoms, abstracts, sables, and multi-patterned Poodles:

  - **Parti-colored:** Parti-colored Poodles are at least 50 percent white, with spots or patches of any other recognized solid color. The head can have a solid color, with a white muzzle, blaze, or white muzzle/blaze combination. (A *blaze* is a strip of white running up the muzzle and between the eyes.) Full or partial saddles are also accepted, as long as they don't exceed the color proportion of 50-50. *Ticking* (small flecks of color) in the white of the coat is acceptable but not preferred.

  - **Phantom:** Phantoms have a solid base color with defined markings of a second acceptable color above each eye, on the sides of the muzzle, on the throat, on the forechest, on all four legs and feet, and below the tail. A phantom without clearly defined face markings or one with its whole face in the second color is acceptable, as long as the coat maintains all the other body markings.

  - **Abstract:** Abstracts have less than 50 percent white, with the remaining percentage being any other acceptable solid color.

  - **Sable:** A sable coat has black-tipped hairs on a background of any solid color. There is no particular pattern for such hairs.

  - **Multi-patterned:** A multi-patterned coat clearly shows more than one acceptable color pattern. For example, a parti-colored dog could have full or incomplete phantom markings. You could also see a phantom with additional abstract markings.

Chapter 3

Deciding Whether a Poodle Is Right for You

In This Chapter

▶ Knowing whether you have what it takes to own a Poodle

▶ Thinking about the time and money you need to own a Poodle

*P*oodles are real people pleasers who have keen intelligence and a sense of humor. But take a minute to really think about what owning a Poodle entails. Not every breed is right for every person.

You can choose from more than 300 breeds of dogs worldwide. That means that everyone can discover a breed that matches an individual's personality. So think about your home, your family, and your finances (among other things), and then think about which breed is best for you.

This chapter helps you to consider what having a Poodle means and whether a Poodle is right for you. If, after careful thought and thorough research, the Poodle seems like the perfect dog for you, chances are he is. (And in that case, head to Chapter 4 for tips on picking the best Poodle out there for you.)

Asking Yourself a Few Important Questions Upfront

You may have had a Poodle when you were growing up, and now you want another dog just like your childhood pal. You may never have owned a Poodle (or any dog for that matter), but you've always liked their looks. These things may, or may not, be good reasons to own a Poodle. In the following sections, I give you a few questions to ponder before you take the plunge with Poodle ownership.

Does a Poodle fit in with your lifestyle?

Poodles are people dogs. They need some quality time with their humans. If both you and your spouse work and the kids are always off playing soccer or attending play rehearsals, when does the dog get some attention? Certainly you can leave a Poodle alone for part of the day, but too much time alone, and he's going to get bored, and maybe destructive.

If you enjoy hiking, jogging, throwing a ball for a dog, playing doggy games, or competing in organized dog events, then a Poodle fits right in. But if your idea of exercise is changing the channel on the television, rethink your breed choice.

Do you have room for a Poodle?

Even a Standard Poodle can be happy in a small apartment, if a lot of exercise is on the daily schedule (and it should be!), but remember, you need to have room in the apartment for your Poodle. Think about whether you have space for a large crate or a plush bed in the living room. Do you even have a living room?

The bigger the dog, the nicer it is to have an entire house. You can generally play games with your dog indoors, such as tag or hide-and-seek, and houses have more room for dog beds and crates. If you're paper training, a house is more likely to have a room that you can close off for training purposes (see Chapter 9 for details).

Many apartments don't have access to a yard; that means that each and every time your Poodle goes out, you have to go, too. A fenced yard also offers a safe place to throw a ball or run a race with your Poodle. If you live in an apartment, you'll need to find somewhere else for your Poodle's daily exercise.

How will a Poodle respond to your children and other pets?

Children and other pets need to be considered before making your final decision. Most Poodles adore children, but if you have younger children, make sure they understand how to handle a dog. No ear or tail pulling allowed. If children are allowed to tease a dog, treat him roughly, or pull his tail or ears, the dog may learn to avoid the children or may even retaliate by biting. Poodles are usually good natured with children, but any dog has limits of tolerance.

Never, ever leave babies unattended with any dog. Babies make high-pitched, squeaky noises that are similar to those of prey animals. They also make sudden, jerky movements — again, like prey animals. These noises and movements can trigger the prey drive in a dog and lead to disaster.

Experienced breeders don't recommend Toy Poodles for children under age ten, as they're just too small to romp and play safely with young children. Standards are large and can be boisterous, especially as puppies, so they need very close supervision when interacting with smaller children. A larger Miniature Poodle, at least 13 inches tall and weighing 15 to 20 pounds, is often the best choice for families with children.

Poodles raised with cats are generally fine with them. Make introductions gradually, and always make sure that the cat has somewhere to go where the dog can't.

If you have smaller furry pets like guinea pigs or rabbits, keep them away from your Poodle. Although some Poodles may get along just fine with the family guinea pig, your Poodle may consider it lunch.

Chapter 6 has detailed information about introducing Poodles to children and other pets.

Considering the Costs of Poodle Ownership

When you fall in love with that adorable Poodle puppy or charming Poodle adult, you're thinking with your heart, which is fine, except that your heart rarely concerns itself with finances and time. Think about what a dog can cost during its lifetime, which can be 12 to 14 years for a Standard and 13 to 17 years for a Toy or Miniature. In the following sections, I explain money and time costs that may affect your decision to adopt a Poodle.

How much is that doggy? Money matters

It's not entirely true that the best things in life are free. There's nothing better than having a dog in the family, but expect expenses:

- Consider the price of a dog, which can be anywhere from $1,000 to $2,000. Think about the everyday costs of food, toys, beds, crates, collars, and leads. (See Chapter 5 for details on the gear you need for your Poodle.)

✔ You need to budget for annual visits to the veterinarian, vaccinations, assorted medicines, and possibly even surgery. If you're not showing in the breed ring, you'll want to spay or neuter, and even the healthiest dog may have an accident or swallow something he shouldn't. An annual tooth cleaning is a good idea, too. (See Part IV for more about health issues.)

✔ Grooming supplies, or professional grooming, comes next for Poodles. Poodles are labor-intensive when it comes to coat care, even though they don't shed. Many Poodle owners have a standing appointment with a groomer. The cost per session is anywhere from $50 to $150 for a Standard, and $35 to $50 for a Toy or Miniature. These prices are for pet clips. Show clips, if a groomer even does a show clip, are much more. Most groomers also charge extra if the coat is matted. Using $50 as an average monthly grooming trip, that's $600 per year for every year of your dog's life. (I cover grooming in more detail in Chapter 8.)

The clock's ticking: Time issues

Before you add a Poodle to your family, consider the following time factors:

✔ You or someone else in the family need to spend time housetraining your Poodle puppy, and that may include being home at lunchtime or cutting an evening out short. See Chapter 9 for more about housetraining.

✔ Plan to spend time teaching your Poodle basic manners, as I explain in Chapter 10. You may also want to go further and train for competitive events (which I cover in Chapter 13).

✔ You need to devote time to weekly grooming in between the full grooming, whether done at home or by a professional. A Poodle kept in a fairly short, simple clip needs brushing and combing once or twice a week. For each session, plan to spend 20 minutes on a Toy, 30 minutes on a Miniature, and as much as 45 minutes on a Standard. If the Poodle is in a long or elaborate clip, he needs more frequent brushing. The time needed to brush a Poodle increases in proportion to the length of hair. (See Chapter 8 for details on grooming.)

✔ You also need time to exercise and play with your Poodle. A game of fetch and a walk around the block once or twice a day may be fine for a Toy, whereas a Miniature will appreciate a mile or more, and a Standard can be your jogging buddy. Exercise amounts will vary, depending on your dog's age and conditioning.

Chapter 4

Choosing the Best Poodle for You

In This Chapter

▶ Choosing a Poodle based on certain characteristics

▶ Finding your Poodle

▶ Making sure you go home with a healthy Poodle

▶ Registering your new pet

*D*eciding that you want a Poodle may have been simple, but you need to do more to make sure that everything goes smoothly as you begin the search for your new family member. This chapter helps you figure out the traits you want in a Poodle pal and find the Poodle of your dreams. I also show you how to check your Poodle's health before you go home and register your Poodle.

Selecting the Traits You Want in a Poodle

Be open to all possibilities as you search for your Poodle pal. You may think that you want a black male puppy when, with a little research, you discover that an adult female apricot Poodle is the perfect match. Consider all the factors in the following sections before you make your decision.

Puppy or adult?

The first step is to decide whether you want a puppy or an adult. Each has advantages and disadvantages, but don't close your mind to one or the other before you've given the subject some thought.

Puppies

Nothing is cuter, or sweeter, than a puppy, no matter what the breed. It's easy to fall in love with a puppy, and when people decide to add a dog to the family, they generally think of a puppy.

Puppies don't come with any "baggage." If you've purchased your puppy from a reputable breeder (see "Beginning with breeders for Poodle puppies," later in this chapter), your puppy has the correct Poodle temperament. She's eager, intelligent, and friendly, and she adjusts quickly to you and your family. You can housetrain your puppy your way and not have to retrain an older dog who someone else taught differently. If you don't want your dog to share the furniture with you, you won't have to retrain an adult who has always napped on the sofa if you begin training at the puppy stage.

On the minus side of the ledger, although it's great fun to get a puppy, to watch her grow, and to be able to teach her the things you want her to know, a puppy also requires much more work than an adult dog. Housetraining takes time and requires someone to be home at regular intervals. It can mean trips out to the yard at 3 a.m. in the rain. (See Chapter 9 for tips on making housetraining easier.)

Puppies also are more likely to get into mischief. They're exploring a new world, and that means chewing chair legs, tipping over wastebaskets, and unraveling the toilet tissue roll. You'll have the joy of teaching everything to your puppy, but you'll also have the frustration.

Adults

Choosing adult Poodles over Poodle pups has some advantages:

- ✔ An adult dog is likely housetrained, or, if not, is easier to train. She can go longer between trips outside and catches on quickly.

- ✔ An adult Poodle is over the chewing stage. She still enjoys a chew toy, but she doesn't use table legs as teething rings and is less apt to eat the fringe off the Oriental rug.

- ✔ An adult Poodle knows English. She recognizes commands and already has a vocabulary, unlike a puppy.

- ✔ Poodles need to be with their people, but an older dog may be more willing to spend the afternoon napping than a younger dog.

A disadvantage to an older dog is that she'll come with some habits that may not fit in with your ideas of how your dog should behave — but dogs *can* be taught new tricks with time and patience.

If you decide that an older dog fits your lifestyle better than a puppy, don't worry that the older dog won't bond with you. Dogs are an adaptable species, and you may be amazed at how quickly an adult dog becomes a member of the family.

Toy, Miniature, or Standard?

Poodles give you the advantage of having the breed you want in the size you want (see Chapter 2 for more about these sizes). To help you choose your perfect Poodle, consider the following distinguishing features of the three Poodle types.

Toy

If you live in a small apartment, have limited mobility, lack much of a yard, don't want to take long walks, and want a dog who cuddles in your lap, the Toy Poodle is ready to move in. Toys are just as smart as the larger varieties, but need comparatively less exercise. At the same time, if you do want to compete, Toys are willing and able to show off in the conformation ring, learn obedience commands, or fly around an agility course. Toys do well in households with adults only or with older children who understand how to handle a dog.

Miniature

The Miniature Poodle gives you a bit more dog, but she still adjusts nicely to apartment living. The Miniature wants a bit more attention from you than a Toy, so be prepared for longer walks and more games. Teach your Mini tricks or train her for performance competition. Give her something to do, or, like most dogs, she may get bored and develop her own games (games you may not appreciate as much as she does).

Standard

The Standard can live in an apartment, but only if you give her a lot of outdoor exercise. Standards need more exercise than either the Toy or the Miniature. If you have a busy family and can include your Poodle in family activities, you'll have one happy dog. Standards can go jogging, play ball, hunt, and compete in organized dog events. A Standard is sturdy enough to be able to roughhouse with the children, too. Just remember that a bouncing adolescent Poodle may be too bouncy for small children and that if you want your lamps to remain unbroken, limit roughhousing to the great outdoors.

Male or female?

Both males and females make wonderful companions. Both Poodle genders are intelligent, fun-loving dogs, so whichever sex you choose, you're getting a wonderful pet. Base your selection on the dog's temperament more than on whether the dog is male or female.

A word of caution: A male may be a bit bigger than a female and an unneutered male may get the urge to roam. An unneutered male may also have a tendency to mark his territory, and that marking may include the corner of your sofa. (See Chapter 14 for more about spaying and neutering.)

One benefit of choosing a male is that males tend to pee quickly on a walk. Just steer him to the nearest tree or bush. Females can sometimes take a long time finding just the right spot, and that's no fun when it's pouring rain.

If you already have a dog of one sex, getting another of the opposite sex can help prevent fights, although most Poodles get along well with other dogs, especially if all the dogs are spayed or neutered.

Which color?

The least important aspect of choosing a Poodle (in my book, at least) is color. You may have heard the saying in the dog world that "a good dog can't be a bad color," but that doesn't stop people from having preferences. With a Poodle, it's easy to satisfy that preference. Poodles come in black, blue, red, silver, brown, café-au-lait, apricot, cream, and white. (You can check out Poodles of these colors in the color section of this book.) If the breeder's dogs are registered with the United Kennel Club (UKC), the dogs may also be parti-colored, phantom, abstract, sable, or multi patterned. (See Chapter 2 for definitions of these terms.)

You can have a color preference, but don't let that preference limit your search. Health, temperament, and personality are much more important in the long run.

Deciding Where to Find Your Poodle

You have several sources of Poodles to choose from: breeders, animal shelters, rescue groups, and pet shops. I cover all these options in the following sections.

Beginning with breeders

People think of puppies when they think of breeders, and a breeder is the best source for a puppy, but a breeder may also have an older dog for sale. In the following sections, I describe the benefits of going to a breeder and give you a list of questions that a breeder should ask you. I also provide you with some questions to ask a breeder and explain the elements of a breeder's contract.

The benefits of breeders

Technically, anyone who has a dog that produces a litter is a breeder, but a good breeder is much more than that:

- ✔ Reputable breeders study the breed and always try to improve it.
- ✔ They run health checks and carefully select the parents of a litter.
- ✔ They pay attention to vaccinations, proper diet, and a clean environment.
- ✔ They socialize their puppies, and they screen buyers to assure the best match between dog and human.
- ✔ With Poodles, a breeder will begin grooming.
- ✔ Puppies from a reputable breeder may have a head start with training.

What some people may consider a negative, such as being on a waiting list for a puppy or having to answer a lengthy questionnaire, is just one more example of a breeder acting responsibly by not producing puppies there are no homes for and by working to assure that puppy and family are well-matched and will stay together. Good breeders feel responsible for the puppies they produce for the life of the puppy.

Finding a reputable breeder

You have a couple of options for locating a Poodle breeder:

- ✔ Start your search for a breeder with the Poodle Club of America Web site: www.poodleclubofamerica.org. You can link to affiliate clubs with contacts for breeder referrals as well as rescues in your area. Affiliate clubs have a code of ethics and members typically run all the necessary health checks on their breeding stock. Another source is the American Kennel Club (AKC) Web site: www.akc.org.

- ✔ If you hear of a dog show scheduled in your area, go and spend the day. You can see all three varieties of Poodles and can talk to the handlers. The owners of all dogs entered in a show are at the back of the show catalog, so you can contact those owners near you to see about the availability of puppies.

Talk to exhibitors after they've shown; they'll be more relaxed and have time to talk. Be sure to always ask permission before you pet a dog.

None of these previously listed methods guarantee a reputable breeder. You still need to see the puppies and the mother in person, and you need to ask questions. But most people who belong to a breed club and who show have made a commitment of time and money to the breed, so these are good places to start.

Answering questions from a breeder

Besides having to wait for the puppy (which can feel like forever), the breeder may have questions for you. He's spent a lot of time and money on the breeding — having health checks done on the parents, studying pedigrees so he doesn't double up on faults, and possibly paying shipping or boarding fees. He wants his puppies to go to the best possible home, and, beyond that, he wants it to be a good match. He wants to make sure you understand the care that a Poodle needs for life. Not every puppy is right for every home, and the breeder wants both the humans and the dog to be happy.

A breeder may give you a questionnaire to fill out. Try not to feel insulted or put upon. A questionnaire is one of the signs of a responsible breeder. Answer the questions honestly and don't try to guess at what you think is the "right" answer. For example, many breeders ask about a fenced yard. A fenced yard is a wonderful thing, but lack of fencing isn't necessarily going to disqualify you. If you live in an apartment, you don't have any yard at all.

In the following sections, I give you some questions the breeder may ask you and the reasons he has for asking them.

Previous experience: Assessing your canine know-how

A breeder's questionnaire gives him an understanding of you and your lifestyle and helps him place the right puppy with the right family. It also lets him know where you may need guidance. If you're getting your first dog, he may recommend training books or books about the breed. If you want a show dog, he may help you choose a more active puppy. Check out the following questions that a breeder may ask about your canine know-how:

- ✔ **Have you owned a Poodle before?** Poodles are high-maintenance dogs when it comes to grooming. If you've had one before, the breeder knows you understand the pros and cons of a Poodle. If you've never had a Poodle, he can explain more about grooming and possible health issues.

- ✔ **Have you read any books about the breed?** This question shows whether you're serious about wanting a Poodle. You've done your homework, and the Poodle isn't just an impulse purchase. (Be sure to mention that you've read this book!)

Personal preferences: Helping you choose the right Poodle

You may think you know just what you want, but what you want may not be the best match. Share your preferences with the breeder and be open to other options. You may hear the following questions:

- ✔ **What are your expectations? What do you want in a dog?** Your breeder wants to understand your lifestyle. If you're fairly sedentary, a Standard may be too much dog for you. If you want a jogging partner, a Toy won't be right.

- ✔ **Do you want a particular sex? Would you take a puppy of the opposite sex?** Tell the breeder if you have another dog in the family, or why else you may want a particular sex. Otherwise, he may match you with the puppy he feels is best for your family, regardless of sex. (See the earlier section "Male or female?" for more about differences between the sexes.)

- ✔ **Would you be interested in an older dog?** Breeders sometimes keep puppies to see if they have show potential. A dog that doesn't meet the breeder's expectations can still make a wonderful pet, and you can have the advantage of all the time the breeder spent socializing and training the dog. If you're willing to take an even older dog, the breeder may have an adult that has earned a championship.

- ✔ **Tell me about your household. Spouse? Partner or roommates? Children? If children, what are their ages?** The breeder wants to make sure everyone welcomes the puppy. If you have children, the breeder wants to make sure they're old enough to know how to deal with a puppy. A Toy Poodle puppy in a house with toddlers may get injured.

Poodle preparation: Gauging your groundwork

There's more to owning a dog than just paying your money and taking her home. A breeder's questions can help you prepare:

- ✔ **Who will be responsible for the care and training of your Poodle?** Your breeder wants to know that no one will neglect the dog. No matter how responsible your children are, an adult is ultimately responsible for the care of the puppy. A puppy is not a lesson in responsibility. A puppy is a living thing.

- ✔ **Have you thought about housetraining a puppy and handling an adult dog? Where will your dog go to eliminate? How will you clean up?** You need to think about this question before you buy a puppy. If you're not sure of what options you have in training and in clean up, talk to your breeder; he is glad to give you suggestions. (Chapter 9 has details on housetraining.)

✔ **Do you live in a house, townhouse, condo, or apartment? If so, how large is your yard and what type of fencing do you have?** Poodles can, and do, live happily in all these places. This question can lead to other questions about how and where you plan on housetraining your Poodle, and where she can get her exercise. You may think the fence around your yard is fine, but your breeder may know from experience that it isn't the best for containing a dog.

✔ **If you rent, does your landlord allow dogs? Please provide landlord contact information.** The breeder isn't going to let a dog go to a home where she's not allowed. He doesn't want you to return the puppy or take her to a shelter. He wants the puppy's home to be _forever._

✔ **In what rooms will your dog be permitted? Do you have any ideas about how you will keep your dog out of certain parts of your home if necessary?** Another question designed to make you think. When your puppy is young, you may want her only in the kitchen or family room. Think about using baby gates or shutting doors. It's okay to have certain rooms off limits, but it's not okay to leave your dog in the basement, in the garage, or outdoors all the time. A Poodle is a people dog. She needs to be part of the family. If that's not going to work for you, the Poodle isn't the right breed for you.

✔ **Can you devote the time to teach your puppy manners and expose your puppy to new experiences? Do you have any ideas about where to go for obedience training?** Training and proper socialization are important to a puppy's development. Your breeder wants to make sure you understand the need to train your Poodle. Ask for his help. (Check out Chapters 10 and 11 for details on training and socializing your Poodle.)

Asking the breeder a few questions of your own

Turnabout is fair play. Here are some questions you want to ask the breeder (and the reasons behind them):

✔ **Have the parents had appropriate health testing?** At a minimum, ask whether the parents have been tested for von Willebrand's, a hereditary bleeding disorder; hip dysplasia; and progressive retinal atrophy (PRA). A breeder may also test for thyroid problems.

✔ **How long have you been breeding? Is this a business or a hobby? How often do you have a litter?** Done right, no breeder is going to be able to make a living breeding dogs. A longtime breeder may make a small profit on a litter, but the costs of health checks, stud fees, proper veterinary care, and medical emergencies don't leave much left over. If a breeder has produced a few litters, he can tell you what to expect as your puppy grows.

✔ **May I meet the parents, or at least the mother, of the puppies?** Meeting the parents gives you a good idea of what your puppy will be like as an adult. The adult Poodles should be friendly, not shy or fearful. You shouldn't hear any growling. The father may not be on the premises, but you shouldn't find a reason not to meet the mother. (See "Choosing a Healthy Poodle," later in this chapter, for tips on what to look for.)

✔ **Where do you raise the puppies?** The puppy area should be clean and near household activity. The puppies should be healthy, and all puppies over six weeks old should have a puppy clip, with the face, feet, and tail shaved (see Chapter 8 for details). If the breeder shows you only individual puppies and doesn't show you where they live, find a different breeder.

✔ **Ask to see the pedigree of the puppy and the registration form.** The pedigree is your puppy's family tree. The registration form ensures that you're getting a purebred Poodle, showing that the parents are registered, and the breeder should give you a registration form for each puppy. You need this slip so you can register your puppy. (See "Registering Your Poodle," later in this chapter, for more details.)

✔ **Will I receive a health record?** The breeder should provide a record showing what vaccinations your puppy has had and the dates the puppy was wormed.

✔ **What happens if I can't keep the dog?** Most reputable breeders take back any dog of their breeding at any time.

Checking out a breeder's contract

When you buy a puppy, your breeder has a contract for you to sign. The contract may be as simple as a bill of sale, listing breeder, new owner, name, and sex of dog, and whether the dog is to be spayed or neutered. Here are a few variations on a simple bill of sale:

✔ Most contracts include a health guarantee, which gives you a set amount of time to take your puppy to a veterinarian for a health check. Forty-eight hours is common, but it may be longer. If, within that time frame, your vet discovers a major health problem, the breeder takes the puppy back and refunds your purchase price. Some breeders offer a replacement puppy at any time if a major problem develops.

✔ Most contracts include a clause that says if, for any reason, you can't keep the dog, you must return her to the breeder. This clause is to prevent dogs from ending up in shelters or in rescue groups. A responsible breeder is just that — responsible for the dogs he breeds for the lifetime of the dog.

✔ Some contracts may specify whether the puppy is show or pet quality. If the pup is show quality, the breeder may set a later date for evaluating the dog. The price of the puppy may be based on whether the breeder gets to use a male at stud or whether the breeder wants a puppy back if you ever breed.

✔ Many contracts include limited registration. *Limited registration* means that you may not register any offspring from that dog with the AKC. (See the later section "American Kennel Club registration" for more info.)

Some breeders want a *co-ownership,* which means that the breeder owns the dog with you. The breeder may sign off, giving you total ownership, after you meet certain conditions. This arrangement can mean that you pay less for the puppy on the condition that you complete the dog's championship, or breed the dog and return a puppy to the breeder. Co-ownerships can work, but make sure you understand it before you agree, or you may be sorry down the road.

If the co-ownership agreement says the dog must become a champion, think about whether you have the time, money, and ability to either show the dog yourself or send it with a handler to finish. If you can't show the dog, will the breeder? Who pays the expenses? Are you willing to send your dog away for six months to a year while she's being shown? Co-ownership contracts can work, but they are frequently the source of disagreements, so make sure that every detail is spelled out, and be certain that you feel comfortable working with the breeder.

If the deal is a lesser sale price in return for a puppy, make sure you understand what breeding entails. After you add in stud fees, health checks, a possible C-section, and time spent raising puppies, that "bargain" sale price may not be such a bargain after all.

Whatever the agreement, make sure you understand it before you take your puppy home.

Considering shelters and rescue groups

If the idea of giving a home to a homeless Poodle appeals to you, scout out your local shelters and give rescue groups a call. In the following sections, I explain the pros and cons of these organizations, provide a few tips on finding them, and give you an idea of what to expect when you visit.

The pros and cons of shelters and rescue groups

You may find your dream Poodle at the local shelter or through a rescue group. The shelter charges you a fee, but it is far less than the price of a puppy from a breeder. While most dogs in shelters and rescue are adults, sometimes shelters take in mothers and puppies, or a pregnant dog may have puppies in a shelter. A rescue group may also have the occasional puppy.

With an adopted adult, you have the advantage of a dog who may have had some training and will understand you when you speak. An older dog may be calmer and will have outgrown puppy chewing. The biggest plus to rescuing a dog is that you are providing a home to a dog who needs one.

One downside is that you don't know your dog's history, and you don't have the support system of a breeder. The dog may come with health problems or bad habits, but if you're willing to spend the time and money, your adult rescue will give you just as much love as a breeder's puppy.

 A rescue dog may have issues you don't know about, but being in rescue or at the shelter doesn't necessarily mean the Poodle is a problem. Many dogs end up in shelters because they aren't wanted. The owners may have divorced, the family may be moving, or a new baby is on the way and the family doesn't have the time needed to care for the dog. Also, many Poodles end up in rescue because the owners can no longer deal with the grooming.

 Most rescue groups and many shelters test the temperaments of rescued dogs and can tell you whether a dog is good around other dogs, cats, and children. Rescuing a dog who is very shy, fearful, or sometimes aggressive is a noble gesture, but the dog will need extensive time, attention, and training, and she may not be suitable for a family with children. If you have children, be sure that the dog is good with children.

A rescue Poodle may be housetrained and may even know many commands, which is a real plus. Remember, though, that even if the dog was once housetrained, she may have reverted to going anywhere. Don't worry. Poodles are very smart, and an adult will housetrain quickly. Just follow the same steps you would with a puppy (see Chapter 9 for full housetraining details).

Locating local shelters and rescue groups

Visit your local shelter on a regular basis to see whether a Poodle shows up. Some shelters keep a list of people who want specific breeds and call you when that breed comes in.

Local kennel clubs or training clubs also may know of a rescue group in your area. Check out www.poodleclubofamerica.org to find an affiliate club.

Knowing what to expect

Before choosing a Poodle from a shelter or rescue group, know what you're getting into. Typically, you may find the following:

- ✔ Most shelters and rescue groups spay and neuter, or insist that you do.

- ✔ Both may have a questionnaire similar to the one a breeder would have (see "Answering questions from a breeder," earlier in this chapter).

   You, too, can ask questions. Ask whether any paperwork was turned in with a surrendered dog. This will help with the health and age of dog, and the paperwork may even include registration papers. Much of the time, though, especially with shelter dogs, no background information is available.

- ✔ Some shelters have a contract that requires you to return the dog to it if you can't care for her for any reason. The contract may also say that you can't have the dog put down without the shelter's permission.

   A rescue group may offer a short health guarantee, but shelters and rescue groups have no way to really know much about a dog's history. They won't know about health clearances or how a dog was raised.

- ✔ Many rescue groups, and some shelters, have foster homes for dogs, so that they can tell prospective owners about how the dog reacts to children or other pets.

Wondering about pet shops

Pet shops make it easy to make an impulse purchase. Puppies, especially Poodles, are so darn cute in the window, and you have no questionnaire, no waiting. Just pay your money and walk out cuddling that adorable puppy. But here is where the good news ends.

The bad news is plentiful: You don't get to meet the mother to know what her temperament was like. You can't ask the breeder if the parents had health checks. You don't usually get a health guarantee. If your puppy gets sick in the next day or two, most pet shops won't take the puppy back, or, if they do, they just exchange it for another puppy, which may have been exposed to the same illnesses as the first one. The pet shop doesn't have a breeder to answer questions about this Poodle in particular or the breed in general. If you buy an older puppy, she has no lead training, no housetraining, and no socialization, and the pet shop price is as much, or more, than that of a breeder.

Choosing a Healthy Poodle

No matter where your Poodle comes from, she should be healthy. You may feel sorry for the sick puppy in the corner, but don't take her home. Start with a healthy Poodle, and look for the following:

- ✔ The coat should be clean and shiny.

- ✔ The dog should move freely, with no limping or wobbling. Puppies aren't always graceful, but a puppy shouldn't be falling down or staggering when it moves.

- ✔ A Poodle shouldn't have open sores, and she should look well fed.

- ✔ The eyes should be clear and bright, with no discharge or swelling.

- ✔ Lift up the flaps (properly called *leathers*). The interior of the ear should be pink, not red, and you shouldn't see swelling or discharge. Sniff gently to make sure you don't detect an odor.

If you're buying a puppy from a breeder, ask to see the mother (and the father, if possible). The mother dog should be healthy as well. She may look a bit thin; having a litter takes a lot out of a dog, but she should otherwise look healthy. You may not be able to examine her as closely as a puppy, but the same criteria apply.

Make sure the dogs are housed in a clean, well-lit, well-ventilated area. The bedding and surrounding area should be clean. The area doesn't have to be sterile, but it shouldn't smell or have an accumulation of dirt, feces, or urine.

Go elsewhere for your puppy if the environment is dirty and the dogs aren't healthy. Don't feel so sorry for the puppies that you "rescue" one. This just encourages the breeder to produce more puppies, and you may not be able to save the sick one. If she doesn't die, she may never be a completely healthy adult. And you'll expose any dog you already have at home to disease.

Registering Your Poodle

The AKC and the UKC are the two major purebred dog registration organizations in the United States. The AKC was founded in 1884 and recognizes nearly 200 breeds of dogs. The UKC was founded in 1898 and recognizes more than 300 breeds. I explain the registration processes for both groups in the following sections; I also describe a pedigree. Chapter 2 has more details about these groups.

All registry organizations are registries (sounds simple, right?). If your dog is registered, it means that she's a purebred. Registration is no guarantee of quality.

American Kennel Club registration

Registering your dog is easy. When you bought your puppy, your breeder gave you the registration form. Fill out the form completely and send it to the AKC with the proper registration fee. The AKC also offers online registration at www.akc.org.

The AKC offers two types of registration, full and limited:

- ✔ *Full registration* places no restrictions on the owner.

- ✔ *Limited registration* means that any offspring of the dog are ineligible for registration with the AKC. A limited registration may be changed to full registration, but only the breeder can make the change. Breeders use limited registration to help prevent faults from being passed on. A contract may require the buyer to spay or neuter, but if the buyer breeds the dog instead, the buyer can't register the puppies.

You don't have to register your Poodle, but if you think you may ever be interested in competing, either in conformation or performance events, it's easier to register your dog as a puppy. (See Chapter 13 for more about competitions.) After the puppy turns a year old, there is an additional fee for late registration.

If you never got your registration papers, you didn't bother to register your puppy, or you got your dog from a shelter or from rescue, you can still compete in performance events with an ILP number. ILP stands for *Indefinite Listing Privilege*. With this number, your Poodle may compete in any AKC event in which Poodles are permitted.

To register your rescue Poodle, go to the AKC Web site for an ILP application (www.akc.org), or e-mail the AKC at ILP@akc.org for the form. You also can call (919) 233-9767. To apply, you need two color pictures of your Poodle, one standing in profile and one head-on, as well as veterinary proof that your dog has been spayed or neutered. The AKC charges you a nonrefundable application fee.

United Kennel Club registration

The UKC registration policy is similar to the AKC's. For example, you must register your puppy before she is a year old, and your breeder gives you the necessary paperwork.

Some advantages to registering your Poodle pup with the UKC include:

- ✔ **Limited Privilege:** The UKC offers *Limited Privilege* for both purebred and mixed-breed dogs. Dogs with a Limited Privilege Card may compete in performance events. The dog must be spayed or neutered.

- ✔ **Temporary Listed Number:** The UKC presents this option for people who want to try a UKC event but don't want to register the dog.

    To apply for a Temporary Listed Number, call the UKC's Dog Events department at (269) 343-9020. A Temporary Listed Number is good for 60 days from the day you purchase it.

Perusing a pedigree after you register your Poodle

A *pedigree* is your Poodle's family tree. If someone says his dog has a pedigree, he means that he knows who all the dog's ancestors are. Generally, the dog is a purebred because people rarely know the specific background of a mixed breed.

When you register your Poodle, you receive an official registration certificate from the AKC. For an additional fee, you can get a certified pedigree for three generations (see Figure 4-1). This form lists your dog's parents, grandparents, and great-grandparents as well as each dog's titles. A certified pedigree also lists each dog's color, and, if she's been DNA tested, it includes the dog's DNA number.

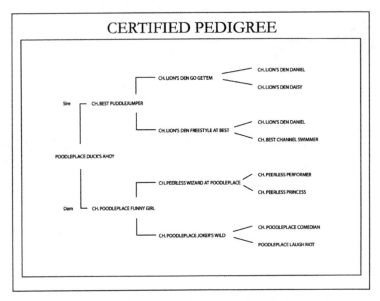

CERTIFIED PEDIGREE

Figure 4-1: A sample Poodle pedigree shows a Poodle with its parents, grandparents, and great-grandparents.

The top part of the pedigree is the *sire's* (father's) family, and the bottom is the *dam's* (mother's). You may see the same name more than once in a pedigree, which is called *line breeding*.

Your breeder should give you a pedigree, and it may go back for more generations, which is fun if you enjoy looking at family trees. One dog I bought had a pedigree that went back almost 40 years! (And in doggy years, that's really saying something.)

The dogs' names on a pedigree are the *registered names*. When you register your dog, you fill in a space for this name. You're limited to 30 letters, and the registered name can't include any abbreviations for titles, like "Ch," which is short for "champion." Frequently, a registered name includes the kennel name of the breeder and may include the kennel name of the purchaser. For instance, the registered name "Best Iron Man of Poodleplace" tells you that a breeder with the kennel name of "Best" bred a Poodle named Iron Man that is now owned by a person with the kennel name "Poodleplace."

A dog's call name isn't shown on the pedigree. The *call name* is what you actually call the dog. It may or may not be part of the registered name. The dog mentioned above with the registered name of "Best Iron Man of Poodleplace" may be called "Sweetie" at home.

Part II

Living Happily with Your Poodle

The 5th Wave

By Rich Tennant

"He's got a sleeping spot, an eating spot, a potty spot, a play spot, and a grooming spot. That's two more spots than I have."

In this part . . .

You've picked out your adorable Poodle puppy or chosen an older Poodle that better suits your lifestyle. It doesn't matter how old your new Poodle is for this part, however; you still need to get ready for his arrival. This part describes what you need to buy, how you should dog-proof your place of residence and yard, how to introduce your new pal to children and other pets, and what to feed your Poodle going forward. I also include a chapter on grooming, which will become a big part of your life with a Poodle!

Chapter 5

Preparing for Your Poodle's Homecoming

In This Chapter

▶ Shopping for your Poodle's everyday necessities

▶ Ensuring that your home is safe for (and from) your Poodle

▶ Setting up your Poodle's special spots

▶ Making an appointment with a vet

*B*ringing home a Poodle is like bringing home a new baby, minus the diapers. You need to make your home safe and to shop for dog beds, toys, dishes, and more. The information in this chapter makes it easy to prepare your home *before* your Poodle arrives.

The easiest way to shop for supplies is one-stop shopping at a large pet-supply store, but if you're not buying everything at once, you have other options. Most supermarkets and discount stores have food and water bowls; some have beds and crates as well. The same goes for dog toys, collars, and leads. You can check out online sites for supplies, too, and dog catalogs sell anything and everything.

Outfitting Your Home with Crates, Gates, and Ex-pens

Before your Poodle arrives in his new home, think about where he'll be spending most of his time. You should have a crate at the ready, and you also may want some baby gates to keep certain rooms off limits. And if you want to give your Poodle some extra space and exercise, an ex-pen provides a little extra stretching room. I cover all three items in the following sections.

Crates

You may not want to buy a crate for your Poodle because you look
at the bars and think *jail*. You're thinking, naturally enough, like a
person. A dog, however, looks at a crate and thinks *den*. The crate
provides many benefits from your Poodle's point of view:

- ✔ He sees a cozy and safe place he can turn to.
- ✔ He can face the opening to observe what's going on without
  worrying about anything approaching him from the back,
  sides, or top.
- ✔ A crate offers a draft-free place to sleep.
- ✔ In cooler weather, the crate helps contain his body heat.

Unfortunately, many people misuse crates. A crate should be a
temporary quarters, not a permanent home. Crate your Poodle
only when you need him temporarily out of the way. You can crate
for a few hours when you need to go out (ideally, for no more than
four to six hours at a stretch). You also can crate for the night.
However, if you plan to routinely leave your dog crated for 8 to
10 hours a day while you work, with no one to give him a break,
you should rethink your decision to get a dog.

In the following sections, I describe the various advantages a crate
has for *you,* and I present the different styles of crates for Poodles.

The benefits of crates to owners

I can't imagine having a dog without a crate. Why? Here are just a
few of the reasons:

- ✔ **Crates make housetraining easy.** Dogs don't like to go to the
  bathroom where they sleep. (See Chapter 9 for more about
  housetraining.)

- ✔ **A crate provides a safe place for your Poodle when you can't
  watch him.** Crates get your Poodle out of the way when you
  have company. You also don't have to worry about someone
  stepping on your Poodle or giving him a forbidden food. When
  you leave the house, your Poodle can curl up with a toy; you'll
  know that he's safe and not gnawing on an electric cord.

- ✔ **In the car, a crate keeps your Poodle in one spot — not
  under the brake pedal, in your lap, or hanging out the
  window.** In case of an accident, your Poodle won't fly into the
  windshield or escape through a door into traffic. (Head to
  Chapter 12 for more about traveling with your Poodle.)

✔ **People who might not otherwise want you to bring your Poodle to visit may allow it if he's crated.** Crating your Poodle in a motel room ensures that he won't cause you to get a bill for damages.

Types of crates

Crates come in two basic styles: solid plastic and wire. A third, less-common style is a soft mesh crate. Figure 5-1 shows these styles; the following list presents the differences between the three types:

✔ **A plastic crate** seems more like a den to your Poodle and will protect him against drafts and keep him warmer. If you plan to fly with your Poodle, and he'll be in cargo, not in the plane's cabin, you need the solid plastic type of crate. Plastic crates are the safest way for your dog to travel in a vehicle. A disadvantage is that they hold in more heat in summer.

✔ **A wire crate** allows for more ventilation in summer. A wire crate will most likely have a removable bottom tray, which can make cleanup easier. Also, many wire crates come with a wire panel that makes the crates smaller for puppies; you can remove the panel when the dog is full-grown. The downside of a wire crate is that it never seems very snug to your Poodle.

If you choose a wire crate, consider buying a special crate cover or covering the top and sides of the crate with a blanket or towel. In the summer, you can flip the sides up on a wire crate to allow more air to reach your Poodle.

✔ **A mesh crate** is an option for frequent travelers. This crate is lightweight and folds compactly; is easy to pack and carry; and allows for quick setup in a motel room. Many dogs do well with these in the short term. People who compete with their dogs in various events find them easy to carry, and they offer good ventilation. They aren't recommended for car travel, though, because they don't offer any protection, and they aren't the best for puppies or for long-term crating, as dogs may try (and succeed) to chew their way out. Also, the bottoms are mesh, so they offer no solid barrier should a puppy have an accident.

If you have a Toy or Miniature Poodle, and you plan to fly with your dog in the cabin, you may consider several brands of carriers designed specifically to fit beneath an airline seat.

A crate must be big enough for your dog to stand up and turn around comfortably. It may make sense to your pocketbook to buy the crate your Poodle will need as an adult, but going that route can make housetraining harder. No dog wants to go to the bathroom where he sleeps, but a crate that's too big may make it possible for him to have a cozy bed at one end and a bathroom at the other. I recommend that you buy or borrow a puppy-sized crate when you first get your Poodle and plan to buy a larger crate later, or buy an adult-sized crate now and insert a divider.

Figure 5-1: You can corral your Poodle in a variety of crates.

Gates

If you have certain places in your home that you want to keep off-limits to your Poodle, baby gates can serve as great barriers to entry. Maybe you have an elegant sitting room with a priceless Oriental rug that you don't want your Poodle to use as a bathroom. Maybe you own an antique desk that won't increase in value if it receives a puppy's teething marks. If you have cats, you may want to keep one room Poodle-free so that your cats can have some privacy. You may have an open staircase, and you don't want to risk your Poodle taking a tumble.

Whatever your reason for wanting an off-limits area, a baby gate makes it easy to keep your Poodle out of certain spaces. Among the types of gates available are the following (see Figure 5-2):

✔ **Metal:** Metal gates are sturdy and less apt to be destroyed.

✔ **Wood:** Wood looks nicer and may blend better with your furnishings, but puppies may find a wood gate the perfect teething tool.

✔ **Mesh:** Mesh is generally cheaper, but that also means that it's easier for a dog to destroy.

Most dog-supply stores and catalogs should sell baby gates. Or, you can use a gate made for human babies. You can assemble and break down many types of gates with no tools and no attachments to a doorjamb. Some gates are more permanent; you can open and close them instead of having to step over them. You can even find some gates made for wider or irregular-shaped openings. Prices can run from $30 to $130, depending on the model you need.

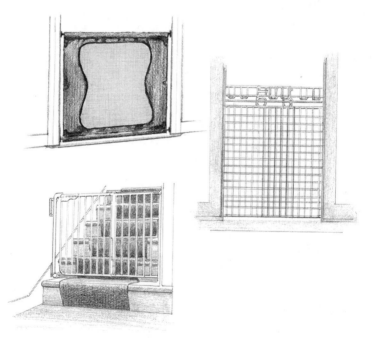

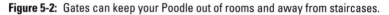

Figure 5-2: Gates can keep your Poodle out of rooms and away from staircases.

When you're scoping out gates, consider the following points:

✔ If you plan to keep certain rooms off-limits when your Poodle puppy reaches adulthood, make sure you buy gates high enough to keep an adult Poodle from jumping over.

✔ Consider the material the gate is made of, as I describe earlier.

> ✔ Consider the size of the gaps between the bars, if the gate has any. Make sure your Poodle can't get his head stuck in a gap. Getting stuck could just frighten your Poodle, or it could cause serious injury. Even small gaps can trap a puppy who's determined to shove through an opening.

Ex-pens

An exercise pen, or an *ex-pen,* is a playpen for your Poodle. An ex-pen isn't a necessity, but it can be a useful piece of equipment. If you want to corral your Poodle in a small part of the yard, an ex-pen is the way to go. It gives your dog more freedom than a lead, but it still limits where he can roam. You also can use an ex-pen indoors. It can act as a gate across a large opening, or you can use it to fence off part of a room for housetraining purposes, if crate training isn't practical for you (see Chapter 9 for more on training). Most ex-pens run between $40 and $90.

Buying Comfortable Bedding

Dog beds come in dozens of different shapes and sizes and can cost anywhere from $20 to $100. If you want to get really fancy, you can buy a four-poster or a French provincial day bed, which cost even more. The style you pick, for the most part, is up to your personal preference.

Whatever you choose, though, you may want to wait until your Poodle becomes an adult before you buy his "good" bed. Why do I say that? Because puppies have accidents and puppies chew. A puppy can chew an expensive bed to pieces faster than you can imagine. Housetraining is another consideration. Most good beds have some kind of padding that makes them warm and comfy for your dog. If your puppy has an accident, it can take two or three days for the "stuffing" to dry.

To keep your Poodle comfortable, make him a bed of old bath towels and some synthetic fleece. Both items are renewable and inexpensive, and you can machine wash and dry them quickly. For untrained puppies, make a nest of shredded paper. They can burrow into the paper for warmth, but there won't be the danger of them chewing and swallowing fabric chunks, which can cause intestinal blockage.

After your Poodle gets beyond housetraining and teething (see Chapter 9), or if you're bringing home an adult Poodle right off the bat, you should enjoy finding the perfect bed for your Poodle. You have many options:

- ✔ You can find basic crate pads if you want to keep it simple.
- ✔ You can buy bumper pads to cushion the sides of wire crates.
- ✔ Some beds are made to fit the corner of a room.
- ✔ Some beds have bolster edges to them for dogs who like to sleep with their heads on pillows.

No matter what style bed you buy, you should get one that has a removable cover so that you can launder it regularly without having to wash and dry the filling.

Staying Attached with Collars and Leads

You can find almost as many types of leads (also known as leashes) and collars as you can beds and crates. And as celebrities and socialites have shown you, many people can combine functionality with personal style. However, you shouldn't invest a fortune in a rhinestone-studded collar-leash combo until your Poodle puppy is fully grown. Starting out with a basic model is the way to go. In the following sections, I discuss the different types of collars and leads you can buy and when you should buy them. Chapter 10 has the full details on fitting different collars and leads on your Poodle and using these items in training.

Shopping for collars

A collar is necessary for your dog so you can control him. A hand or a lead on a collar lets you guide your dog or restrain him. The type of collar you buy depends on how old your Poodle is, how you plan to train your dog, and personal preference. For a Poodle puppy, you should find a basic puppy collar that you won't mind replacing as he grows. Puppy collars are just like "big dog" collars except that they are thinner, lighter, and smaller. Many nylon puppy collars allow you to push the tongue of the buckle through the fabric at any point so you can increase the size of the collar as your Poodle grows. Another choice is an adjustable collar with a quick-release fastener that makes it easy to get the collar off should it catch on something.

When your Poodle enters adulthood (around one year of age), you can consider any of the following collars (see Figure 5-3 for a sampling):

- ✔ **Flat buckle collars:** Typically, these collars are made of leather or nylon. Fancy ones may be made of velvet, decorated with rhinestones.

✔ **Martingale collars:** These join the larger collar with a smaller loop that connects the ends of the larger part. Martingale collars can be tightened, but only to the size of the larger loop. You also can find Martingale collars that have a section that pulls out and acts as a handle. The advantage of these collars is that they can't choke your dog, yet they'll tighten so that the dog can't pull out of the collar. You can't leave a Martingale collar on all the time because the smaller loop can easily snag on things, or a dog can catch a leg in it and be injured.

✔ **Prong collars:** These collars have metal prongs that face inward and pinch the dog's neck when it's tightened. They're typically used on large, strong dogs to keep control; they're not a "general use" collar.

✔ **Training collars:** You don't want to get a training collar until your puppy is at least 6 months old because there is a risk of harming a younger dog whose muscles and bones are still forming.

With the exception of a buckle collar, you should never leave any kind of collar on your Poodle when he's unattended. Collars with attachments can catch on objects and injure or kill your dog.

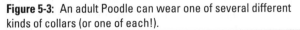

Figure 5-3: An adult Poodle can wear one of several different kinds of collars (or one of each!).

Many dog owners prefer a harness to a collar. Because many small dogs may have sensitive tracheas, a harness replaces a collar that could press on and injure the trachea.

But *don't* use a regular walking harness with a car seatbelt. This type of harness isn't strong enough to restrain a dog in an accident. Use only a harness specifically designed for car travel, and make sure that it's correctly adjusted to the dog and fastened to the seatbelt. Figure 5-4 shows this setup.

I recommend collars over harnesses for walking around. A harness gives you no control over your Poodle and makes it easier for your dog to pull you down the street during a walk. If you're training your Poodle for a competitive event like tracking, weight pulling, skijoring, or sled pulling, get a harness appropriate for that specific activity. Otherwise, stick with a collar.

Figure 5-4: Toy and Mini Poodles may be comfortable in harnesses.

Looking at leads

You need a lead (also known as a leash) right away so you can take your Poodle puppy out into the yard, and a lead will come in handy throughout your Poodle's life — from training (see Chapter 10) to the golden years of leisurely strolls. You have a few considerations when finding a lead for your Poodle:

- ✔ **Length:** A six-foot lead is a good length, no matter the Poodle's age.

- ✔ **Weight:** Buy a weight that suits the Poodle you have. Heavier isn't necessarily better, but a quarter-inch-wide nylon lead that restrains your puppy may be too light for a Standard Poodle. A lead of ¾ inch is nice for a Standard and not too bulky to hold.

- ✔ **Material and color:** You can purchase nylon leads in assorted colors, which frequently have matching collars. You also may find leads made of cotton, and leather is always a good choice. I like leather because it's flexible and feels good in my hand when I take my dogs for walks. It also lasts a long time.

Avoid plastic leads, which have a tendency to crack and break. You also should avoid chain leads. The only way to hold a chain lead comfortably is by grabbing the loop at the end, and many times you need to actually grab the lead itself. Grabbing a chain is uncomfortable, and if your Poodle happens to lunge forward, he'll pull the chain across your hand. Hello, first-aid kit!

Another type of lead you may consider is a retractable lead. This lead consists of a thin, light black line contained in a plastic holder with a handgrip. With this model, you get from 10 to 30 feet of lead. If you walk your Poodle in a wide-open space, a retractable lead is great for allowing him more freedom, and it can give him more exercise. However, a retractable lead isn't as good for a stroll around the block. It doesn't give you as much control as the other models, and it can get tangled in brush, around a mailbox, or around trees. Don't use a retractable lead with a puppy, who can get easily tangled in the cord. It isn't for training, either.

If you opt for a retractable lead, make sure you know your surroundings, and be careful. If you're crossing the street with your Poodle ahead of you by 15 feet or so, you're putting your dog in danger of being hit by a car.

Securing Proper ID for Your Poodle

It doesn't matter how carefully you watch your Poodle, accidents can happen. You may not latch a gate properly, or you may leave a door open a second too long. Bang! Your Poodle is on the loose. You can do your part to help him get back home by outfitting him with proper identification. Your options include the following:

✔ **Have a tag made for your Poodle's collar that features your phone number and any other information you may want to include.** The tag is visible and easy to use. One drawback is that a collar can come off or be removed if someone steals your dog (a worst-case scenario). Most veterinarian offices sell them, as well as animal shelters. Dog shows and carnivals frequently have booths that make up tags as you wait. Tags generally cost less than $5.

✔ **Get your Poodle some ink.** Some breeders tattoo all their puppies for ID purposes. If yours didn't, you may choose to have your Poodle tattooed with his registration number or a phone number (a vet can tattoo your dog). Tattoos usually appear on the inner thigh or on the inside of the flap. The advantage to a tattoo is that it's permanent; the problem with ID tattoos is that they can stretch and fade as a dog grows, and they can be covered by hair. Costs range from $25 to $55.

✔ **Talk to your vet about getting a microchip.** A *microchip* is a small tracking device, about the size of a grain of rice, that a vet implants between your Poodle's shoulder blades. A scanner can read the information on the chip, which allows vets or shelter workers to contact a particular microchip's registry. The registry, in turn, contacts you. A microchip has an advantage over other forms of ID because it will always be a part of your Poodle; it never fades, and it won't get lost. A chip costs between $40 and $50.

Check out Chapter 12 for more information on carrying proper ID when you travel with your Poodle.

Beautifying Your Poodle with the Right Grooming Tools

While you're out shopping for Poodle essentials for your new pal's homecoming, you can't forget grooming supplies. Grooming is an important part of Poodle ownership. Even if you plan to hire a groomer to keep your Poodle looking good, you still need to do some basic grooming between appointments (see Chapter 8 for the full scoop on grooming).

Hair care

For starters, you should pick up a comb and a slicker brush. (A slicker brush has a rubber base, and thin metal wires bent at an angle near the tip are set into it.) Brushes cost between $5 and $30, depending on size and quality. Spend between $10 and $15, and you should be fine.

If you plan to shave your puppy's feet and face, you should talk to your breeder about the proper clipper and the types of blades you need (see Chapter 8 for details).

Nail care

You also need to trim your Poodle's nails. Nail clippers come in several sizes, so you should buy the clippers best suited for your Toy, Miniature, or Standard Poodle. They run in price from $8 to $15. Here are several types of clippers:

- ✔ The guillotine type, with a blade that slides across and slices the nail
- ✔ Clippers that squeeze together to cut the nail
- ✔ Clippers that have small, rounded cutting blades and that cut scissor style

An alternative to nail clipping is grinding the nails. A grinding tool (which costs between $50 and $65) has a wheel that rotates at a high speed to grind away excess nail. Many dogs that fight ordinary clipping happily (or at least willingly) accept grinding. Used frequently, grinders have the advantage of causing the "quick" of the nail to recede so that the nails can be kept shorter.

If clipping and grinding prove too difficult, you can try to just file the nails. Check out all sorts of nail tools — including clippers, grinders, and files — in Figure 5-5.

Self-grooming considerations

Along with a brush, comb, hair clippers, and nail clippers, you may want to think about investing in a grooming table. A grooming table saves strain on your back, and your Poodle may be less apt to fight the grooming process if you have a special table he's used to. Most grooming tables fold up, like a card table, so you can store them easily between grooming sessions. A grooming table, depending on the size of your Poodle, costs between $100 and $150.

If you're doing all your bathing at home, consider investing in a doggy hair dryer. Dryers can cost as little as $50 to as much as $500 for a large floor model. See Figure 5-6 for an example of a grooming table and dryer.

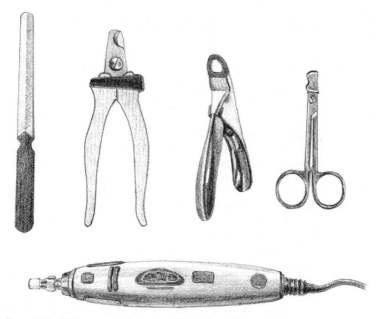

Figure 5-5: Different tools keep your Poodle's nails neat and pretty.

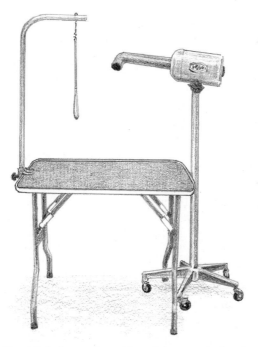

Figure 5-6: A grooming table and dryer can be handy if you plan to groom your Poodle yourself.

Savoring the Details of Food and Bowls

Before you bring home your Poodle, you need to pick up a supply of whatever food your breeder fed the puppy, along with the necessary feeding and drinking tools: bowls. A breeder may be courteous enough to give you a few days' worth of food, but whether she does or not, you shouldn't change the dog's food right away. He's experiencing enough change without having to digest different food. (See Chapter 7 for full details on food.)

When you have the food in tow, you can turn your attention to what to put it in. Bowls for food and water come in plenty of different shapes and materials:

✔ Plastic bowls probably have the most variety when it comes to shapes and colors, and plastic has the advantage of being virtually unbreakable. However, it may be harder to clean plastic, and a dog can develop acne from rubbing his chin on the plastic when eating. Plastic bowls cost between $5 and $10.

✔ Ceramic bowls are heavy, so they prevent easy tipping when your Poodle goes to dine. Many of these bowls come in bright colors and have fun doggy designs on them. The disadvantage of a ceramic bowl is that it's breakable. These bowls cost between $5 and $10 or, for a really fancy bowl, up to around $25.

If you choose ceramic bowls for your Poodle, make sure the glaze on them is lead-free; otherwise, your Poodle can get lead poisoning and become ill, or even die.

✔ Stainless-steel bowls are unbreakable and easy to clean. Some come with rubber bases that prevent tipping, and some are made deeper and with smaller openings to help keep doggy ears from dragging through food or water. These bowls cost between $2 and $15, depending on size and whether you get a bowl with a rubber nonskid bottom.

Whatever your choice of dishes for your Poodle, make sure you wash them after every meal. Just because your Poodle polishes a food bowl with his tongue doesn't make it clean. Wash water bowls daily, too. Wash bowls with soap and water, or put them in your dishwasher.

Getting the Scoop on Cleanup Tools

What goes in must come out, so think about waste management as you shop for your new pet. Invest in pooper-scoopers. These tools are generally made of metal and have large pans at the end of their long handles and a shovel or rake arrangement at the other end. A pooper-scooper makes cleanup easy on you and keeps your living area looking and smelling nice; it costs between $25 and $30.

Of course, after you scoop, you need somewhere to put the waste. Consider lining a small trash can with a garbage bag and keeping this can out of your home! If you're ambitious, you can install a doggy septic tank in your yard with just a bit of digging. Dig a hole deep enough for the unit (about two feet). The top sticks up above the ground and is covered with a lid. Simply scoop the waste and drop it in. The drawback to a doggy septic tank is that you can't use it if your ground freezes solid in the winter. Doggy septic tanks cost between $40 and $75.

You need to be a responsible pet owner and pick up after your Poodle on walks, too. For Toys and Miniature Poodles, plastic sandwich bags work well. If you have a Standard Poodle, you need to graduate to a larger bag. You can save money and recycle by using plastic grocery bags, bread bags, or newspaper bags. (If you decide to use second-hand bags for cleanup duty, make sure they don't have any holes in them — for obvious reasons!) You also can buy special bags for walks at many pet-supply stores. Some come in containers that clip onto your lead, and some are opaque and have easy-to-tie handles.

 If you're a bit squeamish about picking up your Poodle's messes with a bag, you can purchase a small, heavy-duty cardboard cleanup kit. You use the box portion of the kit to pick up, and then you seal it and toss it. If you don't think you can clean up after your dog at all, you should think about getting tropical fish rather than a dog. Responsible dog owners are good neighbors; they clean up after their dogs.

Check out Chapter 9 for more details about the housetraining process.

Finding Toys for Toys (And, Yes, Miniatures and Standards)

The best part of a Poodle-shopping spree is arriving at the toy aisle. Dozens of wonderful toys are on the market for your dog. You can buy cuddly, fluffy toys, latex squeaky toys, flying discs, balls, chew toys, rope toys, and more. You also can make toys out of items you have around the house. In the following sections, I set you up with a few toy guidelines and describe a variety of toys that you can buy (and make!) for your Poodle.

Following a few toy guidelines

Different dogs enjoy different toys. Your Poodle may adore stuffed toys and ignore hard rubber ones. Or maybe your Poodle is a fool for any kind of ball. Consider the following when picking out toys:

- ✔ **Make sure the size of the toy fits the size of your Poodle.** A ball that's just right for a Toy, for instance, may be small enough for a Standard to swallow, and a swallowed ball can mean surgery. On the flip side, a ball that suits a Standard is no fun at all for a Toy who can't pick it up.

- ✔ **Watch your Poodle with toys.** You won't know what kind of toys work best for your dog until you try them. Experiment to find out what's safe and fun for your Poodle.

- ✔ **Consider unstuffed toys if your Poodle likes to be destructive.** Manufacturers seem to be aware of the destructive powers of dogs, so many produce unstuffed toys. These toys still have squeakers, and dogs still rip them open, but at least you won't have to contend with the stuffing.

Gnawing on chew toys

Dogs love to chew, and you'll love it when the objects of your Poodle's affection aren't pieces of furniture or shoes. Chew toys come in many forms, including the following:

- ✔ **Ropes:** Thick rope toys can be both chew toys and tug toys, providing endless entertainment for your Poodle. Supervise your Poodle's chewing so that he doesn't swallow chunks of rope. And if you want to play tug with your Poodle, be gentle so you don't hurt his jaw. With older dogs, stop if the game gets too rough. Some handlers advise that you never play tug with your dog, because it encourages aggression, but others say that the practice isn't a problem if you control the game.

Teach your Poodle the "Leave it!" or "Drop it!" command with a toy like a rope. When you give the command, he must drop whatever he has in his mouth. During play, give him the command. When he drops the rope, tell him that he's a good dog, and then offer the toy again. If the game gets too wild, stop it and move on to something else. (See Chapter 10 for more about commands.)

✔ **Food-stuffed toys:** Some chew toys fall between being toys and being food. You can find several toys on the market that allow you to stuff them with food. These toys make wonderful chews for when you leave your Poodle alone. Some toys dispense bits of kibble or biscuits as your Poodle plays with them, giving him something to think about.

✔ **Rawhides:** Dogs love rawhides, but you need to be careful with these chews. Some dogs swallow chunks of rawhide and end up with impacted bowels. Even a dog who seems to be thoroughly chewing a rawhide can end up with lumps of indigestible material in his stomach. You may be able to pinpoint this if he vomits the material. I give my dogs rawhides sparingly and usually in the form of "bones" made of shredded rawhide; this eliminates the danger of my dogs swallowing large clumps. Always supervise any rawhide treat.

✔ **Animal hooves:** Dogs love to chew on cow hooves, but stand warned that cow hooves smell terrible and can crack your Poodle's teeth. Swallowed chunks can cause intestinal blockage.

Rollicking with retrieving toys

Most Poodles love to retrieve, so retrieving toys like balls make good exercise tools. If you own a Toy or a Mini, you may enjoy a game of indoor fetch, so tennis balls are good toy choices. Tennis balls, indoors or out, make good, inexpensive toys. If you live near a tennis court, you may even be able to get used ones for free!

Dogs also enjoy batting and pushing larger balls, like basketballs or beach balls, even though traditional fetch isn't an option.

A ball that is too big is better than one that is too small. It's easy for a dog to swallow a ball, which can end in tragedy.

Another favorite retrieving toy of the Poodle is the flying disc. Besides the hard plastic versions, there are soft discs made of fabric stretched around a stiff rim. Others may have pieces of rope or a bone shape attached for easy grasping by your dog. Just remember to start out a disc game gradually. Keep the disc low so your Poodle doesn't get hurt leaping and twisting.

Settling on squeaky toys

Dogs love squeaky toys because that squeaky noise sounds like prey. It excites them and makes them want to attack and "kill" the toy. These toys come in latex or stuffed form. Your Poodle may enjoy a latex squeaky toy for its noise-making ability and chewiness. Many dogs eventually chew bits off of latex toys, but these small bits pass harmlessly through their systems. Just make sure that the toy you purchase is large enough that your Poodle can't swallow it whole.

Getting creative with homemade toys

You don't have to buy all your Poodle's toys. You can utilize items around your house to make toys that your Poodle will love (under your supervision, of course). The following list presents some ideas:

- ✔ Open up a paper bag and put it on the floor. Cats aren't the only animals that enjoy the rustle of a bag.

- ✔ Toss your Poodle the cardboard from the center of a roll of paper towels or toilet paper.

- ✔ Let your Poodle bat around a plastic milk carton. You can put a few beans or some dried corn inside so the toy makes an interesting noise. Just make sure you supervise his play.

- ✔ Give your Poodle a whole carrot and watch him play with it and gnaw on it.

- ✔ Tie multiple knots in an old sock and let your Poodle go wild. You also can stuff a tennis ball in a sock and then knot it. If your puppy is teething, wet the toy and freeze it. You also can wet and freeze an old washcloth and let your puppy chew on that.

Don't be afraid that using a sock as a chew toy will teach a puppy that chewing on clothing is acceptable. A puppy will chew on just about anything you leave lying around, whether he's seen the item before or not!

Poodle-Proofing Your Home

Take time to protect your Poodle from himself. Dogs don't have hands, so they use their mouths to explore their world, which can get them into trouble. In the following sections, I show you how to keep your Poodle safe inside *and* outside your home.

On the inside

Puppies are like toddlers: They want to put every object in their mouths, they're faster than they look, and they get into places that seem impossible for them to enter. So, before your Poodle walks through the doors of his new home, you need to take the time to puppy-proof each room. Follow these guidelines:

- ✔ Electrical cords are real threats to your Poodle's safety, so try to use the shortest cords possible. Tuck them behind nearby furniture, or hide them under pieces of carpeting if possible. If you have a cluster of cords, you can run them through a length of PVC pipe to keep them hidden from puppy teeth. Still, nothing works 100 percent. Supervise your Poodle when he's around electrical cords.

- ✔ Make it a habit to keep closet doors closed, and don't leave shoes, socks, or other articles of clothing on the floor.

- ✔ If you want certain rooms or stairways to be off-limits to your Poodle, practice keeping the doors to the rooms shut or get baby gates for the entryways (I discuss gates earlier in this chapter).

- ✔ If you have stair, landing, or balcony railings, be sure you're your Poodle can't get even his head through them. Building codes require them to be narrow enough to protect human infants and toddlers, but puppies are smaller. To keep your Poodle safe, cover railings with wire or fabric mesh, and supervise closely. If your Poodle is a Toy or small Miniature, you may need to leave these coverings up permanently.

- ✔ If you have rugs with fringe edges, you may want to store them away until your Poodle hits adulthood and is beyond his chewing stage. Dogs don't mind chewing on books in a book-case, either, so put your treasured volumes high on the shelves. Keep valuable furniture in a room that's off-limits to your Poodle, or store it where he can't find it.

- ✔ Keep trashcans covered or out of reach. Make sure that house-plants aren't at puppy level so they don't provide a salad (and some houseplants are poisonous — see "Being mindful of particular plants," later in the chapter), and that household cleaning supplies are safely locked away.

Out in the yard

A fenced-in yard is ideal for dog ownership. You and your Poodle have the freedom to run and play without worrying about traffic or your Poodle running off to explore.

You need to make sure that your yard, fenced or not, is free from dangerous plant materials. I go over the details of fencing and removing plants in the following sections.

You can have a Poodle without a fenced yard, but it means never letting him off lead, unless you're in a fenced area, like a dog park. Just like a mail carrier works in all kinds of weather, you'll need to go out with your Poodle each and every time he goes out, though rain, snow, sleet, and gloom of night.

Examining an existing fence

If your yard is fenced and begging for you and your Poodle to use it as a playpen, give it a thorough check before your puppy arrives:

- ✔ Make sure you can't find any gaps or holes. Dogs can wiggle through amazingly small spaces, so, when in doubt, close the gap. Depending on the hole's location, put another piece of fencing over the hole, put a cinder block in front of it, or pull its edges together and wire it closed.

- ✔ Make sure you can't find any sharp bits of wire or wood sticking out that could hurt your Poodle. Bend bits of wire back on itself and wrap tape around sharp points. Remove and replace jagged pieces of wood, or plane them smooth.

- ✔ Check wire fencing to see whether the openings are large enough for a puppy to get through. On the other hand, are the openings small enough to prevent a puppy from getting his head stuck? You may have to replace the fence if its openings are either too large or too small.

- ✔ Make sure the fence is tall enough. Almost any fence can keep a puppy enclosed, but when your Poodle grows up, will your fence contain him? You want to keep other dogs out as well. Four feet tall is good, and five feet is better.

- ✔ Check gaps around gates; if any of them are wide enough for your Poodle's head, fasten stiff wire to the edge of the gate so that it will cover the opening when the gate is closed.

Putting up a new fence

If your yard isn't fenced in, but you want it to be, you have several choices of material you can use:

✔ **Wire:** Chain link is strong and lasts a long time without much maintenance. However, you and everyone else can see through any kind of wire fence. If you have neighbors and a lot of back-yard activity, will your Poodle bark at them? If a dog roams your neighbor's yard, will he and your Poodle bark and forth? Also, children on the other side of the fence may poke objects through that you might not want your Poodle to have.

If you decide to erect a wire fence, you also may want to con-sider planting various bushes and shrubs along the fence line to give your yard more privacy.

✔ **Solid fencing:** This type of fencing cuts down on distractions . . . and barking. Wooden stockade fences are relatively inexpensive, but they need painting or staining regularly. PVC fencing is more expensive, but it requires little maintenance and looks very nice.

If you choose PVC fencing and want to have a gate, make sure you install the gate so that the gap between the gate and the ground is too small for your Poodle to escape.

No matter what material you choose for your fence, make sure you consider other factors besides your Poodle. For instance, the height of your fence shouldn't be based solely on keeping your dog in. You also need to keep other dogs out. Consider installing at least a 4-foot fence. Five feet is even better, and you may even want six.

Some people just don't like the looks of any kind of fence. If you share this opinion, you may want to install an electronic fence. This device relies on a buried wire and a special collar for your dog. As your Poodle approaches the boundary set by the buried wire while wearing his collar, he hears a warning sound. If he con-tinues, he receives a shock. With an electric fence, your dog needs training. Any reputable firm that installs electric fences should also work with you to teach your Poodle the boundaries. If a company you're considering doesn't offer this training, find another company.

The drawback to an electric fence is that, although it keeps your dog in, it doesn't keep out other animals or people. Some dogs get so excited when they see animals or people that they cross the boundary in spite of the shock and then may be unwilling to cross the boundary again to return home.

In addition, some local leash laws don't accept electronic fences as meeting the requirements for canine restraint, so check your local ordinance before buying such a fence.

Before you install any fence, check with your municipality. There may be rules about height, materials, and distance from neighbor-ing properties, and you may need a building permit.

Being mindful of particular plants

Whether your yard is fenced or open to the world, you should take the time to examine the plants in your yard. Many plants and plant materials are poisonous to dogs, although some are more of a problem than others. The following list outlines some dangers to your Poodle:

- ✔ Apple seeds contain cyanide, although your Poodle would have to eat an awful lot of apples to be in danger.

- ✔ Iris, tulip, and daffodil bulbs are poisonous to dogs. These bulbs are underground, though, so the risk is slight.

  If your Poodle enjoys digging, monitor where he digs. Don't leave him in the yard unattended.

- ✔ English ivy is poisonous, as are phododendron, holly, and elderberry. And don't forget poison ivy, which is nobody's friend!

- ✔ Oleander — its flowers, leaves, and stems — is very poisonous.

- ✔ If you have borders and you use mulch to contain weeds, avoid using cocoa mulch. It smells great, but it isn't a good choice for dog owners. Cocoa mulch is made from cacao bean shells and contains theobromine and caffeine — the same ingredients that make chocolate harmful to a dog. If your Poodle eats cocoa mulch, he may get an upset stomach or, depending on the quantity eaten, he may become very ill.

- ✔ Mushrooms can be fatal. Remove any fungus growing in your yard. If your Poodle eats a mushroom, take him to your vet immediately, along with a sample of the mushroom.

If your Poodle ever becomes ill after chewing or eating any plant material, take him to the vet immediately, and be sure to take a sample of the plant with you to be identified; the treatment may depend on what caused the illness.

Each area of the country has its own toxic plants. Check with your local nursery to find out what plants are safe for dogs.

Choosing Special Spaces for Your Poodle

Dogs are creatures of habit, which works to your advantage. You can create special spaces for where you want your Poodle to do his essential duties: eating, sleeping, and going to the bathroom. After you begin teaching, your dog will soon learn where his special places are, or he may even make his own with your help. You should decide before your Poodle arrives what spaces in your home will work best as dog spaces. In the following sections, I show you how to select your Poodle's eating, sleeping, and potty spots. Check out Chapter 6 for details on introducing these spots to your Poodle.

Selecting special spaces doesn't mean your Poodle can't use other places in and around the house. Poodles want, and need, to be with their families. Teaching a spot just means that if you choose your bedroom or a plush bed in the family room as your dog's sleeping spot, he'll be less apt to decide the sofa suits him best.

The eating spot

Many families feed the family dog in the kitchen. The location is convenient, and the floor (commonly tile or hardwood) can take any spills. Your Poodle's eating spot doesn't have to be fancy or take up much space. Your Poodle doesn't need candles, flowers, or a linen napkin. He just needs enough room for his food dish and his water bowl (see the earlier section "Savoring the Details of Food and Bowls"). You can put the dishes on a doggy placemat to catch spills and to prevent the dishes from scooting around on the floor.

Wherever you want to feed your dog, make sure you're consistent. If you are, at mealtime, you'll find your Poodle waiting at his eating spot.

The sleeping spot

For your Poodle's sleeping area, you want a draft-free spot that's out of the main traffic pattern of the house. One of the best places for your Poodle's sleeping spot is your bedroom. You may want him to sleep in his crate or on a bed in the corner, but simply letting your Poodle sleep with you near gives him eight hours in your presence.

If you prefer your dog to sleep out of your bedroom, give him a good bed or a comfortable crate, and put him to bed in his draft-free spot each night. If you're consistent, he'll soon get figure out that he has his own sleeping spot. When I tell my dogs that it's bedtime, they dash for their crates and for the goodnight biscuits they know they'll get!

The potty spot

Your Poodle's potty spot should be outside if possible, which will take a bit of training on your part. The key is consistency. Use the same door all the time for going out, and try to return to the same location in your yard. Your Poodle's nose will tell him that he's gone in that spot before.

If you have a Toy or a Mini and you live in an apartment, you may decide to litter train your Poodle. In this case, the same rules apply. Take your Poodle to his litter box on a regular basis. When you clean up his box, leave a bit of dirty litter to remind your Poodle what the box is for.

Even if you want to use paper training or housetraining pads, the same techniques apply. Just keep the box or papers in the same spot in your home. Good locations are utility rooms and bathrooms. Don't decide after a week that the potty spot should be in a different location. Decide on a good spot and leave the training tools there permanently.

Check out Chapter 9 for full details on housetraining.

Scheduling a Checkup with Your Vet

One important task you should complete before you welcome your Poodle home is to make an appointment with a veterinarian. It may or may not be time for your Poodle to have a booster shot, but you should get your puppy a physical as soon as possible. If he has some minor health issue, the sooner you treat it, the better.

If you have a contract with your breeder that says your breeder will take back the puppy if he has a serious health problem, have a vet check your puppy within the window of time specified in the contract. See Chapter 4 for more information about breeder contracts.

If you already have a family vet, you know whom you'll go to see. Otherwise, try to get a recommendation from a friend, or choose a vet you've already checked out. You may decide to switch vets down the line, but for now, don't delay in getting your puppy looked at. Chapter 14 has full details on selecting and visiting a vet.

Chapter 6

Welcoming Your Poodle Home

In This Chapter

▶ Taking your Poodle home

▶ Showing your Poodle around the house

▶ Introducing family members (of all kinds) to your Poodle

▶ Getting through the first night

▶ Anticipating and solving potential problems

*I*f you're jumping into this chapter, you've most likely chosen the Poodle that's right for you. Congratulations! (If not, you can head to Chapter 4 to find out how.) This chapter gives you tips for picking up your Poodle and introducing her to the rest of the family, to other pets, and to her designated spaces (see Chapter 5), all with a minimal level of stress for both of you. I also show you how to make it through the first night with ease and how to handle any problems that may crop up at the outset.

Picking Up Your Poodle

The big day has arrived. Your wonderful Poodle is finally joining the family. Things may seem a little hectic at first, so take a minute to plan ahead so that the first day at home goes smoothly for both you and the Poodle. In the following sections, I explain how to choose the best day and time for pickup, the items to bring home along with the Poodle, and how to transport your Poodle safely.

Selecting the right day and the right time

Ideally, your Poodle should join the family on a day when you can devote your time to getting her settled. Weekend days are a good choice because no one is rushing to get to work or school, and everyone can help out. If you decide to pick up the Poodle on a

Saturday, try to get her in the morning. That gives you two full days before the Monday-morning routine.

If you want to get your Poodle on a Friday, go as early in the afternoon as you can. If you go too late in the day, your Poodle may only have time for a quick tour before bedtime, which may make it harder for her to get to sleep. Even if you do follow this advice, though, odds are your puppy will cry the first night or two. Even an adult Poodle that you adopt may whine a bit.

Another option for bringing your Poodle home is at the beginning of a vacation. By spending the family vacation at home, you and your Poodle have plenty of time to adjust to each other.

If your schedule is just too crazy for a long introduction, and Wednesday night after supper is the only time you can pick up the Poodle, that's okay, too. In time, you'll all adjust.

Taking home other items besides the Poodle

Most likely, you're picking up your puppy from a breeder (see Chapter 4 for details on places to find a Poodle). At the appointed time, you arrive at the breeder's pickup location, and he gives you your adorable Poodle puppy. However, that's not all you should receive. The breeder should also give you the following:

- A three-generation pedigree
- The American Kennel Club (AKC) registration slip (see Chapter 2 for more information on the AKC and Chapter 4 for more on pedigrees and registrations)
- Your puppy's health record and health guarantee
- A sales contract
- A two- or three-day supply of whatever food your puppy has been eating

As long as you know what kind of food your puppy has been eating, you can get your own if the breeder doesn't offer some. However, you should make sure that you leave with a bill of sale (and/or a contract), the registration slip, and the health information. Don't pay for and accept a puppy without these items.

Whatever else your breeder gives you, the most important extra item you can get is his phone number. Reputable breeders want the best for their puppies and for the people who buy them.

You should be able to call your breeder if you have a question or problem, and he should be happy to help you. Don't just call with problems, either. Your breeder will be delighted to hear that your darling graduated from kindergarten or behaved perfectly at the groomer's office.

If you're picking up an older Poodle from a shelter, you'll probably just get the dog. However, if you ask, the shelter also may give you health records if the Poodle has been vaccinated and/or spayed or neutered. The pickup policies of rescue organizations vary; one may send a dog to a new home with some food and a favorite toy. Others come prepared with registration papers, but most of the time shelters can't provide them.

Traveling home safely

If your breeder gives you a crate, or if you already have a crate, be sure to use it for the ride home. The crate makes the trip home safe and simple. You can line the crate with newspaper to help absorb accidents and add a bit of toweling or a blanket for the puppy's comfort. A cuddly toy may keep the puppy happy. (See Chapter 5 for full details on selecting a crate for your Poodle.)

Is it wise to get a Christmas puppy?

Christmas has long been the one holiday that is *not* considered a good time to get a new puppy. Many breeders refuse to sell puppies two weeks before or two weeks after Christmas. The reason for this reluctance is that Christmas is a hectic time, with a lot of activities, friends, and relatives hustling in and out, leaving little time for puppy care. Puppies need structure, especially as housetraining begins, and the Christmas break may not allow for that structure.

Lately, some shelters have found that if a family fully understands the demands of a new pet, the Christmas break gives the family the time it needs with the pet, and the adoption works quite well.

If you think Christmas break can work, consider the age of your children. For families with very young children, I still say Christmas is a bad time. For homes with older children or adults-only homes, it may work, but Christmas time still wouldn't be my first choice. In fact, I'd prefer getting a puppy when housetraining didn't mean bundling up and wading through snowdrifts every hour or two.

And, no matter what anyone says, Christmas Day is too hectic for getting a puppy. Put a lead and a collar, dog dishes, or a training book (or this book!) under the tree, and pick up your puppy the week after Christmas.

If you don't have a crate yet, you can use a cardboard box and add the same items. Make sure the box is high enough so that your new puppy can't scramble out during the ride home. If your new dog is an adult and you don't have a crate, you should invest in a special seatbelt harness to keep your Poodle secure during the ride. (See Chapter 12 for more tips on traveling with your Poodle.)

Giving Your Poodle the Grand Tour

You shouldn't just turn your Poodle loose to explore when she first gets to her new home. You need to be a tour guide and structure her exploration. Help make the introduction to her new home a positive experience. You can start with a brief visit to the yard so she has a chance to eliminate, which lessens the chance of an accident in the house. After this trip, take your Poodle to the following spots (see Chapter 5 for details on selecting specific places in your home):

1. **The eating spot:** Take your Poodle to the spot you've chosen for her food and water dishes (Chapter 5 lets you know what kind of dishes to buy). Give her a chance to take a drink, if she wants one. Put a few tasty treats in her bowl. Don't worry if she doesn't eat them; she may be too overwhelmed, but at least she knows that she's in the right spot for food. (See Chapter 7 for more on a Poodle's diet.)

2. **The sleeping spot:** The next stop should be your Poodle's bed, which may be her crate at first (see Chapter 5 for info on buying bedding). Wherever you've decided to put her crate, take your Poodle to that spot, and put her in her crate. Depending on how long the trip was from the breeder (or shelter) to your home, you may want to let her have a little rest. Keep people and other pets away from the crate and let her have a nap.

3. **The potty spot:** When the nap is over, take your Poodle directly to her potty spot. If your Poodle went to the bathroom in the yard when you first got home, take her back to that same area. Her nose can tell her that she's in the right spot. If she goes, praise her.

   If you've decided that you're going to paper-train your Poodle or teach her to use a litter box, take her to the appropriate area indoors. Your puppy may have a few accidents before she becomes housetrained, but the sooner you start taking her to the appropriate area and the sooner she starts using it, the faster and easier housetraining is. (Head to Chapter 9 for full details on housetraining.)

Meeting Other Family Members

Having a Poodle come into your home for the first time is a life-changing event for you — and for the other members of your household. Other family members may be children, or they may be different kinds of animals — dogs, cats, guinea pigs, and so on. Your job as a tour guide isn't over yet; you need to introduce your Poodle to whoever and whatever lives beneath your roof.

Kids in the house

Your children were probably in on the Poodle-selection process, because most breeders won't sell puppies to families with children until they've seen the children with the puppies. Besides, how do you manage to keep children out of the selection process after they know about it? Your children also may have gone with you when you picked up your Poodle (see the previous sections of this chapter). If the kids remained at home, however, and haven't seen the Poodle since the selection was made, now's the time to reintroduce them.

If you have young children, have them sit on the floor before you hand them the puppy. Supervise the interaction. Toddlers may want to grab the puppy from a sibling. Teach them that puppies aren't toys, and that they need to be gentle. No grabbing or pulling any part of the puppy.

If you have a baby, have one person hold the baby and someone else hold the dog on a loose lead. Allow the dog to smell the baby. Praise the dog and offer a treat. If you have a puppy, have everyone sit on the floor. Let the puppy smell the baby, but don't let her mouth the baby. (Mouthing is covered in Chapter 10.) Always supervise contact.

Never leave a baby alone with a dog. Babies are even more defenseless than puppies. Dogs can nip, and nails can scratch, and in more serious situations, a baby's high-pitched noises can trigger a dog's instinctive response to nearby prey. Introduce your baby and Poodle, but never leave them alone together.

After introductions, you should teach your children how to pick up the Poodle. A puppy shouldn't be grabbed around the middle like a teddy bear. A person should slip a hand under the puppy's chest and use the other hand to cradle the hindquarters. Hold the puppy firmly but gently against your chest. Very small children may not be able to manage this, so you should have them sit on the floor so you can put the puppy in their laps. Discourage children under the age of 8 from ever picking up the puppy. It's too easy for a young child to drop a squirming puppy and injure her.

Playtime is good for both children and puppies, but remember that all youngsters need naps. Supervise the play between your children and puppy, and then put the puppy in her crate for her nap.

Depending on the age of your kids, you may want to let them help care for the Poodle. Even children under the age of 7 may be able to fill the water dish. A child of 10 or 12 can take the dog out to the yard or feed her. Just remember that your Poodle is a living entity, and that you're responsible for her care. If your children forget their dog chores, you still need to make sure your Poodle is fed, watered, and exercised. If you have a puppy, make sure you leave housetraining chores to adults or teenagers who have a better sense of how to stick to a schedule.

You need to use caution when introducing an adult Poodle as well. A full-grown Standard Poodle can intimidate a small child, not to mention knock him down. Sit the child in a chair, and keep the dog on her lead for introductions. As with puppies, allow no grabbing or pulling of any part of the dog.

Other pets

In the following sections, I explain how to introduce your new Poodle to other pets in your home, including dogs, cats, and smaller animals.

Other dogs

Most adult dogs are just fine with puppies. They seem to recognize that the puppies are young and helpless, but you should still supervise their initial meeting to avoid trouble.

Introduce your resident dog to the new dog out in the yard, not in the house. Your current dog may be more territorial in the house. If you have more than one dog, let them meet the newcomer individually. Supervise the introductions. You don't have to leash your resident dog, but if you feel safer with the dogs on leads, keep the leads loose. Sometimes, a dog on a lead can be more aggressive than one that's loose — especially if the lead is tight.

Even if introductions go smoothly, be careful that the puppy doesn't try to eat from the adult dog's food dish. Even friendly dogs can get cranky if another dog tries to steal their food. Give treats separately for the same reason.

Cats and smaller animals

If you have an adult cat that's used to dogs, he probably can accept the Poodle with no fuss, but you should still make the introduction carefully. A bouncy Poodle may earn a scratch on the nose!

If your cat isn't used to dogs, you should take things even slower. Use the following steps to introduce your Poodle to your feline:

1. Before you bring the Poodle into the house, put your cat in a room and close the door.

2. Let the cat and the dog get to know each other by way of the crack under the door. Let them sniff each other.

3. When you finally open the door, make sure the Poodle is in her crate or in an exercise pen (see Chapter 5). This way, the cat can approach the dog at his own pace, and the dog can't chase or pounce on the cat.

The whole introduction process may take several days, depending on how accepting of the Poodle your cat is. When the cat seems comfortable with the dog, hold your Poodle for the first nose-to-nose meeting. Continue to watch the animals as the days go by. It may take awhile, but eventually your cat and dog will probably become best friends.

If you have a friend with a cat-friendly dog, invite your friend and dog over for a visit before you bring your Poodle home. Your cat doesn't have to actually meet the dog, but it may help get him used to the idea of a dog.

You have a few other tricks up your sleeve to make your house a Poodle/cat friendly place:

✔ Make sure that your cat always has a place to escape the Poodle's attentions. Put a baby gate in a doorway of a "safe room." Your cat can jump in, but your Poodle is kept out.

✔ If putting up a gate isn't possible, make sure your cat has a high area in every room for escaping purposes. Clear off the top of a dresser or a shelf on a bookcase.

✔ Don't let either animal pester the other when they're eating or using the litter box. And speaking of the litter box, you may want to keep it out of your Poodle's reach for another reason. Many dogs consider litter-box contents a tasty treat. (Eeeewwww!)

You've probably seen pictures of a dog snuggling a rabbit or a parakeet sitting on a dog's head, but these images are the exceptions. Protect your other pets from your dog. Put cages up high so that your dog can't reach them, or put them in a room that's off limits to the dog. If you like to let your bird out for exercise or want your bunny out for playtime, put your dog in her crate.

Surviving the First Night

You've given your Poodle a tour of your place and made the proper introductions. Now's the time to settle down for the night. This may be where your adorable Poodle stops seeming so adorable.

Up until now, your Poodle has had her mom and her siblings. She's slept in a pile of puppies, and the humans in her life have always been there. Now she's in a strange house. She's on her own, with no mother and no brothers and sisters. It shouldn't surprise you that she may whine and cry the first night or two (or three).

You can try a few of the following tips to help make your Poodle comfortable and more willing to settle down and go to sleep:

- ✔ Give her a little something to eat. She's more apt to curl up and fall asleep if she's full.

- ✔ Take her out for a final potty break before bedtime.

- ✔ Make sure her bed is warm and cozy. If she gets cold, she may wake up, and if she wakes up, chances are you need to make another trip to the yard.

- ✔ A ticking clock may help to calm your Poodle. Wrap the clock in an old towel or soft shirt. You also can purchase beds and pillows that produce the sound of a heartbeat for up to 30 minutes.

With luck, these tips can help your puppy drift off to dreamland. Or, you may end up with a puppy who's inconsolable. She's warm, well-fed, and has just gone to the bathroom; yet, she's whining or crying loudly and pathetically. It's enough to break your heart! But you need to harden your heart. Eventually, she'll stop crying and fall asleep, and so will you.

Many breeders begin crate training at seven weeks, teaching the puppies to spend time alone in a crate away from the litter. This makes it much easier for a puppy to adjust to a new home away from littermates. Ask your breeder if he does this or can do this with your puppy so that the change of scenery isn't so sudden and stressful.

Anticipating Possible Problems and Planning Sensible Solutions

One old saying states that "an ounce of prevention is worth a pound of cure." It's much easier to teach your Poodle the right way to do something than it is to retrain her or to break her of a bad habit. This section helps you supply the "ounce" of prevention so you'll never need the "pound."

Avoiding bad habits from the outset

Nothing is cuter than a puppy, but if you're not careful, that adorable Poodle can have you wrapped around her paw in no time. Enjoy her puppyhood, but don't let her develop bad habits that you'll have a hard time breaking in the future.

If you're prepared to share your bed for the next 14 years or so with your Poodle, you can welcome her to your pillow top. However, if you don't want to share your bed, especially with a Standard Poodle, don't start this habit.

The same goes for furniture. You can teach your Poodle not to snooze on the sofa. The best way to do that is to never let her up on the sofa in the first place. Decide now what your policy is going to be, and stick with it. Make sure all the members of the family know the rules and obey them.

 If you bring home an adult Poodle, she may already have certain habits. If she's used to sleeping on the couch, but you don't want her to continue this habit, be firm and consistent about removing her. Encourage her to lie in a special spot by giving her treats and plenty of praise. You also can cover your sofa with a washable throw and let her sleep there if the habit proves hard to break.

 You don't have to be an ogre, but be firm and consistent, and start her training immediately. If you have questions about behavior, call your breeder for advice. Put his number on speed dial now. (See Chapter 10 for tips on instilling good manners in your Poodle.)

Handling food issues

Your Poodle should be doing just fine on whatever food your breeder or the shelter recommends, but sometimes that isn't the case, as you can see in the following scenarios:

- ✔ Sometimes, a food that's perfect for all the other puppies in the litter is just too rich for one of them. If your puppy is regurgitating her food, this could be why. If she seems healthy otherwise, she's active, and she has no temperature, her problem may be the food. Gradually (over the span of a week) switch to another food. If your Poodle still has a problem, see your veterinarian. (Chapter 14 has tips on selecting the right vet for your Poodle.)

 ✔ Another consideration is that your Poodle is being too active right after a meal. Let your dog rest or quietly explore right after a meal, and discourage rough and tumble games.

Chapter 7 has full details on feeding your Poodle.

Getting used to grooming

By the time you pick up your Poodle puppy at 8 or 10 weeks, she should've been clipped several times in a puppy clip, which calls for the shaving of the face, feet, and tail (see Chapter 8). The sooner the breeder starts clipping, the more comfortable the Poodle will be with it. If you put off grooming until your Poodle gets older, she'll be very frightened of the clippers and may never be as accepting of grooming practices. As soon as you get your Poodle, make an appointment with a good groomer for no more than four weeks later. If you want to learn how to clip your Poodle yourself, ask the groomer if you can observe.

Grooming is going to be a big part of your Poodle's life. Whether you intend to show your Poodle (see Chapter 13) or just keep her in a pet clip, you have a lot of brushing and trimming ahead of you. Start with the following tips:

 ✔ **Handle your Poodle's feet daily.** You don't need to actually cut her nails, but hold her paws in your hand. Give her treats. If you plan to use a grinder instead of nail clippers, turn on the grinder and hold one of your dog's paw on it. Let her feel the vibration and get used to the noise.

 ✔ **Brush your dog daily.** This beauty routine doesn't have to be a full grooming session. Just run the brush over her body. Start teaching her to hold still while you brush. She can either stand or lie down for these brief grooming sessions. As an adult — especially if your dog is a Standard Poodle — grooming takes some time, and she may be more comfortable lying down. If you intend to groom your Poodle yourself, invest in a grooming table.

If you adopt an adult Poodle, you can safely assume that she's used to the grooming process. You can play it safe by applying these same tips to your adult Poodle. Chapter 8 gives you more detailed information about grooming, but for now, just start slow and get your Poodle comfortable with the process.

Chapter 7

Providing Your Poodle with a Nutritious Diet

At first, you feed your Poodle whatever food your breeder recommends, but as time goes by, you may decide to change to another brand of food. This chapter discusses your choices when it comes to offering your dog a balanced diet. I also explain how to create a feeding routine, show you how to alter your Poodle's diet as he grows, and point out foods that all Poodles must avoid.

Knowing the Nutrients that Your Poodle Needs

Although you may think of your Poodle as a carnivore, needing primarily protein and fat in the form of meat, that's only half right. Dogs also need carbohydrates, vitamins, and minerals to stay healthy.

In the wild, carnivores eat "the good stuff" first, which isn't muscle meat and fat, but the internal organs. They eat the stomach and intestines and get vegetable matter from that, and they eat heart, liver, kidneys, and brains, which are full of vitamins and minerals, as well as protein. (Sounds tasty, doesn't it?)

You can cruise the pet aisle at the supermarket and find a ready-made food that meets your Poodle's dietary requirements. Whether you decide to go with dry, canned, or semi-moist dog food (all of which I cover later in this chapter), read the label so you understand just what your Poodle is getting at mealtime. Figure 7-1 shows a typical dog food label.

Ingredients: Chicken, Corn Meal, Chicken By-Product Meal, Ground Grain Sorghum, Ground Whole Grain Barley, Chicken Meal, Chicken Fat (preserved with mixed Tocopherols, a source of Vitamin E, and Citric Acid), Dried Beet Pulp (sugar removed), Natural Chicken Flavor, Dried Egg Product, Brewers Dried Yeast, Potassium Chloride, Salt, Choline Chloride, Calcium Carbonate, DL-Methionine, Ferrous Sulfate, Vitamin E Supplement, Zinc Oxide, Ascorbic Acid (source of Vitamin C), Dicalcium Phosphate, Manganese Sulfate, Copper Sulfate, Manganese Oxide, Vitamin B_{12} Supplement, Vitamin A Acetate, Calcium Pantothenate, Biotin, Lecithin, Rosemary Extract, Thiamine Mononitrate (source of Vitamin B_1), Niacin, Riboflavin Supplement (source of Vitamin B_2), Pyridoxine Hydrochloride (source of Vitamin B_6), Inositol, Vitamin D_3 Supplement, Potassium Iodide, Folic Acid, Cobalt Carbonate.

Guaranteed Analysis:
Crude Protein not less than 26.0%
Crude Fat not less than 14.0%
Crude Fiber not more than 4.0%
Moisture not more than 10.0%

Animal feeding tests using Association of American Feed Control Official's procedures substantiate that this product provides complete and balanced nutrition for adult dogs.

DOG'S LIFE
DOG FOOD®

Figure 7-1: A label tells you a lot about the nutrients in your Poodle's food.

The first five ingredients are important. Ingredients are listed by quantity, from most to least. Somewhere in those five, and preferably in first place, should be a meat protein. This ingredient can be beef, chicken, turkey, or lamb. Meat byproducts may also be listed in the first five ingredients. *Byproducts* may not sound too appetizing to us, but your dog loves them. Byproducts include organ meat, and they're full of vitamins and minerals for your dog.

Next on the label is a grain filler. Manufacturers use grain to add bulk to the food. A grain filler is fine, as long as more meat than filler is in the food. Filler grains are corn, wheat, soy, and rice. Fillers supply carbohydrates and smaller amounts of protein and vitamins. You may want to take note of the following filler facts:

✔ **Corn** is in most dog foods because it's cheap.

✔ **Wheat and soy,** along with corn, may cause allergies, so pay attention to how your dog reacts to his food.

If he's scratching or biting and chewing at his paws, he may be allergic to something in his food. In this instance, you should consider trying another brand of food that uses a different grain or protein source. If the problem continues, consult your veterinarian. (See Chapter 15 for more on allergies.)

✔ **Rice** causes fewer allergic reactions and has become a popular filler for that reason.

Vitamins and minerals, such as B vitamins, vitamin A, vitamin C, vitamin D, calcium, iron, and zinc, are frequently added to dog food to make the food a complete and balanced diet for your dog.

The meaning of AAFCO

On every dog food label you examine, you can see the acronym AAFCO. That stands for American Association of Feed Control Officials, the governing body for all animal feed products. AAFCO sets the guidelines for pet food manufacturers. For instance, under AAFCO regulations, byproducts may not include hair, horn, teeth, hooves, feathers, or manure.

AAFCO regulations also state that all ingredients must be listed, and they must be in order, from the largest amount to the smallest, including preservatives.

Keep in mind, though, that AAFCO regulates quantity, not quality. It's still up to you to decide which food offers the best nutrition for your Poodle. For more information about AAFCO, check out www.aafco.org.

Fat in dog foods usually comes from the protein source. A food containing chicken will have chicken fat. This isn't always true, but the label will specify the type of fat, such as beef, chicken, or lamb.

You may also see preservatives listed on the label. Preservatives are added to the food to give it a longer shelf life and to keep the food from spoiling.

Your dog food label includes a *guaranteed analysis,* which tells you the percentage of ingredients, such as protein, fat, and fiber. The more active your dog, the higher protein content you want. If your dog is overweight, consider foods with less fat. The food may have a higher percentage than the analysis lists, but it can't have less.

Dishing Out Main Meals

Snacks and training treats are a part of your dog's daily diet, but most of your Poodle's nutritional needs are met during his scheduled meals. In the following sections, I go over several options for a Poodle's regular meals.

Choosing among dry, canned, and semi-moist foods

Most Poodle owners opt to feed their pooches dry, canned, or semi-moist food. In the following sections, I explore the pros and cons of each of these doggy dishes.

Many foods may come in separate varieties for puppies, adults, or seniors. Puppy foods tend to have more protein, and senior foods contain both less protein and less fat. Even adult foods may vary as far as protein goes. You can find foods for active dogs that contain more protein and fat than food for the average pet.

Dry food

Dry food is a popular option for many dog owners. It's relatively inexpensive and keeps for a long time. If you have multiple dogs, this option is the easiest and cheapest. Dry food gives your dog something to chew, if he doesn't just inhale his food like my male, and if you decide to free feed your dog, that is, leave food out all the time, dry food won't spoil. (See "Having food available all the time," later in this chapter, for more about free feeding.)

Dry food varies in quality. While the cheap brands may have the necessary nutrients (listed on the label), these foods may not always be in a form that is readily absorbed by your Poodle. They may keep a dog alive, but many are barely adequate nutritionally.

Kibble size, that is, the size of each individual piece of food, does make a difference to your Poodle. Small dogs like Toy Poodles need more calcium and phosphorus than large dogs like Standard Poodles and have higher energy needs than large dogs. They can get what they need with a smaller, denser piece of food.

Canned food

Dry food may be the choice of humans, but if your Poodle could talk, he'd probably vote for canned food. Canned food smells great to your dog — if not to you — and tastes great, too (at least that's what my dogs tell me). Most canned foods have a higher meat content by volume and less grain filler. (See the previous section for more on dog food ingredients.)

Canned foods are more expensive. And after you open the can, you have to use it within a day or two and refrigerate the unused portion. Canned food can spoil if you leave it out all day, so it's not a good choice for free feeding.

If you like the convenience and price of dry food, but your Poodle adores canned, consider adding a bit of canned food to the dry when you feed your dog. Just mix in a spoonful or two of the canned, and your Poodle can get the great flavor he loves at a fraction of the price. Another trick is to soak dry food in beef or chicken broth to make it more appealing.

Semi-moist food

Semi-moist food is the most expensive of the three types of food. The shape of semi-moist food generally looks like people food — like a hamburger patty. While this food may have the vitamins and minerals your dog needs, it may also have added food coloring, sugar, flour, and preservatives to keep the patty in a desirable shape. The sugar and flour are empty calories your dog doesn't need. Semi-moist food may also contain more artificial preservatives.

Semi-moist food does have the advantage of coming in little pouches, so it's convenient if you're traveling.

Doing some home cooking

If you want to feed your Poodle a natural diet but aren't comfortable with feeding raw (see the following section), you can cook for your dog. Puppies, as well as adult Poodles, can thrive on a properly balanced home-cooked diet.

To give your Poodle the benefits of fresh meat and bones, you can feed him chicken, but you need to kill all the harmful bacteria and soften the hard bones that splinter or become impacted in the dog's digestive tract. Here are some ways to provide healthy protein:

- ✔ Put chicken legs in a slow cooker, cover with water, and cook on low for 24 hours. This reduces the bones to mush.

- ✔ Cook chicken wings in a pressure cooker, with 15 pounds of pressure for 75 minutes for a pint jar of wings.

You also need to cook up vegetables and grains and add supplements to make sure your home cooking offers a balanced diet. Oatmeal, barley, and rice are all good grains to use, and you can use a wide range of vegetables. (Just stay away from onions as they can cause hemolytic anemia.) Cooking the vegetables helps break down the cell walls so your dog gets the benefits; otherwise, dogs can't break down the cellulose. Add vitamin supplements after you've cooked the food (liquid baby vitamins are an easy way to add vitamins). Some people like to feed meat at one meal and the veggies and grains at another; others mix everything all together. As with raw, you can freeze individual portions for later use.

Before you decide on either a raw or a home-cooked diet for your dog, make sure you have the time, as well as the desire. Cooking up large batches and freezing them saves time, but remember that this isn't a short-term project. You're cooking for the life of your Poodle, which can be anywhere from 14 to 18 years. Also, you may need to invest in a freezer.

Getting the scoop on raw foods

BARF is the unfortunate acronym for a raw food diet. It stands for Bones And Raw Food, or Biologically Appropriate Raw Food. Either way, it means you reject processed dog foods in favor of raw foods, similar to what a wild canine eats. In the following sections, I help you evaluate whether a raw diet is appropriate for your Poodle and explain how to start one safely.

Deciding whether to use a raw diet

People are either enthusiastic supporters or totally against feeding raw. Those devotees who feed raw report healthier, more-energetic dogs with whiter teeth and shinier coats. On the other hand, critics say that the harmful bacteria in uncooked food present a danger. Supporters say that the dog's short digestive system doesn't let those bacteria stay in the body long enough to cause harm.

While many feeders of raw food are convinced their dogs are healthier on this diet, to date, no controlled research indicates that this is the case. You should give serious consideration to the risk/benefit ratio before deciding on this or any other diet for your Poodle. Both salmonella and E. coli may be in raw foods, and even if your dog can handle these, you run the chance of spreading them to your own foods if you don't maintain strict sanitary conditions when preparing the food. Always clean preparation surfaces thoroughly and wash all utensils in warm, soapy water.

If you decide to try the BARF diet with your Poodle, remember that it's more than just meat and bones. No matter what kind of food you give your dog, the diet still needs to be balanced. People who feed raw may add supplements (such as B vitamins, vitamin C, vitamin E, fish oil, flaxseed oil, cod liver oil, kelp and alfalfa powders, and unsulphured blackstrap molasses) to their dog's meals, and they also feed the pooches a variety of foods.

Talk to your veterinarian before starting a raw food diet. If she approves, she may have suggestions for making the diet balanced. If she's against raw diets, but you're going to feed raw anyway, have her do a blood scan on your Poodle before your start, and then schedule one every six months. A blood scan allows your vet to monitor the effects of the diet, and you continue working with her, which may be a better option than finding a new vet.

Putting your Poodle on a raw diet

Typically, dogs on a raw diet are fed raw, meaty bones each morning. If you have a Toy Poodle, that may be one chicken neck. A Miniature may eat two or three. For a Standard, you can use something larger, like turkey necks. The evening meal alternates between muscle meat, organ meat, and vegetables. If you start your puppy on raw foods, crush or grind bones to make chewing, swallowing, and digesting easier.

The "raw" in a raw diet refers to the meat and bones. Vegetables need to be processed in a blender or food processor or lightly cooked to break down the cellulose. Dogs don't produce the necessary enzymes to digest cellulose, so, unless you start the process, the vegetables pass through your dog's system untouched. If you're adding grains, like rice or oatmeal, to the diet, cook those first. Cook potatoes as well, if you want to add a few for variety.

Most people who feed raw cook up a large batch of vegetables and grain and then freeze individual portions. You need freezer space for those individual portions, as well as space for the raw foods.

Find a good butcher who can supply you with the meaty bones and organ meats that you need. If you live in a larger city, a pet supply shop in your area may stock frozen raw bones, turkey necks, tripe, and packages of raw meat mixed with vegetables.

Steering clear of table scraps

Before the advent of commercial dog foods, many dogs lived on table scraps. Today, people have a better understanding of what a dog needs for a balanced diet, and table scraps aren't the recommended choice for your dog.

It's fine to add a bit of lean meat or a few vegetables to your Poodle's dinner bowl. Just make sure that you're just adding a tasty treat and not making those leftovers your dog's entire meal. As much as you consider your dog a part of the family, a dog isn't a person, and he needs a different diet to stay healthy.

Keeping water, water everywhere

Fresh, clean water is as important a part of your Poodle's diet as the vitamins and minerals he needs. Keep a clean bowl full of water where your dog has access to it at all times. I keep a bowl in the kitchen, and my dogs always have fresh water in their crates, too.

If you have an outdoor run or you're in the yard playing with your Poodle, make sure that he has water available. In hot weather, I increase the number of ice cubes I give my dogs as well. They may not stop to have a drink, but they always happily munch down an ice cube or two.

Check the water level in bowls during hot weather. Poodles enjoy playing in water and may paw and splash in the bowl. You may also want to set the bowl on a folded bath towel to catch the overflow.

Giving Snacks and Treats Smartly

Technically, your Poodle will do just fine with his regular meals, eating nothing in between, but realistically, most people feed their dogs goodies at other times. Food rewards are useful for training, and resisting those pleading eyes when you're enjoying a bowl of popcorn in front of the television can be on the verge of painful. In the following sections, I give you some tips on feeding snacks and treats to your Poodle.

Giving out snacks

It's easy to say that dogs should eat their regular meals, and that's it. No added goodies are necessary. Easy to say, but very hard to follow. My dogs all get a dog biscuit when they go into their kennels, a piece of carrot after breakfast, a morsel of cheese at lunchtime, and, if we have pizza, they're in line for a bite of crust. My male is passionate about mashed potatoes, and who am I to deny those pleading brown eyes a spoonful of potatoes?

It's easy to see that snacking can get out of hand. You need to set some rules, like the following:

✔ Snacks and treats should never make up more than ten percent of your dog's total diet.

✔ Avoid too much people food. A sliver of turkey at Thanksgiving is fine, but hold off on the rich gravy. A spoonful of canned pumpkin makes a fine low-cal treat, but pumpkin pie can be too rich and spicy. Almost any vegetable adds a low-calorie treat to the food dish. (Check out "Avoiding Certain Foods," later in this chapter, for people food no-nos.)

Trying treats

Most dogs eat anything and everything, so it's up to you to provide snacks that are both good and tasty. I cover several types of treats in the following sections.

Tasty rewards

The pet aisle in the supermarket is lined with all kinds of doggy treats, from hard, crunchy biscuits to treats stuffed with cheese or peanut butter to chewy jerky-type treats. Any or all of these morsels make good rewards for your Poodle, and some of the softer treats can be broken down into a good size to use when training (which I cover in Chapter 10). You want to give a lot of rewards, not a lot of calories, when you train, and your dog is perfectly happy with smaller morsels.

The softer treats, especially, may have more added sugars, salt, and preservatives, so make treats a treat, not a full meal.

Many types of rubber toys on the market have a place to put a treat. Some even come with a chewy treat. These toys offer play and chewing exercise. A great combo for you and your Poodle!

Rawhide and nylon chews

Rawhide chews are also on the shelf. Many dogs enjoy rawhide chews and never have a problem. In others, the rawhide can sit in an indigestible mass in the stomach or can block the intestines.

Supervise chewing. If your dog is the kind who bites off chunks and swallows, give him a different kind of chew toy. I prefer the rawhide bones that are made of shredded rawhide. The bits of shredded rawhide are too small to do damage, but even those should be given sparingly, especially if you have a dog who chews rapidly.

For long-lasting chewing pleasure, my dogs like the nylon bones. The tiny pieces of nylon pass harmlessly through the system, and the bones are too hard for the dogs to bite off chunks.

If your dog is a very vigorous chewer, he could crack a tooth on a nylon bone.

Establishing a Feeding Routine

In the following sections, I discuss feeding your Poodle at regular times, choosing to have food available all the time, and portioning food correctly.

Feeding at set times

If you're feeding a prepared commercial food, the number of feeding times doesn't make much difference, but raw diets require twice-daily feedings. No matter what you choose to feed your Poodle, he expects his meals regularly. You decide whether you feed your adult once or twice a day or whether you plan to leave food out all the time (see the next section).

Consistency is key! Dogs are creatures of habit, and your dog will anticipate his meal, which means that his digestive juices will begin to flow. An advantage to feeding at regular times, whether once or twice a day, is that if your Poodle isn't feeling well and skips a meal, you know right away.

I prefer twice-a-day meals for all sizes of Poodles. Part of that reason is my feelings. I'd want two meals a day (at least!), so I feel better giving my dogs two. The other part of my reasoning is practical. With Standards, two meals a day can help to prevent bloating, and with Toy dogs, it prevents dangerous dips in blood sugar levels. Toy dogs have a higher metabolism rate than larger dogs as well as smaller stomachs. One meal a day may not give a Toy the nutrition or energy he needs. Twice a day also makes it easier to sneak medications into the food as well.

Having food available all the time

Free feeding, or leaving the food down all day, may work well if you have one dog. If you have more than one, it's harder to keep track of how much food each dog is getting. The more dominant dog may be gobbling it all. Also, you can't really free feed canned, cooked, and raw foods, because they spoil if they sit out all day.

If you do decide to free feed, still ration your Poodle's food. Put down a set amount each day (see the following section for details). When it's gone, it's gone. Don't keep refilling the bowl. That's a good way to get a very pudgy Poodle, and an overweight dog runs a greater risk of arthritis, heart disease, and diabetes.

Knowing how much food to feed

If you read the label on your dog's food, you can generally find a chart suggesting how much food you should give your dog, based on his weight. You can start with that, but it's been my experience that I need to feed less than the recommended amount.

Depending on weight, activity, and age, different size Poodles eat different amounts:

- A Toy may eat between ½ and ¾ of a cup a day
- A Miniature about one cup a day
- A Standard between two and three cups a day

Whatever you feed for an entire day of meals is how much food you would put down if you were free feeding your dog. For instance, if your Standard Poodle eats one cup of food in the morning and another cup at night, you'd put down two cups of food all at once for free feeding. If you feed multiple dogs and the system works for you, add all your daily amounts and offer the food in several dishes.

Changing Your Poodle's Diet as He Grows

You probably start out by feeding your Poodle puppy a specially formulated food only for puppies, but you may wonder just when to make the switch to adult food. For a while, the trend was to feed a puppy food for a full year, but then it turned out that larger dogs do better growing slower. Rapid growth can lead to joint problems, so most breeders and veterinarians recommend making the switch at six months, or even three months of age. Even for Toys and Miniatures, it's fine to start feeding adult food at six months of age, and some people never feed puppy food at all.

If your Poodle, no matter what his size, is a house pet getting an average amount of exercise, regular adult food should be just fine. If, however, you're competing in dog shows or performance events (see Chapter 13 for more about these events), consider a food with a higher protein level to match the energy your dog is expending.

After age seven or so, your Poodle may show signs of aging. Even if he still seems as active as ever, his metabolism can be changing. Talk to your veterinarian. She may run blood tests and, depending on the results, suggest a senior food. Senior foods typically have less protein and fat, and may include supplements such as glucosamine and chondroitin, as well as omega-3 fatty acids to help control arthritis. A senior food may also have omega-6 fatty acids for healthy skin and coat. See Chapter 17 for more about easing your senior Poodle into the golden years.

Avoiding Certain Foods

Your Poodle can share a lot of people food with you, but several foods can cause serious problems and can even be fatal. Here's a list of some foods to keep away from your Poodle:

- ✔ **Alcohol:** No alcoholic beverages, ever. A drunken dog isn't funny, and even a small amount of liquor can cause alcohol poisoning, which can kill your dog.

✔ **Chocolate:** Hold the bon-bons when it comes to treating your dog. Chocolate contains theobromine, which can be fatal. The darker the chocolate, the greater the danger, so while the occasional, accidental M&M may not be harmful, baker's chocolate can be deadly. Guard against cacao shell mulch in the yard, as well. It, too, contains theobromine.

✔ **Coffee and tea:** Both of these items contain caffeine and theobromine, which can cause serious harm to your Poodle.

✔ **Egg whites:** Raw egg whites contain avidin, a protein that binds up the B vitamin biotin, making it impossible for a dog to use the biotin. Cooked egg whites are fine, because cooking changes the character of the avidin, so it can't bind to the biotin.

✔ **Grapes and raisins:** While the occasional grape or raisin may not be cause for alarm, if your Poodle eats an entire bunch of grapes or a box of raisins, call your vet. Raisins or grapes can cause acute renal failure. Your dog may start vomiting within two hours of eating the fruit, or he may have diarrhea, lethargy, or be thirsty. He may also have abdominal pain.

✔ **Macadamia nuts:** Eating too many Macadamia nuts can cause paralysis in your dog. Symptoms include a mild fever and upset stomach. Depending on the size of your Poodle and how many nuts he eats, within 12 to 24 hours his back legs can become paralyzed. The front legs are either unaffected or minimally affected. Within 72 hours, the dog will be fine.

While eating these nuts causes no lasting damage, some dogs may be euthanized because they're misdiagnosed as having a severely injured disc. So, keep the Macadamia nuts away.

✔ **Onions:** It's not just onion breath that is a hazard. Onions can cause hemolytic anemia. Symptoms include pale mucus membranes, loss of energy, and lack of appetite. Your Poodle may also feel the cold more and try to find a warm corner. The dog may have a fever or a rapid heart rate. Treatment may include a blood transfusion and/or vitamin B-12.

✔ **Xylitol:** Xylitol (*zahy*-li-tawl) is an artificial sweetener that can cause a sudden drop in blood sugar, resulting in depression, loss of coordination, and seizures. The most common use for this product is as a sweetener in gum, and even two or three pieces of Xylitol-sweetened gum can be fatal.

Although nicotine isn't a food as in the previous list, tobacco products are just as deadly if your dog ingests them. Keep all tobacco products — cigars, cigarettes, snuff, and chewing tobacco — away from your Poodle.

Chapter 8

Keeping Your Poodle Clean and Attractive

. . . .

In This Chapter

▶ Outlining a grooming schedule

▶ Choosing who will groom your Poodle (or grooming yourself)

▶ Homing in on hair-care concerns

▶ Styling your Poodle in different clips

▶ Caring for your Poodle's nails, eyes, ears, and teeth

. . . .

I can give you some good news and some bad news about your Poodle's curly locks. The good news is that Poodles don't shed. The bad news is that their hair grows continuously. Therefore, grooming is a large part of Poodle care. No matter what size Poodle you own, your dog is definitely not a "wash and wear" breed. This chapter explores all the grooming options for your Poodle pal.

Drawing Up a Grooming Schedule

How often you groom your Poodle — or take her to a professional — depends on the type of clip you want her to have and the length of her hair. For example:

✔ Any size Poodle sporting a show clip (such as continental or English saddle; see the later section "Showing off with show clips") needs grooming every four weeks or less.

✔ A Poodle in a pet clip may be able to go as long as eight weeks, although six weeks is generally the maximum between grooming sessions. (I discuss pet clips in the later section "Keeping it simple with pet clips.")

When I say grooming here, I mean a full grooming session: clipping, scissoring, bathing, and brushing. In between your Poodle's full grooming sessions, you still need to thoroughly brush her, and you also may need to shave her face and feet.

Each Poodle presents different variables that affect grooming schedules. Here's an example grooming schedule for a Poodle in a pet clip:

- ✔ **Brushing:** Brush your Poodle's coat thoroughly two to three times a week, depending on coat length. If the trim is very short, and your Poodle has a harsh coat, once a week should do the trick.

   The texture of your Poodle's coat plays a role in how much grooming attention she needs. The softer the coat, the more likely it is to mat and tangle, meaning you need to groom her more often.

- ✔ **Bathing:** If you take your dog to a professional groomer, he'll take care of bathing. Otherwise, you should bathe your Poodle before any major clipping or scissoring, or every four to six weeks.

- ✔ **Clipping:** If you want to clip the hair between visits to the groomer, once a month should suffice.

- ✔ **Nails:** Nails grow at different rates, but trimming them once a week is a good idea. See "Trimming your Poodle's nails" later in this chapter.

- ✔ **Eyes:** Check your Poodle's eyes at least once a week. If you notice your dog blinking, pawing at her face, or squinting, check her eyes to see if you notice any debris or scratches. See "Keeping an eye on your Poodle's eyes" later in this chapter.

- ✔ **Ears:** Check your Poodle's ears weekly. Clean out excess hair, and make sure they aren't infected. Those lovely earflaps prevent air circulation, providing a perfect atmosphere for yeast infections. Check out "Examining the ears" later in this chapter.

- ✔ **Teeth:** Brush your Poodle's teeth to keep them shining and healthy. Daily is terrific. Two or three times a week is splendid. Once a week isn't bad.

A Poodle in a show trim needs more frequent brushing and trimming than a dog in a shorter pet clip. A dog in a short pet clip may need brushing out only once a week, but a dog in a show trim needs a full to-the-skin brushing every two or three days. Depending on how active the Poodle is, she may need brushing every day.

If you want to keep your Poodle in show trim, but you don't want to groom her yourself, make sure you can find a suitable groomer before you start letting that hair grow. Many grooming shops won't do a show trim on a Poodle. (See the section "Ushering your Poodle to a groomer" later in this chapter.)

Deciding between Professional and Personal Grooming

You need to decide how much, if any, grooming you want to handle on your own. The pros and cons of your options pretty much balance out. If you enjoy grooming and have the time and necessary tools, you can do it yourself. If grooming seems like a chore, and you'd rather spend your money than your time, find a qualified professional groomer. I cover both options in the following sections.

Grooming in your personal Poodle salon

So you're interested in grooming your Poodle on your own. Here's to hoping it goes better than grandma cutting your hair as a child! In the following sections, I describe the pros and cons of grooming your Poodle yourself and list the necessary equipment.

If you do decide to groom yourself, ask your breeder if he can teach you the basics, or study a grooming book, like *Dog Grooming For Dummies* by Margaret H. Bonham (Wiley).

The pros and cons of grooming at home

Grooming your Poodle yourself saves you the regular costs of a professional, but it also requires serious commitment. You need to invest in quality grooming tools, and you need to devote the time to keeping your Poodle properly groomed.

- ✔ It can take six hours to properly brush, bathe, and trim a Standard Poodle.

- ✔ A Miniature Poodle with a moderately long clip can take up to three hours to bathe, dry, and trim. Drying alone can take 30 to 40 minutes.

- ✔ A Toy Poodle will take slightly less time than a Miniature, but give yourself three hours in the beginning.

Grooming is a major commitment of time and effort, but it gives you one-on-one time with your Poodle and can be a wonderful way to bond with your Poodle. With time, you'll gain both confidence and speed in your grooming. Grooming is also a good chance to feel your dog all over and to catch cuts or lumps and deal with them before they become a problem.

The gear you need

Most folks opt to have groomers clip their Poodle pals. But if you plan to do all your own grooming, or if you want to do touch-up work between appointments, get the best equipment you can. I cover different types of combs and brushes in Chapter 5, but if you plan to clip your Poodle, you'll also need clippers and scissors. What's the difference?

- *Clippers* are electric shavers for dogs. They have assorted clipping heads that determine the closeness of the shave.

- *Grooming scissors* are just like the scissors that your barber or hairdresser uses.

Cheaper models of clippers and scissors need sharpening more often and won't last as long. Dull clipper blades are more apt to nick or cut your Poodle, and dull scissors won't give you the even, finished look you want. You can buy high-quality clippers and scissors through dog catalogs, at some pet-supply stores, and at specialty booths at dog shows. You also can talk to your groomer or your personal hairdresser or barber.

Clipper blades can get hot after extensive use. Be careful not to let the blades get so hot that they burn your dog. If the blade is warm, switch blades or spray it with a special blade coolant. (You can find the coolant wherever you got your clippers.) Another option is to wrap a block of artificial ice in a towel, and lay your blades on it to cool. If you use two or three #40 or #50 blades and swap them for a cooled one as they heat up, you can do the close shaving much faster.

Besides all the necessary grooming tools, you'll need a grooming table or another firm, nonslip surface for grooming. Dog-supply stores and catalogs sell special grooming tables, or you can create your own with a sturdy table and a rubber mat. In a pinch, you can put a mat on a countertop or a clothes dryer. Don't even think about home grooming without some kind of a raised surface. Your back and knees will never survive. A table also makes it easier to control your Poodle.

It's ideal if you have room in your home for your own permanent grooming area. It's much easier to follow a regular schedule if you don't have to set up the table and gather all your tools every time you groom.

Ushering your Poodle to a groomer

In the following sections, I explain the pros and cons of taking your Poodle to a groomer, and I give you tips on how to find a good groomer for your Poodle.

The pros and cons of professional grooming

When you take your Poodle to a groomer, you know that your pet will be washed, bathed, trimmed, have a pedicure, and have her ears cleaned. The grooming will be done properly and on a regular schedule (that you may set with your groomer; see the earlier section "Drawing Up a Grooming Schedule"). Necessary tasks won't slide because you're too tired, want to go out, have to work late, or have to report for carpool duty.

You need to keep regularly scheduled appointments no matter what. If you need to cancel, it may be hard to reschedule before your Poodle's coat gets a bit wild. If you forget to cancel and don't show up, you'll likely have to pay for the appointment anyway.

Here are more benefits of calling on the services of a groomer:

✔ If you want to try a new look, the groomer can give you some options and will know what to do. You aren't stuck with the simple pet clip that your breeder showed you how to do.

✔ You really don't need to buy a grooming table, a dryer, or clippers, although you still need a brush and a comb to keep your Poodle looking presentable between visits to the grooming shop.

Conversely, a groomer will, over the years, cost you more money than grooming yourself. The cost will be anywhere from $50 to $150 for a Standard and $35 to $50 for a Toy or Miniature. These prices are for pet clips. Show clips are much more. Most groomers also charge extra if the coat is matted. You have to decide if the fees are worth it for what you save in time and in grooming supplies. Also, you may find that the groomer closest to you doesn't work with many Poodles or does only pet clips, so you may have to drive farther to search for a suitable groomer.

If you're considering showing your Poodle, remember that most grooming shops don't do show trims. You may have to do the trimming yourself or send your dog to shows with a professional handler.

Finding a good groomer

Finding a good groomer for your Poodle may be harder than you think, depending on where you're located, so you need to find some good resources. Start by asking your breeder for recommendations. If you have friends or know of people who own Poodles, ask them whom they use. Your veterinarian may have some suggestions. You also can look online or in your phone book.

When you have a prospective groomer in your sights, visit the shop to investigate and talk to the owner before you make an appointment. Keep your eyes peeled for the following:

- ✔ Grooming shops should be as neat and clean as possible. Make sure the shop doesn't smell. If a groomer is working on a dog, hair will fall on the floor and the table, but someone should sweep it up in between sessions.

- ✔ Watch how the groomers handle the dogs. A groomer may need to be firm with a dog, but that doesn't mean jerking on the animal or hitting it.

- ✔ Visit at the end of the day, when groomed Poodles are going home. Do they look the way you want your Poodle to look?

- ✔ Do the dogs seem happy (or at least calm)? Watch the groomers at work. Are they gentle?

Getting to the Root of Hair Care

Keeping your Poodle's coat healthy, clean, and tangle- and mat-free are important parts of grooming. The process may be time consuming, but it isn't particularly hard. In the following sections, I show you how to brush, comb, bathe, and dry your Poodle — tasks you need to complete whether you take your Poodle to a groomer or groom her yourself.

Brushing and combing

Before you take on the task of brushing and combing your Poodle's coat, you need to have the right tools. You need a good slicker brush and a good comb to keep your Poodle's coat looking its best.

You also need a handy spot to do the grooming. A grooming table or a countertop with a nonskid mat are good choices. (See the earlier section "The gear you need" for details.)

The following steps take you through the process of brushing and combing your Poodle's coat once you're prepared:

1. **Lightly spray your dog's coat with water, or a water/conditioner mix, before you brush.**

   This spray helps prevent the hair from breaking as you brush.

2. **Choose a method and start brushing.**

   Some people do the body first, then the ears, legs, and tail. I prefer this method, but the important thing is to brush the same way every time so that you groom the entire dog and don't skip an area.

   Depending on the length of your Poodle's hair, you can brush it straight, or you may need to brush it in sections. With longer hair, make sure you brush all the way down to the skin, not just over the top of it (see Figure 8-1). Top brushing doesn't break tangles, and eventually the coat will mat. Regular brushing to the skin eliminates the potential for mats.

Figure 8-1: Get all the way down to the skin when you brush your Poodle.

3. **Use your comb and fingers to work out any tangles or mats.**

   Be gentle and try not to pull. Scissors or clippers should be your last resort for getting rid of mats. If you're growing a show coat for your Poodle, mats could undo months of work. Even if you don't plan to show your Poodle, you don't want her to have a bald spot where you had to remove a mat.

Bathing and drying

In the following sections, I walk you through the process of bathing and drying your Poodle.

Gathering the bathtime goods

Finding a bathing oasis for your Poodle is the first order of cleaning business. Bathing your pet is much easier if you don't have to bend over a bathtub. Where you bathe may depend on the type of Poodle you own:

- ✔ If you have a Toy Poodle, you may be able to give her a bath in a sink.

- ✔ For a Miniature, a laundry tub works well, or if your kitchen sink is large enough, that will work, too.

- ✔ For a Standard, you have to put her in the tub, which is, unfortunately, a pain in the back. That is, unless you install a tub just for your dog!

Sinks and laundry tubs may have a sprayer, which can help with rinsing off the shampoo — a definite advantage. If you plan to use your bathtub, hand-held showerheads work, or you can buy dog-washing kits at almost any pet-supply shop. I have a kit that diverts the water from my showerhead to the flexible hose and sprayer head of the dog washer. Some kits attach directly to your faucet. If you don't get a special kit, you need a large pan or a non-breakable pitcher to pour water over your dog, but this setup doesn't work well with a Standard. It's almost impossible to thoroughly wet and then rinse a Standard without some kind of a sprayer.

No matter where you wash your Poodle or what type of kit you may use, after you pick a location, you need to gather all your supplies before you add your dog to the mix:

✔ Grab your Poodle's shampoo and conditioner, vinegar, cotton balls, and plenty of towels. Get more towels than you think you need.

✔ Place a rubber mat in the tub so your dog won't slip.

✔ Have a handful of dog treats at the ready.

✔ If you have to use a bathtub, get something to kneel on. I use a rubber pad intended for gardening. Gardener's kneepads are ideal. A pillow works, but make sure you won't ruin it if it gets wet. You can also use a towel or two, but your knees will appreciate something with more give.

✔ Wear clothes that you can get wet, including shoes, because I guarantee you'll get wet!

Preparing your Poodle for her rinse

When you have all your tools assembled, go get your dog. Don't call her if she hates baths. Go and get her. Give her some of the treats you've prepared to help her see things your way.

Close the door. If you have other pets, you want to keep them out of the room, and if your Poodle should escape from you, closed doors prevent her from spreading water and soap throughout your house. When the bath is over and your dog is shaking, you want the water to sit in one area for easy cleaning.

If you're doing your bathing in a basement, there won't be any furniture or carpeting to worry about and you can shut any other dogs upstairs. If you're using the kitchen sink, and your kitchen doesn't have a door, close other pets in another room. If possible, you can use a baby gate in a doorway to keep your wet Poodle from running through the house. Another alternative is to put a lead on your Poodle before you release her from the bath.

If your Poodle's hair is lengthy, brush her out before you put her in the water (I cover brushing earlier in this chapter). If you don't, any snarls she has will get worse when you add water, and you may have mats to contend with after the bath.

Spending time in the tub or sink

Run the water to the desired temperature before you put your Poodle in the tub or sink. You don't want the water hot enough to burn your dog's feet. The water should be lukewarm. Use the inside of your wrist to test the temperature. You also don't want to have to hang on to your dog while you adjust the taps.

With the water at the right temperature, your Poodle and bathing tools in tow, and the room sealed off, follow these steps to execute the perfect bath:

1. **Put your Poodle in the tub or sink and wet her all over.**

2. **Apply shampoo and lather.**

   Squeeze the suds through her coat; don't rub or scrub, an action that can cause mats. Make sure you clean her paws, between her elbows and body, her tummy, and around the tail. In other words, don't miss anything!

3. **Rinse and repeat.**

   Make sure you get all the soap off. Dried soap can irritate your dog's skin, causing her to itch and scratch.

   Adding half of a cup or so of vinegar in the final rinse helps get rid of all the soap. If you want to add conditioner to the coat, this is the time to do it. Follow the directions on the bottle.

Drying your Poodle's lovely locks

After the bath is over, expect to have a hyper and restless dog on your hands! Follow these steps to transition from wet and anxious to dry and happy:

1. **Hold your dog in the tub or sink a minute or two to see if she'll shake.**

   I'm working on teaching my dogs to shake on command. Just before you think your dog is about to shake, give the command. When she shakes, tell her she's wonderful, and give her a treat.

2. **Wrap a towel around her body and lift her from the tub or sink.**

   If you can't physically lift your Standard, support and guide her over the edge of the tub. Don't let her leap unassisted; she could fall and hurt herself.

3. **Squeeze and blot your dog's coat with the towel.**

   Don't rub. Let your dog shake a few times, and then blot again.

4. **Repeat Step 3.**

   It's amazing how much water a Poodle's coat can hold.

5. **Start drying.**

   You have a couple of options for drying your Poodle's coat:

- If she has a short coat and you don't mind if it dries curly, you can let her air-dry. In the winter, keep her inside until she dries completely. In the summer, you can let her outside, but be warned that she'll probably roll. A roll in the grass isn't so bad, but she may also choose the middle of your garden. Now you have to start the bath all over again!

- If she has a longer coat, you may opt for a dryer and a brush. Depending on the texture of your dog's coat, you may be able to let her air-dry without fear of mats and tangles. If her coat tangles, you'll need to brush her after she dries.

If you want to clip or scissor your dog after her bath, you definitely need to use a dryer and brush. You can't do a good trimming job if your Poodle's coat is all curly. As one groomer told me, "It will look like you used a weed whacker."

6. **If you opt for a machine dryer for your Poodle's coat, use a moderate power dryer and brush constantly up and away from the skin.**

You can dry your Poodle with a human hair dryer if it has a warm setting and isn't too hot. Just keep it moving and don't hold it still on the same spot.

Stand dryers are expensive but do an excellent job and are a necessity on show coats, as a force dryer will tangle long hair. Some stand dryers come with hose attachments so they can be used as force dryers as well.

Clipping Your Poodle

Your Poodle needs to be clipped on a regular schedule (see the first section in this chapter) — whether you do the clipping yourself or pay a professional. The following sections describe some possible clips for your Poodle in two categories: pet clips and show clips.

Keeping it simple with pet clips

Any clips other than the required show ring clips (which I cover later in this chapter) are pet clips. You can clip a pet Poodle in many ways; you're limited only by your imagination and preferences. Most pet Poodles are kept in fairly simple, easily maintained clips. When deciding on a clip for your Poodle, go with your preferences, but remember that the longer the coat is, the more brushing and combing you'll need to do.

The following sections describe different types of pet clips that may fit your vision for your Poodle's coat.

The kennel clip

The kennel clip is the shortest clip and the easiest to do and maintain. It's ideal for Poodles who hike in the woods, play on the beach, or go swimming. The Poodle's face, feet, and tail are shaved; she also has a scissored topknot and a tail pompon. The body and legs are the same length and quite short, usually under ½ inch in length. The ears may be full, shortened, or completely clipped.

The sporting clip

The sporting clip is similar to the kennel clip, but the legs are longer than the body and scissored to blend into the body. The body is often as much as one inch long, with the leg length in proportion to the body length.

The lamb trim

The lamb trim is a longer version of the sporting clip, with the body and legs as long as you wish, often as long as two or three inches.

The puppy clip

In the puppy clip, the Poodle's face, feet, and tail are shaved, with a pompon left on the tail and the rest of the coat left long. The hindquarters, chest, and legs are shaped with scissors to blend in with the longer hair on the rest of the body. These areas should blend smoothly into the body and show no abrupt change in length. If the body hair is shortened, it isn't a true puppy clip.

Show Poodles may be, and usually are, kept in a puppy clip until they are a year old (I cover show puppy clips later in this chapter). Pet Poodles are usually clipped into a shorter pet clip when the long hair becomes more work to keep brushed.

The modified puppy clip

The modified puppy clip is similar to the true puppy clip, but the topknot is shaped and the entire body is shortened with scissors.

The teddy bear clip

Strictly speaking, the teddy bear clip isn't a clip because clippers aren't used; the entire body is shortened and shaped with scissors. The body, legs, and tail are usually a couple of inches long, with no changes in lengths on different parts of the body. The topknot is shortened and rounded, but not in a cap as in other clips. The face, feet, and tail are scissored to blend with the body, not shaved.

This trim can be very cute, especially on smaller Poodles, but it's high maintenance and needs frequent brushing. You'll need to check your Poodle twice a day to be sure that the rear is clean and to wipe her face with a damp cloth and dry it to keep it clear of food and dampness.

Showing off with show clips

If you've decided you want to enter the world of conformation dog shows, your Poodle needs to be in a specific, accepted clip. Or maybe you just want to see your Poodle in a fancier clip! I describe several types of popular show clips in the sections that follow. (Check out Poodles in these clips in the color section, too.)

The puppy clip

A poodle under a year of age may be shown in a true puppy clip as I describe earlier in this chapter. (You may show a puppy in an adult clip, but it's rarely done because puppies are still immature in body and coat.) See Figure 8-2 for an example of a puppy clip.

Figure 8-2: The puppy clip features shaped long hair.

The continental clip

The continental clip is the clip most people think of when they think "Poodle." It's one of two approved clips a Poodle can wear in the conformation show ring (the other is the English saddle clip). In the continental clip, the face, throat, feet, and base of the tail are shaved, as are the hindquarters and the legs. Pompons on the hips are optional. The hind legs have bracelets, and the front legs have puffs. ("Bracelets" and "puffs" are the same thing, but the Poodle world uses two different words). A pompon is on the end of the tail. The shaved feet are visible, as is part of the shaved front legs. The rest of the body is in a full coat. Figure 8-3 shows the continental clip.

Figure 8-3: Part of a Poodle's body is shaved in a continental clip.

The modified continental clip

Competitors who enjoy showing in the breed ring and also are interested in entering performance events may show their Poodles in a modified continental clip or a historically correct continental clip. People use both terms. This trim is the same as the continental clip (see the previous section), but the hair is cut to about one inch. The topknot is shaped into a cap, and the hip rosettes are shaved off. See Figure 8-4 for an example of a modified continental clip.

Figure 8-4: A modified continental clip features a shorter cut than a continental clip.

Wearing the latest coat style: Cords

Some Poodles have corded coats, which look like dreadlocks and take years to form (you can see a Poodle with a corded coat in the color section). If you look at old photos of Poodles, you'll find some of them wearing this look; however, you won't see many of today's Poodles sporting cords. Cords take years to create and are harder to keep clean than uncorded coats. If you've ever seen a Puli or a Komondor, you've seen an example of a corded coat.

You need to separate the hair and shape it as it grows. The longer the hair, the more work it takes as you hand-separate sections of hair. After you have your dog's coat in cords, you need to trim the ends and maybe even tie them up in bunches to keep them clean. You still want to shave your Poodle's stomach and around the genitals to help keep the cords clean.

And speaking of clean, a Poodle with a corded coat needs more frequent bathing, and you can't air-dry a corded coat. You need a dryer and plenty of time to thoroughly dry the cords. This coat takes a lot of work to maintain and isn't recommended for pet Poodles.

The English saddle clip

You rarely see the English saddle clip in the show ring, because the continental clip (see the previous sections) is relatively faster to do and easier to maintain. As with the continental clip, the face, throat, feet, fore legs, and base of the tail are shaved. Instead of shaved hindquarters, however, they're covered with short hair, except for a curved shaved section on each side. Each hind leg has two shaped bands. The rest of the body is in a full coat, similar to the continental clip. See Figure 8-5 for the English saddle clip.

Figure 8-5: Unlike the continental clip, the English saddle clip covers the hindquarters.

The sporting clip

The sporting clip is a great clip for a pet, but it can also be seen at dog shows in Stud Dog and Brood Bitch classes and in an exhibition-only Parade of Champions. These classes are typically held at specialty shows (shows featuring only one breed, such as the Poodle). See Figure 8-6 for an example of the sporting clip.

As I describe earlier in this chapter, the Poodle's face, feet, throat, and base of the tail are shaved, with a scissored topknot and a tail pompon. The rest of the coat is one-inch long all over the body. Leg hair may be slightly longer.

Figure 8-6: The sporting clip is great for both pet and show Poodles.

Fresh from Head to Toe: Tackling Other Grooming Tasks

Good grooming isn't just about hair, as any makeover show will tell you. You need to keep your whole dog neat, clean, and tidy so she can enjoy the best life possible. And during the grooming process, you'll examine your dog to catch health problems while they're small. In the following sections, I show you how to care for your Poodle's nails, eyes, ears, and teeth. You need to address these areas regularly in between visits to your professional groomer (if you hire one).

Trimming your Poodle's nails

Dogs' nails grow at different speeds, so your Poodle may need her nails trimmed once a week or once a month. As a quick gauge, if you can hear your Poodle's nails clicking across a bare floor, it's time to clip. The nail shouldn't have much of a curve at the end; if it does, time to clip. If you do a lot of walking on cement sidewalks, you may never need to trim her nails. All that contact with the rough cement does the job for you. Most people need to trim their dogs' nails, though.

You can find different types of nail clippers (see Chapter 5 for details on clippers and other nail tools). Your breeder or groomer may recommend a style, or you can just choose whatever style you're most comfortable with.

Nail clipping the old-fashioned way

If you have your nail clippers in hand, follow these steps to take your dog's nails from "ouch!" to smooth:

1. **Put your Poodle on a grooming table or another raised surface.**

   You'll be able to see better and have more control over your dog. Enlist help if you can't hold your dog and cut the nails at the same time. And have treats ready so that your Poodle considers nail trimming to be a good thing.

2. **Clip the tip off each nail, being careful not to hit the *quick* — the blood vessel that runs down the center of the nail.**

   If your dog has white nails, you can see this vein. If your dog has black nails, try to cut just below the point where the nails curve. Gradually, with regular trimming, the quick recedes, so you have a lesser chance of cutting it. See Figure 8-7 to find out exactly where to cut a Poodle's nail.

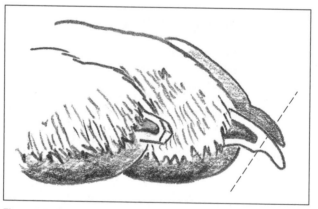

Figure 8-7: Cut where the nail curves to miss the quick.

If you do hit the quick, don't panic. Applying bit of styptic powder will stop the bleeding. You can find styptic powder at pet-supply stores or drugstores. If you don't have any styptic powder handy, cornstarch will work. Some dogs hardly flinch if you hit the quick, and others scream, but either way the mistake isn't life threatening.

Alternative nail-clipping options

If you're like me and just hate cutting nails, or if you're afraid of hitting the quick, you have some nail-cutting alternatives. One is to take your dog to a groomer. Many groomers accept walk-ins for clipping nails. (I discuss taking your Poodle to a groomer earlier in this chapter.)

Another possibility is to use a grinding wheel. Grinding wheels grind the nails down (no joke!). Many dogs who fight having their nails cut don't mind the grinder at all. However, you should get your dog used to the grinder gradually. Just follow these steps:

1. **Hold the body of the grinder against her foot to get her used to the vibration.**

2. **Grind a nail or two.**

3. **Give her a treat.**

4. **Stop *before* she starts fidgeting.**

5. **Later in the day, or the next day, try a couple more nails.**

   Within a week or two, depending on your dog's temperament, you should be able to grind all the nails in one session.

The Web site www.DoberDawn.com has excellent instructions and illustrations to show you how to use an electric grinder on your poodle's nails.

You can also file your Poodle's nails, which gives you the advantage of never hitting the quick, and you don't need to rely on electricity or batteries. You can file anywhere!

Keeping an eye on your Poodle's eyes

Generally, there's not much you need to do about your Poodle's eyes. You just need to hold your dog's head firmly with one hand over the top of the head. Then you can clean away matter, if necessary (see Figure 8-8). Never poke at your dog's eyes; just take a look at them to make sure they appear clean and clear, not cloudy or bloodshot. Gently clean away any gunk you see in the corners with a tissue, soft cloth, or baby wipe. If you notice a problem, such as swelling, or if your dog is blinking and/or pawing at her eyes, you need to take a trip to the veterinarian.

One issue you may see with your Poodle's eyes is *tearing*. Tear stains may be evident on white and cream Poodle's as reddish stains running from the eyes down along the sides of the muzzle. Not all Poodles will have tear stains, but if they do, the stains are harmless. So, if you don't mind them, you can just leave them alone. If, however, you want to eliminate the stains, talk to your groomer or veterinarian about stain-removal products. If your Poodle's eyes are constantly tearing, have your vet check her eyes to make sure that the tear ducts aren't blocked.

Figure 8-8: Do a visual check of your Poodle's eyes for redness, swelling, or tearing.

Examining the ears

Regular examination of your Poodle's ears is an important part of the grooming process. Dogs with drop ears, like the Poodle, have a greater chance of developing problems. Those flaps that make your dog so lovely also prevent air from circulating, and your Poodle may end up with a yeast infection.

To examine one of your Poodle's ears, just grasp her head over the top of her skull, with the flap lifted and in the grasp of that same hand. Use the other hand to clean the ear, if necessary (see Figure 8-9).

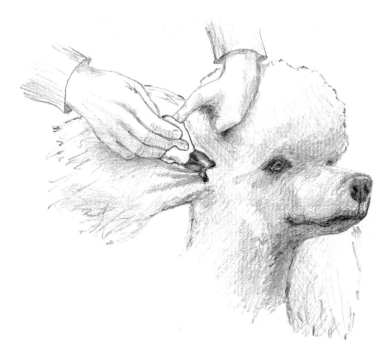

Figure 8-9: Hold your Poodle's flap out of the way for cleaning and hair removal.

Look into your dog's ears. If you see just a bit of wax buildup, use an ear cleaner for dogs (which you can buy at a pet-supply store or from your veterinarian) on a cotton ball and clean the flap and the inside of the ear. If your dog's ear is full of gunk or smells (or both), you may need medicine from your veterinarian to cure the problem.

Don't poke, prod, or push into the ear canal, or you may end up pushing wax and dirt further into the ear.

You also should remove the hair from inside your Poodle's ears. Hair prevents air circulation and holds in dirt. You can use a little medicated powder and pluck the hair with your fingers or use hemostats, which look a bit like a pair of scissors, except that instead of cutting blades, serrated inner edges grip and hold. Medicated powder is available from your vet and from pet-supply stores and catalogs.

Completely plucking a Poodle's ears monthly with a medicated powder, especially one containing iodoform, is sufficient for most Poodles. More frequent plucking can cause irritation of the ear canal. Some folks prefer not to pluck ears; instead they flush weekly with half vinegar and half water and dry the ear canal well.

Doing some dental work

Keeping your Poodle's big teeth clean should be a part of your regular grooming routine. Dogs don't get cavities the way humans do, but plaque can build up on their pearly whites and harden into tartar. A heavy tartar build-up can cause gum abscesses. The bacteria from said abscesses can circulate through your dog's system and lead to pneumonia, or it can cause heart, liver, or kidney problems. In short, don't let it get to that point! In the following sections, I discuss home and professional cleanings and give you a few signs of potential tooth problems.

Brushing your Poodle's pearly whites yourself

If you start cleaning your Poodle's teeth when she's a puppy, she'll get used to it, even though it may not become the highlight of her day. If you can fit brushing her teeth into your dog's daily schedule, that's great, but you're also doing well if you brush her teeth two or three times a week. Even once a week is better than never.

Follow these steps to keep your Poodle's smile bright:

1. **Wrap your finger in a piece of gauze.**

2. **Put your hand over the top of your Poodle's head, with your thumb and fingers on either side to pull up the lips (see Figure 8-10).**

3. **Gently rub your dog's teeth and gums with the gauze.**

    After your dog gets used to you putting your finger in her mouth, you can advance to a doggy toothbrush. You have your choice of pretreated wipes, small plastic brushes that fit over your finger, or special toothbrushes that look much like your own (available from your veterinarian or from a pet-supply shop catalog). You can use a special flavored paste as well.

Never use human toothpaste on your Poodle. Fluoride and artificial sweeteners in toothpaste are toxic to dogs.

Springing for the occasional professional cleaning

Your veterinarian may recommend an occasional professional cleaning for your Poodle's teeth. You brush and floss your teeth, but you still need the attention of a dentist to do a more thorough cleaning. You dog's teeth also benefit from professional attention.

How often a dog needs a professional cleaning depends on the individual dog. I have a male whose teeth need attention every six months, but I've also had other dogs that could go years between cleanings. Your vet can advise you on the proper cleaning schedule for your Poodle.

Your vet may want to do a blood test before a teeth cleaning, especially if your Poodle is older. The test ensures that your dog can be anesthetized without worry. Make sure your vet also goes over any pre-cleaning guidelines you need to follow — with food and drink, for example.

During a cleaning, your vet gives your dog anesthesia and then he, or a technician, removes any tartar build-up and cleans and polishes your dog's teeth. If your vet discovers any broken or cracked teeth, he'll pull them at this time.

Figure 8-10: Besides regular cleaning, check your dog's teeth for tartar build-up and any broken teeth.

Knowing when your Poodle may have a dental problem

Your Poodle's teeth may look fine to you, but that doesn't mean they're problem-free. Take your Poodle to the vet in the following instances:

✔ If your dog's breath is bad or smells different than normal

✔ If she's drooling and/or pawing at her mouth

✔ If she has trouble eating hard food or no longer wants to play with toys or chew on bones

Part III

Training and Having Fun with Your Poodle Pal

The 5th Wave   By Rich Tennant

"Okay, this is getting ridiculous! Either teach your dog not to run away, or name him something other than 'Fire.'"

In this part . . .

The time has come to start training your Poodle so he's not an annoying, albeit adorable, companion. This third part starts with housetraining tips. Next, I move out of the house to address good manners, socialization, and travel. Finally, I include a chapter on all the activities you and your Poodle can enjoy together. Your pal can earn a Canine Good Citizen certificate; he can become a certified therapy dog; he can show off in the breed ring; and he can have fun flying over, under, and through obstacles on an agility course. Prepare to have fun!

Chapter 9

Housetraining Made Easy

· ·

In This Chapter

▶ Understanding the basics of housetraining

▶ Surveying the different housetraining methods available to you

▶ Tidying up after your Poodle

· ·

*Y*ou can't live outdoors for as long as your Poodle is in the picture, so you need to housetrain him. In other words, you need to teach him where to "go." The task may sound daunting, but if you're patient and consistent, it won't be that hard. In this chapter, I explain the basics of housetraining, describe several methods you can use, and give you tips for the task of cleaning up.

This chapter focuses on housetraining Poodle puppies. If you adopt an adult Poodle, hope that you're lucky enough to find one that's already housetrained and that needs to see the potty spot in his new home only once to know where to go. However, if you adopt an untrained adult Poodle, treat him like a puppy and follow the guidelines in this chapter.

Littering Your Brain with Housetraining Basics

No matter what housetraining method you use with your Poodle, the basics of the process are the same. You use the tools available to you to achieve the goal of creating a schedule, sticking to it, and molding a well-behaved, potty-trained pup!

The purpose of housetraining is to teach your Poodle where to eliminate. Whether you're teaching your Toy or Miniature to use a litter box or your Standard to use the backyard, the process and the purpose are the same. Your dog will figure out that he has an acceptable area for eliminating, and that area isn't the *entire* house.

In the following sections, I explain how to draw up a housetraining schedule, keep your routine consistent yet flexible, and how to recognize the signs that your Poodle needs to go. You can check out "Mastering Effective Housetraining Methods," later in this chapter, for full details on different housetraining methods.

Setting up a housetraining schedule for your Poodle

Poodles can learn what their masters want them to learn quickly, as long as the masters are diligent. Your Poodle can become housetrained even faster if you stick to a housetraining schedule. Puppies don't have adult-sized bladders, but they can still "hold it" for a reasonable amount of time — a time you set on a schedule. In the following sections, I show you a typical training schedule and provide tips on working with the schedule you create.

Looking at a typical schedule

You make up your own housetraining schedule to fit your family's lifestyle, but some elements of the schedule won't change. Your puppy needs to go to the bathroom when he first wakes up — from a good night's sleep or from a short nap. He also needs to go 10 to 20 minutes after eating, as well as after any play session.

A good housetraining schedule for an untrained Poodle may look something like this:

- ✔ **6:00 a.m.** Take the puppy outside or to his indoor "potty spot" if you choose to keep him inside (see Chapter 5 for more about selecting a spot).

    Lift your puppy and carry him to the yard; don't put him on the floor and coax him to follow you to the door. He may not be able to make it that far without going, and the more accidents he has in the house, the longer the housetraining will take.

- ✔ **6:15 a.m.** Feed your puppy.

- ✔ **6:30 a.m.** Take your puppy to his spot.

- ✔ **6:40–7:00 a.m.** Play with your puppy.

- ✔ **7:00 a.m.** Take your puppy to his spot. This time, when he's finished, pop him into his crate so he's safe and out of the way while you get ready for work or school.

- ✔ **8:00 a.m.** Take your puppy to his spot once more before you leave the house, then crate him or put him in his enclosed space.

- ✔ **Noon.** Take your puppy to his spot that you've designated.

- ✔ **12:10 p.m.** Feed your puppy, and prepare your own lunch. Crate your puppy while you eat.

- ✔ **12:45 p.m.** Take your puppy outside or to his indoor spot again. If you have time, play with him for a bit, take him to his spot again, and then put him back in his crate or space.

- ✔ **3:00 p.m.** The kids get home from school! Now they get the chance to take the puppy to his spot, play with him, and take him to his spot again.

- ✔ **5:30 p.m.** Take your puppy outside or to his indoor area when you get home and then feed him.

- ✔ **5:45 p.m.** Take your puppy to his spot again. Put him in his crate or training space while you fix dinner and your family eats. After dinner, take your puppy to his spot again.

- ✔ **7:00 p.m.** Take your puppy to his spot and then get ready for some playtime!

- ✔ **7:15 p.m.** Take your puppy to his spot after you play.

  For the rest of the evening, depending on your puppy, he may snooze, or he may want to play. Watch him for signs that he needs to go outside (I cover telltale signs later in this chapter).

- ✔ **11:00 p.m.** Take your puppy outside one more time before bed.

Again, this example schedule isn't a carved-in-stone guide that you must follow. If your puppy sleeps until 7:00 a.m., great for you! If your family members are all early-to-bedders, you don't need to stay up with your pup until 11:00, but you should be prepared for some trips to your puppy's spot in the middle of the night.

Adapting training to your schedule

Puppies adapt quickly, so as long as you're consistent and the times between potty breaks are reasonable, your Poodle will learn the routine. Not everyone has the same lifestyle, so modify the training schedule as needed:

- ✔ Post the housetraining schedule on your refrigerator door so that all family members can see when your puppy needs to go out or be put in the litter box (I cover this method later in this chapter).

- ✔ If no one in your house can get home at noon, find out whether a neighbor is willing to take your puppy out. On the other hand, if someone in your family stays home all day, your puppy will get more playtime and more trips out to the yard. You could also hire a pet sitter or professional dog walker, which would probably cost between $9 and $20 a visit.

If everyone in your family leaves home early and gets back late, your schedule doesn't prevent you from having a puppy, but it does mean that you can't crate train, all the time. Use an ex-pen (see Chapter 5) during the day and the crate on evenings and weekends. The whole process will probably take longer. But Poodles are both smart and adaptable, and with time, you'll have a housetrained dog.

Staying consistent (yet flexible) in your training routine

Be consistent in your housetraining routine . . . and stay flexible at the same time. If this paragraph were an e-mail, I'd put a smiley face here. My advice may seem contradictory, but I assure you that it isn't. So, what do I mean by consistent *and* flexible?

- ✔ **Consistency:** As much as possible, you should follow your housetraining schedule (see the previous section). Dogs are creatures of habit, and your puppy will soon learn when you let him out. If you don't stick to a schedule, your puppy will get confused, and housetraining will take longer.

- ✔ **Flexibility:** However, your puppy isn't a machine. He may have his own ideas, or his needs may not match the schedule you've chosen. He may always need a 2 a.m. outing during the first couple weeks at his new home. Or you may discover that your puppy doesn't have to go outside for 45 minutes after eating.

  No matter what kind of pattern your puppy seems to have, remember that it can change over time. Try to be consistent, but stay alert to any changes you may need to make.

Speeding up the training process

Besides creating a routine for your puppy, you can do other things to speed up the housetraining process. The following list presents some of these actions (most of these tips pertain to methods in which you take your Poodle outside instead of keeping him inside):

- ✔ **Always use the same door to go outside.** Make sure all your other family members or roommates use that door, too. When your puppy is old enough to signal to you that he needs to go out, he'll always use that door (see the following section for a list of telltale signals).

- ✔ **Use the same spot in the yard.** Your puppy will smell urine and know that he's come to the right place. Use his sense of smell to your advantage.

WARNING!

The exact spot is your choice, but remember that vegetation in any spot that gets frequent visits from a dog will suffer a bit, both from doggy paws and from urine.

✔ **Praise!** When your puppy goes where you want him to go, praise him. Your neighbors may think you're strange if you're outside clapping and spouting baby talk, but pay no mind; make a big fuss when he goes in the right spot, and give him a treat. You may even reward him with a play session.

However, always save the play session for after he goes. Puppies are easily distracted, and if you play first, he may forget that he has to go until he gets back to your new carpet.

✔ **Always go out with your puppy.** Don't just open your chosen door and shove your puppy out. Giving your dog some privacy may be fine if he's an adult, but with a puppy, you need to take him to the right area and praise him.

✔ **Take out your puppy on a lead.** Not only does a lead help you guide your puppy but also keeps him from scooting away. Puppies are faster than you! You don't want to be on your hands and knees, crawling under a lilac bush to retrieve your puppy at three in the morning or when you're dressed for work. (See Chapter 5 for more on the right tools to have for your Poodle.)

✔ **Make mealtime a part of the schedule.** When your Poodle becomes an adult, you may decide that you want to free feed him, and that's fine (see Chapter 7 for details on free feeding). But for now, regular meals make it easier to schedule bathroom breaks and reduce the chance that your puppy will go while you're away.

Recognizing the telltale "I gotta go!" signs

Following a housetraining schedule you create and being consistent go a long way toward preventing accidents in the house (see the previous sections), but you can do more in your quest to housetrain your Poodle. Use your eyes to discover how your dog acts before he goes to the bathroom. With a very young puppy, you may get no warning at all. He'll just stop and go.

As he grows, though, your Poodle will give you some telltale signs that now isn't the time to watch television or take a picture of how cute he is. The following list presents some "I gotta go!" signals:

✔ **The "potty dance":** You may see your dog do a short little "dance," shifting his front paws back and forth.

- ✔ **The sniff and circle:** Many dogs sniff around and circle a spot before they go. Puppies often grow out of this phase, but it may become quite a ritual for some adults.

- ✔ **Pacing:** Generally, with dogs that pace back and forth, the pacing area gets shorter and shorter until they finally go.

- ✔ **Whining:** Whining is a sound cue that may mean, "I gotta go!" Adult dogs frequently stand by doors and whine to signal you for a bathroom break.

- ✔ **Standing by the door:** Some dogs never whine; they just wait patiently by their doors until their humans come along to open them. If you haven't seen your Poodle in a while, check in front of your door.

- ✔ **Staring:** Staring isn't as common as some of the other indicators, but some dogs use it as a signal. Generally, when your Poodle sits in front of you and stares, he wants to remind you that it's dinnertime, but some dogs stare when they need to go out.

Mastering Effective Housetraining Methods

You have several different options for housetraining your Poodle, depending on your lifestyle and personal preference. You can opt for crate training, paper training, litter training, and so on. You may even want to use a combination of certain methods. Whatever method you choose to use from the following sections, however, remember to be consistent, and always praise your puppy for his successes! (Check out Chapter 5 for a rundown of the many tools you need for training, including crates, leads, and so on.)

Poodles are smart enough to be both indoor and outdoor dogs when it comes to bathroom habits. Although it may be easier and preferable to teach your Poodle to go either outdoors or indoors, apartment dwellers who train their Poodles to go outdoors, for example, may have times when they want their dogs to go indoors. A dog trained with litter or paper that experiences a move outside will quickly learn that when his owner provides paper or litter, he has permission to go indoors.

Sleeping the day away: Crate training

Crate training is my all-time personal favorite method for house-training a puppy. Crate training doesn't mean that your puppy never leaves the crate, but it does mean that when you can't watch

A dense, curly coat is an easily recognizable trait of a Poodle.

Poodles are happy to curl up and relax at the end of a busy day.

© ALICE SU

Blue is just one of several unusual colors that Poodles come in.

You have a variety of grooming options for your Poodle; some owners choose to accessorize their Poodles with ribbons.

© JEANMFOGLE.COM

© ELIANE FARRAY-SULLE/ALAMY

Toy Poodles are the smallest variety of Poodle; they measure 10 inches or less at the shoulder.

Poodles, like this apricot Miniature, are famous for their dignified, elegant look.

Straight, parallel front legs, like those of this gorgeous red Poodle, are ideal.

Stylish puppy clips are reserved for Poodles under 12 months of ag

The continental clip is one of several traditional clips that Poodles

During competition, Poodles can strut their stuff in an English saddle clip.

Poodles excel at competitive events. This Poodle selects an object during an obedience exercise.

Poodles show great form while navigating tire obstacles during an agility event.

Poodles love water and were originally bred to hunt and retrieve.

For a striking look, you can keep your Poodle's coat corded rather than brushed out.

Poodles can perform any activity you teach them. This Poodle is earning its keep as a draft animal.

Poodles come in three sizes; Standard Poodles are the largest variety.

Poodles love to play and can never have too many toys.

Poodles are smart and versatile; this Poodle is ready to help in a garden.

Breeders are the best source for healthy, adorable Poodle puppies.

your puppy every minute, he should be in his crate. He should be in his crate when he's home alone or when you're trying to fix dinner. He shouldn't be loose unless someone is watching him. Follow the schedule earlier in this chapter for successful crate training.

Crate training isn't possible if you or others in your life can't come home for long stretches of time. You can't expect your puppy to hold it for more than four hours at a time. No puppy wants to go in his bed, but he will if he must. And when your puppy does start to go in his crate, he starts a hard habit to break.

If your lifestyle and preferences make crate training a viable option, you enjoy two big housetraining advantages:

- ✔ Your puppy doesn't want to go in his bed, so he learns to hold it — especially if you follow a schedule and he knows he'll be able to go soon (see the section "Setting up a housetraining schedule for your Poodle").

- ✔ If your puppy does have an accident in his crate, you have only a small, easy-to-clean area to worry about — not a big spot in the middle of the living room rug.

See Chapter 5 for more on crates and other tools.

Putting pee to paper: Paper training

Paper training is how pet owners housetrained in the "good old days," before crates came along to change our thinking. The method still works if you can't crate train your Poodle; it just takes longer. You still take your dog out at regular intervals when you're home, but otherwise, your dog learns to "go" on newspapers spread out to cover the floor. More work is involved because you have more clean up of papers and the spreading of clean ones.

Here are the steps you take to paper train your Poodle:

1. **Set up an exercise pen, in a large area of your home.**

   A bathroom, laundry room, or corner of the kitchen can work; these areas typically have linoleum flooring, which makes cleanup easier. If the room has a door, that will keep the puppy in, or you can put up a baby gate across the doorway. In a large area, with no doors, consider using an exercise pen to contain your Poodle.

2. **Remove any chewable items from the area.**

   Chair and table legs make great toys for puppies. Make sure no electric cords are visible in the housetraining area.

3. **Put your puppy's crate in the area; leave the door open for naps, and supply water and a few toys.**

4. **Cover the entire floor with several layers of newspaper inside the pen.**

   Depending on the flooring, you may want to put down a large piece of plastic to protect it. A shower curtain makes for an inexpensive barrier. Figure 9-1 shows a setup for paper training.

5. **Whenever you notice a puddle or a pile, you should clean the area; to clean, remove the top layers of newspaper, but leave a lower layer or two.**

   When you cover the area with more newspaper after cleaning, you'll leave enough odor to tell your puppy that this is the spot to go.

6. **After several days, remove some of the newspapers, leaving a smaller area of the floor covered.**

   If your puppy consistently uses the paper rather than the uncovered floor, you can reduce the papered area even further. Continue this process until you've removed all the paper. Be sure to take your time; you want your puppy to fully understand that the paper is the proper bathroom spot.

   During this process, you can begin the transition to going outside. You can use a piece of the soiled newspaper you clean up to mark an appropriate spot in the yard. Weigh the paper down with a rock, and when you're in the yard, walk your puppy to the paper and let him sniff.

Figure 9-1: A paper-training arrangement gives your Poodle a specific potty area and a place for naps.

Continue to take your puppy outside on a regular schedule when you're home (see the section "Looking at a typical schedule"). By the time you reach the no-paper stage, your Poodle should be old enough to control his bladder, and he'll have made the connection that outdoors is the place to go. This doesn't necessarily mean that you should give him the run of the house, but you should trust him to keep his training area clean.

Scratch and sprinkle: Litter training

Litter training is exactly what it sounds like: You train your Toy or Miniature Poodle to use a litter box for bathroom breaks instead of taking him to a specific spot in your yard or relying on newspaper and an enclosed area. You may find it easier to clean a litter box instead of patrolling your yard with a pooper-scooper or replacing messy newspaper.

You can train your Poodle with a litter box both outdoors and indoors:

- ✔ If you have a small balcony off your house or apartment, a corner of it could serve as a doggy outhouse.

- ✔ You can use a litter box without a cover at any convenient spot in your home (see Figure 9-2).

You train your Poodle to use a litter box the same way you paper train him (see the previous section). The difference is that you place the litter box in your puppy's enclosure and cover the newspaper on the floor with a thin layer of litter. You should gradually reduce the area covered by the paper and litter until the only space left is the litter box. Your Poodle will be litter-trained when he consistently uses the box to eliminate. That means *you* can eliminate barriers.

 You may decide to use a cat litter box, which is fine, but some litter boxes are made especially for dog litter. If you decide to use litter, make sure you use dog litter, not cat litter. Dog litter doesn't fly around as much if your Poodle wants to scratch and scuff after going. Other boxes may use sod or artificial turf, or may even come with a post for male dogs. Sod or turf look more like grass, but can be more expensive to replace. Artificial turf needs to be cleaned frequently to prevent a build-up of odor and germs. Litter is easier to replace and store.

Figure 9-2: Litter training is a convenient option for housetraining your small Poodle indoors.

You also can crate train your puppy to use a litter box. You follow the same steps you do when utilizing a crate and the outdoors, but instead of taking the puppy outside, you take him to the litter box. The goal of this method, like the others, is for your Poodle pup to learn to use his litter box when nature calls. (I cover crate training earlier in this chapter.)

Surveying additional indoor training options

Most people train their dogs to go to the bathroom in the great outdoors, but for some people this just isn't practical. Apartment dwellers or people with physical handicaps may prefer training their Poodles to use specific spots indoors. With this approach, you must train your Poodle so that he understands just one small part of the house is his bathroom, not the entire home. In this section, I cover a couple strictly indoor options for training your Poodle.

All indoor training methods are best suited for Toy or Miniature Poodles. However, if you have plenty of space, your Standard can learn these methods just as quickly as the smaller Poodle varieties (see Chapter 2 for more on variety distinctions).

Permanent paper training

If you can't take your Poodle outside for bathroom breaks for whatever reason, and you don't want to use a litter box, you can permanently paper train your Poodle. Follow the paper training instructions that I give in the section "Putting pee to paper: Paper training," only never eliminate all the papers. Your goal should be to train your Poodle to use only a small area of paper.

Before beginning this type of training, make sure you plan ahead and start the training in an area that's fit to be your Poodle's permanent bathroom. You can create a small wooden or plastic frame to help define the area and contain the papers if you like.

Pads

Many Poodle owners use puppy pads rather than paper or litter for indoor housetraining. These pads, which look a bit like disposable diapers, have plastic backings and are scented to attract your dog to the spot where you want him to go.

Use these pads the same way you'd use paper or a litter box (see previous sections on these topics). Select the area of the house that will be your Poodle's bathroom. The scent of the pads will encourage your Poodle to use them.

Pads are more absorbent than paper and are easier to put down and pick up than paper. Because they are usually scented to encourage use, you have less of a chance of your Poodle having an accident. The pads also have a moisture-proof barrier so the chance that flooring will get dirty or stained isn't as great.

Many people who use pads opt for disposable pads, but washable pads also are available. Here are some characteristics of these pads:

- ✔ You can wash these pads approximately 300 times each.
- ✔ You need four or five pads at least because they need to air dry before reuse.
- ✔ Washable pads are generally larger than disposable pads; they come in sizes of 2 feet x 2 feet, 3 x 3, and 4 x 4.

A pad, whether washable or disposable, looks pretty much the same. Figure 9-3 shows a pad that you can use to train your Poodle.

Figure 9-3: A pad for your Poodle can help with indoor training.

Getting the Scoop on Cleanup Duty

Unfortunately, when your Poodle makes a deposit, you can't holler for cleanup on aisle six. Cleanup is part of your responsibility as a dog owner, both inside and outside your home. It isn't the most pleasant job, but it became yours when you got your Poodle, and it will be yours for the lifetime of your companion. If you're still on the fence with your decision to buy a Poodle, and you aren't willing to pick up after a dog, get guppies instead.

The good news about cleanup is that you can buy products that make the process a bit easier. In the following sections, I explain how to clean up after your Poodle, both inside and outside.

Cleaning up inside

After you housetrain your Poodle, indoor cleanup is mostly a thing of the past, unless your dog gets sick. The two enemies you must deal with are stains and odor. Some products work better at fighting one than the other, and some miracle products can handle both.

When you're cleaning feces or vomit, follow this short list of steps:

1. **Your first goal is to pick up the feces or vomit.**

   You can use a plastic bag or paper towels to pick up the feces. For vomit, you can use a dustpan or a couple of paper plates to scrape it up. If you use plates, fold the first plate in half and crease the fold. Do the same with the second plate, and then use them both to scoop and trap the vomit.

2. **When you have all the extra liquids and solids off the floor, you can tackle cleaning with your product of choice.**

   Your favorite carpet cleaner or floor cleaner will suffice. However, the old standbys are club soda and white vinegar. The soda is supposed to prevent staining, and the vinegar should take care of the odor. I've had mixed results with this combination, but in a pinch, these two products will help.

If your pup leaves you a puddle, follow these steps:

1. **Blot as much of the puddle as you can, pour on some vinegar, and then blot it all up.**

   No matter where the accident occurs, never use ammonia-based products to clean it. Urine contains ammonia, and a faint whiff of the chemical will tell your puppy to return to that spot the next time he needs to go.

2. **Create a large pad of paper towels, place the pad over the wet spot, and step on it.**

3. **Rock back and forth. Repeat. Repeat.**

   Keep going until you don't pick up any more moisture. You'll use a lot of paper towels, so you may want to buy stock in a paper company now!

4. **Repeat the process with some club soda to minimize staining and let the area dry.**

Urine-Off is an amazing product that handles both stain and odor. It works! I've never used it on any accidents other than urine, but you may want to give it a try. Your local pet-supply stores may have Urine-Off. Where I live, it's available at a carpet store. Oxygen cleaners also can effectively remove stains and odor. You may be able to find products available through pet-supply catalogs and at pet-supply stores that will work to some extent. You can easily find oxygen cleaners in your grocery store with other cleaning supplies.

A hand held wet/dry vacuum is also an excellent tool for dog owners. First remove any solid matter, and then vacuum up any liquid from the carpet or floor. Use your disinfectant or cleaner as liberally as needed, and vacuum that up, leaving the carpet almost dry.

These vacuums come in both corded and rechargeable models, and some even have motorized scrub brushes.

If your Poodle goes on linoleum, use any disinfecting cleaner. You won't have to worry about odors or stains, as you would with carpet.

Cleaning up in the great outdoors

You may think that if your Poodle heeds the call of nature outdoors, you're off the hook as far as cleanup goes, but you're wrong! Many people use public property, and your kids or roommates would love to be able to use your yard, and they have the right to use it without worrying about stepping in whatever your Poodle leaves behind. Not even other dog people approve if you don't pick up. I've had dogs for over 30 years, and I still hate scraping poop off my shoes.

I just know you'll do the right thing with your Poodle's accidents, as soon as I tell you how easy it is. Just follow these guidelines:

- ✔ **Your yard:** You may like to take your Poodle on hikes or for jogs around the block, but first thing in the morning and last thing at night, your Poodle will use your yard for exercise and bathroom breaks. To clean up, use a pooper-scooper on a regular basis, and dispose of the waste in a lined trashcan or in a doggy septic system (see Chapter 5 for more on these items).

- ✔ **Public areas:** You can't easily carry a pooper-scooper on a walk, which is where plastic bags come in. For Toys and Miniatures (see Chapter 2), small, plastic sandwich bags work well. And for any size Poodle, this is your chance to recycle. You can recycle the plastic sleeves that cover your newspapers, use plastic bread bags, or use the plastic bags your groceries come in. Just make sure the bags don't have holes in them!

To pick up after your Poodle in public areas, follow these steps:

1. **Put the bag over your hand.**

2. **Pick up the droppings.**

3. **Pull the bag edge forward, over the mess in your hand.**

   I also carry a small brown bag in which to drop the plastic bag for the trip home. It's a bit more aesthetically pleasing to others.

A benefit of picking up after your Poodle is that you soon know what your dog's normal stool looks like. If you see a change — you notice mucus, blood, or a drastic change in color — you may want to plan a trip to the vet's.

Chapter 10

Instilling Good Manners in Your Poodle

* *

In This Chapter

▶ Beginning with basic training principles

▶ Working with a collar and lead

▶ Teaching basic commands to your Poodle

▶ Conquering common behavior problems

▶ Acquiring the help of professionals

* *

Dogs are pack animals, which means, in report-card language, that they "play well with others." Dogs don't function well as loners; they do well with structure, routine, and rules. You want your Poodle to be a socialite, but you don't want her to be the boss or to annoy your acquaintances. An untrained dog may be an unhappy dog, because she doesn't know what you expect of her. Your Poodle doesn't have to be a champion obedience dog, but she should have good manners — for your sake and for hers.

This chapter gives you some training tips to turn your Poodle into a model citizen. I also tell you when and how to get professional help if you need it. For more information, check out *Dog Training For Dummies,* 2nd Edition, by Jack and Wendy Volhard (Wiley).

Getting a Grip on Some Disciplinary Basics

There are many different ways to train a dog, and not all methods work with all dogs. You may find that part of one training method works well with part of another. The following list gives you basics that will help you no matter what particular method you choose:

✔ **Have your equipment handy.** A plain buckle collar and a lead are all the equipment you need, and for some training, you can work without them. (I discuss collars and leads in the next section.) If you decide to train with food rewards, have a good supply of treats on hand, and keep them small. Your objective is training, not overfeeding.

✔ **Keep your training sessions short.** You can make more progress if you train four times a day at five minutes per session than if you hold one 20-minute training session.

✔ **Have a release word that tells your dog she can stop acting on your command.** Make the release word short, and say it happily. Many owners use "okay." No matter what word you choose, be consistent. Don't say "okay" today and "good job" tomorrow.

✔ **Try not to laugh at mistakes.** Poodles are very intelligent, and they have good senses of humor. They seem to enjoy making people laugh; therefore, if you laugh at your Poodle during training, you'll find that she's likely to repeat whatever behavior made you laugh.

✔ **Be flexible with your training methods.** Not every training method works for every dog every time (which is why I list many in this chapter). Be consistent with your commands and methods, but if a technique isn't working, don't be afraid to try something different.

✔ **Never punish your dog for obeying.** You may be furious that she ran away from you, but you need to praise her if she obeyed your "stay" command. Poodles aren't stupid. They won't obey any command that gets them punished.

✔ **No losing your temper, and no hitting, ever.** Don't scream uncontrollably or hit or kick your dog. If you get frustrated, take a break. Go somewhere far away from your Poodle. Take a walk. Count to 100. Meditate. Distract yourself until you can approach your dog calmly.

✔ **Always end on a positive note.** For example, if your Poodle knows the "sit" command and always follows it promptly, but she hasn't quite mastered "down," end your session with a sit.

Handling a Collar and Lead

A collar and lead (also known as a leash) are the first, most basic training tools you need. You can train your Poodle with many commands that don't require a collar and lead (see the later section "Training Your Poodle with Basic Commands" for details), but she needs to be able to accept a collar and walk nicely on a lead.

Otherwise, trips to the vet's office, obedience class, or just around the block will be pretty darn difficult, if not impossible. In the following sections, I explain how to navigate collar and lead training with your Poodle. Chapter 5 has the full details on buying specific collars and leads.

Collaring your Poodle

A collar is an essential part of your Poodle's wardrobe. She will wear a buckle collar with her ID tags all the time. If the worst happens and she gets lost, those tags will help see that she gets home. The collar also gives you an opportunity to accessorize. Poodles are often considered glamour dogs, so have fun with velvet and rhinestones, or a little something from Tiffany's. However, the collar serves a functional purpose for your Poodle, and the one you choose and train with depends on many factors. I explain how to fit your Poodle with different collars in the following sections.

Beginning with buckle collars

You should start with a simple buckle collar for your Poodle puppy. The collar should be tight enough that your dog can't paw it off over her head, but not so tight that it chokes her or rubs a sore on her neck. Here's a good test: You should be able to slide two fingers between her throat and the collar. And remember, your puppy is growing all the time, so a collar that fit her perfectly last week may be getting too tight this week. You can leave a buckle collar on your dog all the time, so make sure she's comfortable!

If your Poodle always wears a buckle collar, think about adding a small bell or two — especially if you have a Toy or a Miniature Poodle (see Chapter 2 for more on the distinctions). Small dogs have to worry about people stepping on them or tripping over them. A bell announcing your dog's presence may help reduce injury risk.

Fitting other types of collars

A *martingale collar* is made with two loops. The loop that goes around your Poodle's neck stays loose. Another loop is attached to the loose loop, and you secure the lead to this loop. When you pull the lead on the smaller loop, the loop around your Poodle's neck tightens, preventing escape. Many owners like martingale collars because they can be tight enough to give a correction and to keep the dogs from pulling out, yet they can't strangle the dogs.

On the negative side, that extra loop can easily catch on something, or your Poodle could get her paw or jaw tangled in the loop and injure herself. You should use the martingale collar only when you're with your dog on a walk or during a training session. Take it off afterward.

All this advice is doubly true for training collars (also called slip collars). *Training collars* are lengths of chains, leather, or fabric meant to tighten around your dog's neck to give a correction. This type of collar gives you more control over your Poodle, and if she has figured out that she can pull out of a buckle collar, you can use a training collar and pull it tighter.

If you leave a training collar on your Poodle, and the ring on the end of the collar catches onto something, your dog could die. Never tie your dog outside with a training collar, and never leave your dog unattended while she's wearing a training collar.

You must put on a training collar properly in order for it to work. If you put the collar on backward, it will tighten around your Poodle's neck. In that position, it will be uncomfortable, and it won't work as intended. With your dog sitting on your left, hold the collar so that it looks like the letter "P" on its side. The loop of the letter hangs in front of your dog's head, and the long side runs parallel to the ground. Slide the loop over your Poodle's head. See Figure 10-1 for an illustration of the correct way to put on a training collar.

Figure 10-1: You must put on a training collar properly for it to work.

It's also important to fit a slip collar correctly. When you gently pull it snug, it should have no more than 2½ inches of excess length on a large poodle, and no more than two inches on a small one, so that it will tighten and instantly release as it should.

Gaining control with harnesses or halters

Many small dogs have problems with their tracheas, so a training collar could cause more problems. To combat this, some owners of Toy Poodles don't like to put any kind of collar on their dogs. If you don't want to put a collar on your Toy or Mini, you need to use a harness.

A *harness* can be made of leather or fabric, and it adjusts around a dog's chest and legs, generally fastening with a strap around the body as well. It should have a ring on the back for attaching your lead. The most important thing is to find one that fits snugly. If the harness is too tight, it will pinch; if it's too loose, it will chafe.

Another option for training is a *head halter.* These devices fit on your dog's head and over her muzzle. You attach the lead to a ring on the halter. Head halters can give you more control during training — especially if you have a larger, more exuberant Poodle (probably in the Standard category) that's difficult to handle with a collar and lead. The halter should fit very snugly. There should be no looseness, as with a buckle collar, but it shouldn't be so tight as to cut into the flesh or leave an indentation or ridge.

At first, dogs fight head halters. The secret to faster acceptance is to keep your Poodle's head up as she tries to paw off the halter. Try not to let her succeed; if she knows she can get it off, it will take longer to convince her to leave it alone.

Head halters come with detailed instructions on their use, which should be followed carefully. Head halters should *never* be pulled or jerked with the leash, as this action can jerk the dog's head around and cause serious neck injury. An injury can also occur if the dog makes a sudden lunge that causes her head to be pulled back or to the side. It's best to learn the use of a head halter under the direction of an experienced trainer.

Leading on

The lead (or leash) is what connects you to your Poodle and keeps her safe during walks while giving her some freedom to move around. When your puppy is ready to head out into the great outdoors, try to familiarize her with the lead first with these steps:

1. **Start by attaching a lightweight, short lead to your puppy's collar (collars come with a ring just for this purpose).**

   Many show leads are ideal for puppies, because they're lightweight and shorter than a regular lead.

2. **Let your puppy drag the lead until she gets used to it.**

Always supervise when the lead is attached to your puppy's collar. You don't want it to catch on an object and panic your puppy.

3. **After your puppy gets used to dragging the lead, pick the lead up and walk with her.**

The desired position when you walk a dog is to have the dog on your left side, but at this point, don't worry about that. You want the dog walking on a slack lead and at this point, that's all.

4. **If your puppy keeps getting distracted, encourage her to walk with you by slapping your leg and calling her.**

Having a treat or two on hand is also a good idea.

Here's a tip to teach your Poodle not to pull or to follow you when you want to change directions: Every time she wants to go somewhere you don't, stop. Just stand still. She'll likely look back to see what's going on, and then you can start walking again. Or, after you have her attention, you can turn and head in the direction *you* want.

When your Poodle gets older and has figured out the concept of walking nicely, you can get a longer lead; six feet is a good length. If you have a Toy or a Miniature, get a lighter, thinner lead so the clasp isn't dragging at the dog's neck. You can get a heavier lead for a Standard.

You also can walk an older Poodle on a retractable lead, but be courteous if you use one. Be aware of other people and dogs, and don't let your dog dash up to strangers, just because the lead is long enough to allow it. You have much less control of your dog with a retractable lead, although they do have the advantage, in an open area, of allowing your dog more freedom.

Training Your Poodle with Basic Commands

Basic commands can help keep your Poodle safe and make her a pleasure to be around. In the sections that follow, I describe a variety of commands you can teach to your Poodle to become master of your domain. (At least you'll think you're the master. Poodles tend to teach their "masters" quite a bit.)

Come!

Come is the first command you should teach your Poodle. You'll need it in many everyday situations, whether you're in your home, on a walk, or at the vet's office. Before you start training, though, remember these tips:

- ✔ Always praise your Poodle for coming to you.

- ✔ Never call your Poodle to you for punishment or for any activity she may find unpleasant, like nail clipping. For these situations, go and get her.

- ✔ Never call your Poodle if you can't enforce the command. For example, if your dog is bounding across the yard after a squirrel, don't start hollering "Come!" Doing so just teaches her that she doesn't have to obey.

In the following sections, I explain how to use treats and train outside when working on the "Come!" command with your Poodle.

Tempting with treats

Start your "Come!" training with treats; most dogs have never met a treat they didn't like. Just follow these steps:

1. **Start with your dog on lead.**

   You can use a long rope as the training advances, so you always have the option of reeling your dog in. That way, she learns that even at a distance, she must obey the command.

2. **Train close up at first so your Poodle can see and smell the treat.**

   Don't pull her in with the lead unless it's absolutely necessary.

3. **When your Poodle reaches you, take hold of her collar before you give her the treat.**

   If you really need to catch your Poodle, you don't want her to run in, snatch the treat, and take off again, so include holding the collar as part of the deal. If you want to, you can let go and allow her to go back to whatever she was doing before you called her. Mix the training up so that the command to come doesn't always mean that playtime is over.

 If your dog is less than enthusiastic over the treat you're using, switch to something more tempting, like a ball or a squeaky toy. Use whatever it takes to get your Poodle running to you when you say her name and "Come!"

It's a snap: Clicker training

Clicker training is a technique that uses the sound of a clicker and positive reinforcement to produce a desired reaction in an animal. The sound of the clicker marks a behavior the minute the behavior occurs, and the sound is followed by the giving of a treat. Soon, the animal discovers that she gets a reward when she follows an order like "Sit!"

The advantages of clicker training include the lack of delay in the process, and the fact that the clicker sounds the same to the animal every time. Giving commands with your voice can be inconsistent, because you may produce variations in volume or tone that will confuse your Poodle. You also use the clicker only for training purposes, unlike your voice.

One disadvantage is that you need to have your clicker with you at all times, and it can take awhile to be coordinated enough to click and then give your dog a treat. Many beginners treat and then click, or they click too late. Don't worry; dogs are forgiving, and soon both you and your Poodle will master the process.

If you're interested in using clicker training with your Poodle, you first must get her used to the idea that the sound of the clicker means a treat is coming. Click the device and give a treat several times. It shouldn't take long for your Poodle to make the connection. You can buy clickers at pet-supply stores, from catalogs, or online. You also can use the top of a ballpoint pen. It doesn't produce as loud a sound, but it does work.

You have three ways to train your Poodle with a clicker:

✔ To *lure* a dog into an action like sitting, take a treat and hold it over her head, moving the treat back out of her sight. As your dog goes into the sit position, click and treat.

✔ To *shape* a desired behavior, watch your Poodle and click when she begins to do something you want her to do. For example, if you want her to lie down on her bed on command, click and treat when she walks near or over her bed. After she realizes that being near her bed gets her a treat, treat only when she actually moves onto the bed. After that, treat only when she sits. Finally, give out a treat only when she lies down.

✔ When you *capture,* you click for a final result. Say your Poodle does something cute, like sneezing just before you set down her food bowl. Arm yourself with your clicker and treats just before you feed her. As you set the bowl down and she sneezes, click and treat! Every time she sneezes, click and treat. Name the action, and with click training, your Poodle will be doing it on command.

As with all training techniques, you need to be patient and consistent with clicker training. Don't get frustrated if you can't seem to coordinate clicking and treating all the time. It isn't unusual for owners to treat and then click at first, but you'll get it eventually.

Note: You'll need many treats for this training, so cut them up small when you get them. Your dog will work just as happily for a tiny piece. The idea is to train your Poodle, not make her fat!

Check out *Dog Training For Dummies,* 2nd Edition, by Jack and Wendy Volhard (Wiley) for more details on clicker training.

Moving to the great outdoors

When you're ready to move your "Come!" training outdoors, keep your Poodle on lead and follow the steps in the previous section. Use lots of praise and treats, and let her go back to playing after she's come to you.

Don't rush the training. A dog in hot pursuit of a squirrel isn't going to listen to you. Keep a lead or a long rope attached to your Poodle's collar until you're certain that she'll obey the command to "come."

Another technique you can use to get your Poodle to come when you're outside is to play the chase game. Follow these simple steps:

1. **Wait until your Poodle becomes interested in something else around her.**

2. **Call her name and then say "Come!"**

3. **When she looks at you, turn and run the opposite direction.**

   It's a rare dog who won't dash after you at this point. When she catches you, praise her and hold her collar. Then, either snap on the lead or release her for another play session. Your Poodle will think this is a wonderful game.

Years ago, my family lived near a schoolyard that offered plenty of room for an early morning romp. To get to the schoolyard, though, we had to walk a short distance up a busy road. One morning, our two dogs got loose and started for the yard on their own, trotting right down the middle of the road. They were too far away to grab, so I yelled their names to get their attention and then turned and ran back to the house. My heart was in my mouth, but I didn't stop until I reached the house. When I got there, both dogs were dancing around my feet, excited to play this great new game.

Sit!

"Sit!" is another basic, useful command. You have many reasons to want to teach your Poodle to sit:

- ✔ You'll have an easier time putting a collar or lead on a dog that's sitting rather than bouncing with excitement at the thought of a walk.

- ✔ Having your Poodle sit before you put down her food dish reduces the risk that she'll jump up and knock the dish out of your hand.

- ✔ A sitting Poodle is much nicer for guests to pet than one that acts like she's on a pogo stick.

To train your Poodle how to sit, follow these simple steps:

1. **Grab a small treat from your collection.**

2. **Hold the treat in front of your Poodle's nose, move it back over the top of her head, and then tell her to sit.**

   She should sink into a sit as she lifts her nose to follow the treat. Don't hold the treat too high, though, or she may try to get it by jumping.

3. **The minute your Poodle sinks into a sit, give her the treat and praise her.**

Down!

"Down!" is a basic command you can use if you want your Poodle to lie down. If you plan to do most of your Poodle's grooming yourself (see Chapter 8), teaching her to lie down on the grooming table makes the process easier for both of you. She doesn't have to stand the entire time, and you can reach all of her body more easily. Also, when you combine "Down!" with the stay command in the next section, you can leave your Poodle for an extended period of time and be sure that she's in a comfortable and relaxed state.

You can teach most anything in multiple ways, so if one method of teaching "Down!" doesn't work, try something else. Here are a couple of methods you can try:

✔ Take a treat, put your dog in a sitting position (see the previous section), and then lower the treat in front of her while simultaneously moving it slightly forward. Say "down." Ideally, your Poodle will sink into the down position as she follows the treat. If this works for you, terrific!

✔ I've found that with smaller dogs, as their heads move forward, their rears pop up. So, in this position with a smaller dog, show her a treat and then bring your closed hand down. If she slides into a down position, terrific! If not, keep your closed hand, holding the treat, on the floor. Your Poodle may paw or nibble at your hand, but be patient. Eventually, she'll lie down. The minute she does, praise her and give her the treat. It won't take her long to figure out that down is where she needs to be if she wants a treat.

Stay!

"Stay!" can be just as important as "Come!" You'll be happy to have a dog that will sit and lie down on command, but "Stay!" can save your Poodle's life! How, you ask? Here are a few examples:

- ✔ You can teach your Poodle to stay when you open a door so she won't bolt out into traffic or go after another animal.

- ✔ If your Poodle does get away from you and crosses the street safely, you don't want to call her back through traffic. Give the "Stay!" command so you can go and get her.

- ✔ I use "Stay!" to keep my dogs at a safe distance when I'm removing food from a hot oven.

"Stay!" can also serve practical purposes. For example, you can combine "Down!" and "Stay!" so you don't have to banish your Poodle to another room when you put snacks on the coffee table.

You can teach "Stay!" with your Poodle in a standing, sitting, or lying position. I've always started with my dogs sitting, so that's how I describe the steps here, but the choice is yours:

1. **Attach the lead to your Poodle's collar and have her sit by your left side.**

2. **Holding the lead in your right hand, extend your left arm so that your left hand, palm facing the dog, is in front of your Poodle's muzzle.**

3. **Give the "Stay!" command, and take one step in front of your Poodle, pivoting as you step so that you're standing directly in front of her and facing her.**

4. **Step back into your original position: beside your dog and facing forward.**

   If your Poodle stays, praise her and give her a treat.

Gradually, I increase the amount of time between when I give the command and when I give the treat. I also try to take an extra step or two back. As your Poodle gets better at staying, you can start to move around before you return to her side.

When you feel that your Poodle fully understands the "Stay!" command, start trying it with her off the lead. Leave the room for a second or two and then return. Just remember not to rush the training.

If you plan to compete formally in obedience (see Chapter 13 for details), start walking all the way around your Poodle. Walk past her left side, behind her, and then stop next to her right shoulder.

Leave it!

I couldn't live without the "Leave it!" command. Okay, I could live, but life wouldn't be as pleasant. You can teach your dog to "leave it" so she doesn't eat or carry around undesirable items. When she drops something she shouldn't have to the floor, you can get rid of it right away. I can think of many situations that "Leave it!" rescues:

- ✔ When your Poodle has one of your best shoes in her mouth, she'll spit it out before she takes another bite.

- ✔ You can prevent an episode from turning into a lovely game of chase or a tug-of-war with your lingerie.

- ✔ When the day comes that your precious darling tries to bring a dead chipmunk into the house, you won't have to pry the animal from her jaws.

- ✔ I also use the command when I'm playing fetch with my dog. I prefer having her drop the ball at my feet instead of wrestling the slimy thing away from her.

An easy way to teach "Leave it!" is with a trade. Have some kind of yummy treat ready; when your Poodle has a toy in her mouth, tell her to leave it at the same time that you show her the treat. She should willingly trade! After she eats the treat, give her the toy back. If she has a piece of clothing like a sock in her mouth, make the trade with the treat and then substitute an acceptable toy for the sock. For these situations, some people teach the word "trade" as well so their dogs know for sure that they'll replace whatever they have in their mouths.

My male dog knows the "Leave it!" command, but he also knows a toy when he has it clenched between his jaws. He enjoys destroying stuffed toys, so when I want to end a play session, I tell him I want to "trade." If he obliges, I get the toy and he gets a dog biscuit. He's gotten so clever, though, that he sometimes picks up a toy, goes over to the counter, and looks up at the treat jar, waiting for a trade!

Heel!

"Heel" is a formal position, where your Poodle appears at your left side with her muzzle even with your knee. Your dog should maintain this position when you walk, run, or halt. When you stop, your Poodle should do an automatic sit, without hearing the command.

You may not need your dog to heel in most situations, but it can be a useful command. When you're walking in a crowd or near other people and dogs, having your Poodle next to you makes it easier to avoid others. If you need to go up an escalator or ride in an elevator, you'll want your Poodle at your side.

Follow these steps to teach your Poodle to heel:

1. **Start with your Poodle on your left side in the sit position.**

2. **Give the command to "Heel!" and start walking.**

   When you first start out, you can hold a piece of food in your left hand to keep her in position. If you're coordinated enough, you can drop a piece of food into your Poodle's mouth every now and then as you go along.

   If your Poodle lags, speed up the walk. If she forges ahead, stop dead or turn around and run in the opposite direction. Change direction without warning. All these behaviors make her keep an eye on you to see what you're going to do next.

3. **Whenever you stop, even if only for a moment to get her to stop walking ahead of you, tell her to sit.**

   Eventually, your Poodle will sit automatically, because you always tell her to sit when you stop. Praise for the automatic sit, but keep it low key. This isn't the time for a "dance of joy." That would make your dog break the sit. A pleasant "good dog" will do.

 If you've taught your Poodle to sit by standing in front of her, you may need to teach her to sit all over again for the heel command. To a dog, sitting in front of you and sitting beside you are two entirely different behaviors.

Overcoming Common Canine Behavior Problems

As much as we all want to believe that our wonderful dogs are perfect, we know that none of them are. You don't want others to expect you to be perfect, so you shouldn't expect the same of your Poodle. I discuss some imperfect behaviors in the following sections.

 You can correct many of the behaviors, or at least lessen them, with training. If you can't seem to do it yourself, and none of the methods are working, you can find a professional who can help (I cover getting help in the final section of this chapter).

Barking at the mailman, at neighbors, at squirrels, at . . .

Dogs bark for many reasons. Sometimes, you want your Poodle to bark to let you know if a stranger is walking in your yard or if an unwanted animal is digging through your trash. Other times, though, your Poodle's barking can get out of hand. It can annoy you and your neighbors if your Poodle barks at every jogger or squirrel in the yard. If the bad outweighs the good, you need to figure out a way to lessen, if not stop, the barking. The following sections cover ways you can curb outdoor and indoor barking.

Some people have had luck with bark collars; these devices release a puff of citrus scent every time the dog barks. The theory is that the surprise, plus the smell that many dogs dislike, will correct the habit. This may work, but some dogs are smart enough to catch on that the collars have a limited supply of the spray, so they just bark nonstop until they use up the spray. At that point, they're free to bark as much as they want. If your dog figures it out, you have one smart puppy!

Outdoor barking

Your dog may love to bark at animals in the yard. If you have rabbits, squirrels, or other critters on your property, try to supervise your Poodle's yard time. Join her for a game, or give her a toy packed with treats to draw her attention away from the bunnies.

Animals aren't the only things that trigger barking, though. The following list gives you some causes and tips of outdoor barking:

- ✔ Your Poodle could be bored. Your solution may be a game of fetch. If you play hard enough, she may want to find a shady corner and snooze. Another trick is to not leave your dog outdoors for so long that she gets bored. If you suspect this is the case, when she starts barking, call her in at once.

- ✔ If your Poodle barks every time someone walks by, consider erecting a solid fence. Dogs are less apt to bark if they can't see what's on the other side of a fence.

- ✔ Maybe your Poodle is barking because she wants to come inside. She may be hot, cold, wet, or lonely. Let her in!

Indoor barking

Indoor barking may not drive the neighbors nuts, but it will test your sanity. A frequent culprit is noises outside. A loud truck may be rumbling by, an emergency vehicle may have its siren going, or children may be playing in the street. A softly playing radio or tele-vision may be enough to mask the sounds, and drapes or blinds may help to prevent your Poodle from barking at the kids.

Another frequent culprit is the doorbell, which tends to set most dogs off. Even a doorbell ringing on TV can start my dogs woofing. Just about every dog-training book ever written has a solution for this problem. You may have to try more than one method before you find the one that works for you and your Poodle.

Here's my two cents: When the doorbell rings and your Poodle barks — or, if you're fast, just before she starts — tell her to bark. When she follows your command, which is to bark, praise her and give her a treat. Soon, she may stop barking in anticipation of the treat. Otherwise, after she knows the command "bark," add "quiet," "stop," or whatever word you want to use as the command to stop barking, and give the treat when she stops.

What worked for me with my male dog was to have a handful of treats in my closed hand. When he started barking, I held up my fist, said "Quiet," and released a treat when he looked at me. It didn't take him long to make the connection between my raised fist and a treat, and he was more than happy to stop barking.

It's also helpful with many Poodles to put them on a down and stay when the bell rings. Most won't bark under this command. You may release your Poodle to calmly greet the visitor when he enters.

If you're at home and your Poodle is barking, you can distract her with an indoor game, or you can run through the obedience com-mands she knows. However, if your dog is indoors and you're away, she may bark because she's suffering from separation anxi-ety. Videotapes of dogs left alone have shown that they're most anxious during the first 10 to 15 minutes of alone time. Before you leave home, try to give your Poodle some strenuous exercise. Go on a brisk walk, or play a game of fetch. When you finish, give her a treat-stuffed toy just before you leave. The combination of fatigue and having something to occupy her while you're gone may be enough to keep her calm.

If your Poodle isn't anxious and just loves to bark, try these steps:

1. **Go through your normal routine of getting ready to leave the house.**

2. **Leave.**

3. **Count to ten and then go back in the house.**

4. **Leave again.**

5. **Try to gradually extend the amount of time you're gone.**

6. **When your dog starts barking, go back in immediately; otherwise, continue to extend the time.**

This procedure may take days or even weeks, so be patient.

I beg you — no begging!

Begging, to me, is worse than barking. Begging means you have a dog in your face just when you want to enjoy a meal or relax with a snack. At best, begging takes the form of a silent stare with those big pathetic eyes. At worst, your dog is pawing at you, jumping on you, or actually stealing a morsel from your hand. As Barney Fife used to say, "Nip it. Nip it in the bud!"

Unfortunately, begging is a hard habit to break. Canine survival over the years has been dependent on knowing where the food is. If you catch a rabbit once by the pine tree, that's the spot to revisit. If you feed your adorable little puppy once from the table, you'll have an uninvited dinner guest forever. You may think, "Oh, just this once won't hurt," but once is all it takes to start the begging habit. You need to follow Barney's advice and nip it in the bud.

The best approach to overcoming a begging problem is to not let the begging habit start in the first place. Make it a firm family rule to never feed your Poodle from the table. If you absolutely must give the little dear a taste of your Thanksgiving turkey, add the treat to her food bowl; don't slip it to her under the table. The same goes for evening snacks in front of the television.

If the begging habit is in place, you can break it, but it will take time and patience. Stop feeding whatever the Poodle is begging for. The dog will make a pest of herself and may increase her begging behavior. She may jump up, bark, paw at you, and whine, but don't give in. It's common for the behavior to get worse before it's eliminated. It's up to you to stop rewarding the behavior. Then all you can do is live through your dog's efforts for that reward. Eventually, she'll stop trying.

It also helps to put your Poodle on a down and stay if she begs, and then ignore her. For the very persistent beggar, simply remove her from the room at the first sign of begging.

Chewing on everything

Dogs love to chew on most any object. Why a dog chews may depend on her mood. Some dogs chew because they feel relaxed and happy (think a bone by the fireplace). Some dogs chew because they feel anxious (think your new shoe by the front door). Young dogs chew because they're teething, and the act of chewing massages their gums and makes them feel better. Chewing is natural, so you don't want your Poodle to never chew. What you want is to make sure that what your Poodle chews, she doesn't choose the fringe on your rug, the rung of an antique chair, or your good pair of shoes.

No matter how old your Poodle is, supply chew toys for her. Some dogs enjoy stuffed toys; some prefer nylon bones; and others like the hard, rubber toys that you can stuff with peanut butter or cheese. Having acceptable chew toys on hand gives your Poodle more appealing options. If you find your Poodle in the act of chewing on something off-limits, trade him for an acceptable toy (see the earlier section "Leave it!" for more on trading). You should also make sure the shoe's owner doesn't leave the shoe where the dog can reach it. (There's nothing better than a puppy to teach everyone in the family to pick up all items of clothing!) See Chapter 5 for examples of good chew toys.

A teething dog benefits from anything cold, so to supply acceptable chewing objects, wet and freeze a tennis ball or an old washcloth. You also can give your Poodle an ice cube now and then.

Nipping and mouthing

Nipping and biting aren't the same actions. Biting implies an act of aggression (which I cover later in this chapter). Nipping also can indicate aggression, but I think of nipping in a separate, more benign category. That doesn't make it pleasant, however — just less Cujo-like.

Puppies nip. Most likely, they learned not to bite too hard while they were still playing with their littermates. However, their play bites may be too much for a human hand or ankle to handle, due to their needle-sharp baby teeth. If your Poodle puppy nips you, say "Owww" in a high-pitched voice. Stop playing. Your pup will soon figure out that if she bites, the fun stops.

If your adult Poodle, who has always been well mannered, is now nipping, schedule a visit to your veterinarian's office to make sure she has no physical problems. An older dog with arthritis in her joints may start nipping when you touch her, because the touch hurts. If she's fine physically, you may need to consult an animal behaviorist (see the later section on finding professional help).

You may have a Poodle that mouths, which can certainly startle people who don't know what your dog is doing. Some dogs just like putting their mouths around hands or wrists. I have a dog, who, when excited, grabs my hand. To prevent her from mouthing on a guest's hand, and to prevent her from accidentally tearing skin when she falls back, I've trained her to get her toy when she gets excited. This game is a variation of fetch. She knows the word "toy," so getting her to retrieve it was easy.

Digging up some trouble

Poodles aren't diggers in the way that other dogs, such as terriers, are diggers. The activity isn't their life work. Your Poodle may, however, be a recreational digger, for many reasons:

- Poodle puppies often dig and then outgrow the practice.
- A Poodle may dig if she's hot, because lying in a cool hole is a real treat in the summer.
- A Poodle may dig if she's chasing a rodent or any critter that disappears down a hole or under a fence.
- Heck, maybe your Poodle is just bored!

If your Poodle digs only now and then, you can just fill in the holes and forget it. You also can keep a sharp eye on your Poodle and, if she starts to dig, distract her with a game or a trade (see the earlier section "Leave it!" for more on trading). Telling her no in a firm voice is fine, too.

If your Poodle seems to have a passion for digging, you should consider giving your dog her own special digging spot. Follow these steps:

1. **Select a fitting area of your yard and mark it off with low boards.**

2. **Add sand or soil to the boarded area, or dig up the area to provide your Poodle with some digging material.**

3. **Bury your Poodle's favorite toy or some tasty treats in the area, and guide her to her new digging spot.**

   Another trick is to drip a bit of bacon grease on the surface.

4. **If she starts to dig up another part of the yard, bury a few more treats and guide her to the spot.**

   It shouldn't take long for your Poodle to figure out that the boarded area is her own private excavation site.

Jump, jumping around

Most dogs are great jumpers; otherwise, you wouldn't see those cool animal-trick bits on late-night television shows. If you have a Toy or Miniature, you may not consider jumping such a terrible habit, but even smaller Poodle varieties can get mud all over good clothes or ruin a pair of nylons. Standard Poodles, however, can knock people over with their exuberance. You may love the joyous leaping greetings your Poodle gives you, but not all your visitors will feel the same way — especially if a child or older person gets injured.

The simplest way to teach your Poodle not to jump is to ignore her when she jumps up, starting when she's a puppy. It's hard to ignore an adult Standard when she jumps! When you walk in the door and your Poodle jumps up to greet you, turn sideways and totally ignore her. Don't pet her, talk to her, or make eye contact with her. Don't even push her away. When she doesn't get the attention she wants, she stops the ineffective behavior; that's when you use the sit command (which I cover earlier in this chapter) and pet her. Giving the cold shoulder is tough, but you'll be glad you did!

 Make sure everyone in your family understands the no-jumping rule. It isn't fair to your Poodle to be allowed to jump up sometimes but not always. She'll get confused. Explain your system to any visitors ahead of time to make sure that they, too, ignore your Poodle when she jumps up.

 When your Poodle understands that she must sit for attention, you can teach her to jump up on command. Lure her up with treats held to chest level (or whatever height your Poodle can reach), or pat your chest or leg, while giving whatever command you choose, such as "hup" or "stand tall." Give plenty of praise and a treat when she obeys.

Aggression against others

Aggression against a burglar is something you'd approve of in your Poodle, but unprovoked or indiscriminate aggression is a problem you can't condone. Generally, Poodles, as a breed, don't show aggression for no reason, but any individual dog can have a problem. The dog's personality and the way she was or wasn't socialized can have a bearing on how aggressive she is (for more on socializing your Poodle, see Chapter 11).

 If your Poodle shows unprovoked aggression toward people, get professional help, as I explain later in this chapter. You're not going to be able to correct this on your own.

On the other hand, your Poodle may be fine with people and still show aggression toward other dogs. Toys and Miniatures can go on the offensive against larger dogs out of fear. A male of any size that hasn't been neutered may show aggression toward another male. You can nip the problem in the bud with early socialization around other dogs, or you can count on a good obedience class to lessen, if not eliminate, the problem. For more on finding the right class, see the following section.

If you decide on training your Poodle with a class, make sure the instructor knows that your dog is aggressive toward other dogs. You also should make sure that the instructor has experience dealing with this problem and is comfortable with the situation. If you enter your Poodle in the class without divulging all the info and a fight erupts, your Poodle may be seriously injured or even killed, not to mention that a lawsuit is possible if your dog attacks another. If you let the instructor know, the worst that could happen is that he'll refer you to someone else.

If your Poodle has always been a lover but is now showing aggression for no apparent reason, you need to rule out any physical problems by visiting your veterinarian. At that point, you should run, not walk, to the nearest source of help.

Finding Professional Help

You can find many wonderful books that deal with the subject of training your Poodle, as well as training DVDs that aim to help you mold a well-mannered canine companion. I include extensive advice on training techniques throughout this chapter (and book, really). However, you also have other training options at your disposal, such as classes, lessons, and visits to animal behaviorists. I describe these options in the following sections; you shouldn't hesitate to take advantage of any of these options. I've always used a combination of classes and books. Find out as much as you can in any way that you can.

If you have a problem of any kind with your Poodle, act to correct it before it grows to uncontrollable proportions. The sooner you deal with a problem, the less likely it is to grow worse.

Attending classes

You can find all kinds of formal classes to enroll your Poodle in, from puppy classes (see Chapter 11 on socializing) to novice obedience to advanced training. For Poodles old enough for formal training, as opposed to puppy classes that are for socialization, you should look for an obedience class. Most instructors won't accept a dog in class until she's had all her shots, which is generally by the age of three months. An obedience class helps your Poodle adjust to other people and dogs and teaches her the basic commands that will make her a good citizen (see earlier sections in this chapter for more on teaching commands).

You should be able to find an obedience class for your Poodle at one of the following places:

- ✔ Your local YMCA or YWCA
- ✔ Your community's animal shelter
- ✔ A boarding kennel (also a good place to get a referral)
- ✔ A local pet-supply store
- ✔ The bulletin board at the local pet-supply store or the one at your vet's office

You also can ask your veterinarian, your breeder, and your friends for recommendations.

The price of a series of classes varies, and classes generally run for eight weeks. Look for small classes; the larger the class, the less personal attention you and your dog will receive. And always observe an instructor at work before you sign up.

Taking private lessons

If you have a specific problem with your Poodle's behavior, such as dog aggression (see the earlier section "Aggression against others"), you may want to hire a professional trainer to come to your home for some one-on-one attention. In a classroom setting, the instructor won't have the time to focus on specific problems; the goal of a class is to teach everyone particular behaviors.

To find a qualified trainer to come to your home, ask for recommendations. Many people may know how to train basic commands, but if you've got a problem, you need someone experienced in dealing with that problem. Get references and check them out. A qualified trainer may be a member of a professional organization, such as the Association of Pet Dog Trainers (APDT; www.apdt.com).

Look for a trainer who is calm; he shouldn't yell or scream. Some trainers use only positive reinforcement; others may tell a dog "no" or give a collar correction. There should never be a correction until the dog knows what she's supposed to do. Dogs shouldn't be forced into positions.

If any instructor, whether from a class or in the personalized field, tells you to hit, drag, or "hang" your dog, look for another trainer.

Seeking out animal behaviorists

Most Poodles have stable temperaments, but if you're having problems with your Poodle — problems that go beyond high spirits and annoying habits that you can correct (or have corrected) with proper training and regular exercise — you may want to consider hiring an animal behaviorist.

An animal behaviorist helping your Poodle is a bit like a psychologist or psychiatrist helping a person. His job is to figure out the reasons behind your dog's behavior and to work to modify that behavior, based on the causes. A behaviorist, like a psychiatrist, should look at the possible causes of bad behavior, not just trying to train your dog not to engage in that bad behavior. He works with you and your dog in your home.

You can talk to your veterinarian for a referral to an animal behaviorist, as well as other dog owners who may have consulted with behaviorists. No national standards govern animal training, but here are some sources that may help you locate a behaviorist:

- **American Veterinary Society of Animal Behavior (AVSAB):** This organization consists of a group of veterinarians who share an interest in teaching training techniques and treating behavior problems in animals. Head to www.avsab.us for more info.

- **Animal Behavior Society (ABS):** Members of the Animal Behavior Society have degrees ranging from psychology to biology, zoology, or animal science, but they all have demonstrated expertise in understanding and treating animal behaviors. Go to www.animalbehavior.org for more details.

- **International Association of Animal Behavior Consultants (IAABC):** This organization works to help animals and their people by teaching people how to correct behavior problems. Head to www.iaabc.org for more information.

A trainer also may be an animal behaviorist but not necessarily. A trainer may have trained hundreds of dogs, and he may call himself a behaviorist, but that doesn't mean he is one. Make sure you check the credentials of the supposed "therapist" so you aren't duped into paying high fees for amateur help.

Chapter 11

Socializing Your Poodle

In This Chapter
▶ Getting your Poodle used to new folks
▶ Dealing with new situations, objects, and noises

*F*aces, places, and things that go bump in the night: You want your Poodle to be comfortable with all of these things. This chapter helps you socialize your Poodle so that he's not a "scaredy cat."

Acclimating Your Poodle to New Faces

Your Poodle needs to feel comfortable in the world beyond his immediate family, and the only way that's going to happen is to introduce him to as many different people as possible while he's young. (You can socialize an older dog, but it's much harder.) I give you some pointers in the following sections.

Meeting the neighbors

Give your Poodle a few days to get used to his new home and family (see Chapter 6 about welcoming your Poodle home) and then start introducing him to the wide world. Until he has all his shots, you don't want him running at the local dog park, but he can start to meet the neighbors — both human and canine.

Let your children bring home their friends to play with your Poodle. Supervise their play so no one gets hurt. Make sure younger children, especially, understand how to be gentle with a puppy, and keep the play sessions short and quiet. Very young children don't understand that tugging on an ear or a tail can hurt a dog, so you may have to remove either the puppy or the child from the group. Chapter 6 has more details on introducing a Poodle to children.

To a dog, all humans aren't created equal. A dog differentiates between men, women, and children and needs to meet and be comfortable with all three categories:

- If you're childless, ask the neighbor children to play with your puppy.

- If you have no men in your household, ask a few male friends to stop by to meet your puppy.

- If your household is all male, find a female or two who can help socialize your puppy.

Many experienced dog trainers recommend that a puppy meet at least 100 people by the time he's 12 weeks old. Here are some guidelines for introducing your Poodle to new people:

- If you have a fenced yard, invite friends and neighbors over to meet your Poodle while he's off his lead. If you don't have a fence, keep your Poodle on a lead for the meetings. Have plenty of treats handy for the visitors to give.

- If your Poodle is full of energy and likely to jump up, be cautious around small children, who can get knocked down. Keep your dog on a lead when meeting children, and encourage children to approach him quietly.

- Carry treats with you on walks. If you meet someone, ask if they'll pet your Poodle and give him a treat.

My adult female is a bit shy, but she never hesitates to approach a stranger at a dog show because she's learned that almost everyone has a pocketful of liver!

- Keep greetings low key, and let your Poodle approach people on his own. Don't drag him up to people and force him to hold still for petting.

Setting up play dates

Play dates are a good way for your puppy to meet other dogs in a controlled setting. If you know someone with a puppy of any breed, or with a smaller adult dog, arrange a play date. Plan the date for a secure area. At first, it's best to have two or three dogs in the group so it'll be easier to control them should things get out of hand.

While your Poodle is still a puppy, stay away from larger adult dogs who may be too rough for a puppy. If your dog's play date is with an adult dog, make the introductions gradually. Most adult dogs are fine with a small puppy, but it's better to be safe than sorry. Keep the dogs on loose leads for the introduction.

Don't tighten the leads. The tension of the lead can translate as tension, which can lead to aggression, instead of a friendly greeting.

Most adult dogs understand that puppies aren't a threat, and they'll accept things from puppies that they would never allow in another adult dog. Still, if you notice the hair on the adult dog's neck and back going up or feel a growl through the lead, or if the adult lifts his lip, it's time to separate the dogs before a fight breaks out.

You can organize neighbors to meet an older Poodle, too, but you may need to be more cautious. An older dog may already be leery of children or men, and you need to proceed slowly and with care to overcome your dog's fear.

Enrolling in puppy kindergarten or other classes

If you don't have any children in your neighborhood and can't find a friend with a dog for play dates, puppy kindergarten is a wonderful way to socialize a puppy. Animal shelters sometimes hold puppy kindergarten classes, or they may know someone who does offer classes. Call area boarding kennels or contact your local kennel club or dog training club to find a puppy kindergarten near you.

Although your puppy may discover a few basic commands in class, formal training isn't the point of puppy kindergarten. The goal is to socialize the puppies and make them happy to see people and other dogs. One common kindergarten exercise is to have people sit on the ground in a circle, with a puppy in the middle. Taking turns, the people call the puppy, using a high, happy voice and giving lots of treats and pats when the puppy responds. This exercise teaches a puppy that people have good things to offer. The puppy also realizes that responding when called is a good thing.

If you've adopted an older dog, ask around about basic obedience classes. A beginner's class may be the perfect way to introduce your older Poodle to strange people and dogs.

Visit any training class before joining. Look for a class that uses positive training methods. Poodles don't respond well to harsh training methods.

Talk to the instructor ahead of time if your dog is shy or fearful around other dogs or if you think your dog may be aggressive, either with dogs or with people. A good instructor can help with these issues without endangering anyone.

Handling Strange Situations, Objects, and Noises

Getting your Poodle used to different situations, objects, and noises doesn't mean your dog may not be startled by something, but it does mean that he can recover quickly and return to normal — and not cower or bark. In the following sections, I explain how to prepare your Poodle for car rides, get him used to new situations and objects, and handle a fear of loud noises.

Going for car rides

Most puppies adjust easily to car rides. Occasionally, a puppy can be carsick, but he generally outgrows this, especially if you make sure that rides are a pleasant treat (make sure you don't always end at the veterinarian's). If your puppy gets carsick, keep rides short and carry a roll of paper towels for clean up.

If you have an older dog, and he only enters the car kicking and screaming, take it slow and be patient. Open doors on both sides of the car and coax your dog in with treats, and then let him leave by way of the opposite door. Don't try to keep him in the car.

After he's comfortable getting in and out of the car, shut one door. Get him in the car, give him a treat, and get out of the car. Gradually, stay in the car with him, until he's comfortable sitting with you. Shut the door and sit awhile, offering tasty treats.

When your Poodle is happy with this arrangement, take a short drive. The important word is *short* — which may mean the length of your driveway and back. Gradually increase the length of the ride. Drive around the block or to a neighborhood park.

Offer treats and keep your tone of voice upbeat during a car ride. Take your Poodle with you when you do your banking. Many tellers keep dog treats at the drive-thru window. Stop by the local fast food restaurant for a snack. Sometimes they also have dog biscuits at the take-out window, or you can order a burger. . . hold everything. It won't take your dog long to associate car rides with goodies.

Did I mention that you need to restrain your Poodle in some way while he's in the car? You can crate your dog, or you can secure him with a special seat restraint (see Chapter 5 for more about these items). As with children, your dog should always be in the back seat. Not only is it safer for the dog, but also he can't interfere with the driver, which makes the back seat safer for everyone.

Adjusting to unfamiliar situations and objects

Introduce your Poodle to as many unfamiliar things as possible in a controlled setting, so you can make the encounters positive and reward his positive reactions.

To help familiarize your Poodle with a variety of people, places, sounds, and situations, try these helpful tips:

✔ Start introducing the unfamiliar when your Poodle is young and let him be a part of family life. Put his crate or pen in the kitchen or family room where he can get used to pots and pans banging or a timer beeping. Let him hear a radio or television, and if no one else does, ring the doorbell occasionally.

✔ Give your Poodle different surfaces to walk on. Put down a piece of carpeting or linoleum. Lay a section of screen on the floor. Put a milk jug in his pen or out in the yard. Outside, make a small playground. Cut the bottom from a box to form a small tunnel. Give him steps to go up and down.

✔ Take your puppy with you whenever you can (prepare him with the information on car rides in the previous section). Most banks allow dogs, and having the tellers make a fuss over your puppy and offer treats helps him think of strangers in a positive way. Weather permitting, sit on a bench outside a shopping mall. It's an easy way for your puppy to meet all kinds of people, dressed in all kinds of outfits, as well as being exposed to shopping carts and strollers.

✔ Get your Poodle used to people wearing different kinds of hats, as well as glasses. Place an open umbrella near your puppy and let him get used to it.

✔ When you're adding something new to the environment, invite your puppy to sniff the object. I tell my dogs to "smell," and when they do, I praise and, if possible, give a small treat.

✔ If your Poodle is already a member of the family when a new baby arrives, make introductions. Some people will bring home a garment from the hospital that the baby has worn to get the dog used to the smell before the baby ever comes home. Hold the baby and let your Poodle smell it, and then praise him. A new baby needs a lot of attention, but don't ignore your dog. Try to make time for regular walks and play. Let the dog join you as you care for the baby. The more your Poodle is included, the easier he'll accept the new addition to the family.

The more you can introduce to your puppy, the fewer problems you'll have when your dog grows up. You can get an adult dog used to new situations using the same techniques you use with a puppy, but it takes longer if he hasn't had a history of discovering new situations as a puppy.

Easing a fear of loud noises

Sometimes, in spite of all your efforts, something frightens your dog. Don't cuddle your Poodle and tell him everything is all right. You just reinforce his behavior, and he begins to equate a loud noise with your attention.

 The first dog I ever had was terrified of thunder and felt much more secure in the bathtub or shut in the car. (I didn't know about crates then.) As my male has aged, he's become more sensitive to thunder. If I notice he's becoming nervous or if he's pacing or whining, I distract him with a toy or a treat or try to interest him in a game.

Some dogs react to thunder; others pay no attention at all. If your dog is truly bothered by thunder, you can work to desensitize him. Get a recording, or make your own, of a thunderstorm. Play this on very low volume. If your dog doesn't react, turn the volume up a bit. As soon as your dog reacts to the sound, distract him with a game or make him work for a treat. Just say a quick "down," "sit," or "come," so that he's rewarded for doing something. You can also try a toy that holds food or dispenses it, so that your dog can focus on getting goodies and not on the noise. With each session, try to increase the volume until your dog ignores even the loudest thunderclap. This technique can be used with other loud noises, too, such as fireworks.

 If your Poodle is still bothered, try putting some cotton in his ears to muffle the sound. He may just shake his head until the cotton falls out, but it's worth a try!

The change in air pressure can bother a dog more than the actual noise of the thunder. Try to distract your Poodle with games or toys until the storm has passed. Try a peanut-butter-filled Kong or a similar toy that dispenses treats as your Poodle rolls and bats it around.

Chapter 12

Hitting the Road with Your Poodle

· ·

· ·

*Y*ou, the proud parent, will want your Poodle with you at all times, which is great (unless you're in the shower or at work). But, as I show you in this chapter, you need to know some things before you go traveling with your best buddy by land, air, or sea — like when it's better for everyone if your Poodle stays home!

Checking Out Your Traveling Options

The easiest way to travel with your Poodle is by car, but that doesn't mean you can just grab your dog and hit the road. You need to plan ahead and pack for your dog as well as yourself. Air travel is another way to go with your canine pal, but this takes more advance planning, and you need to think about whether your dog will travel as cargo or, if you have a Toy or a Miniature Poodle, whether she'll travel in the cabin with you. I go over the details of car and air travel with your Poodle in the following sections.

By car

Traveling by car gives you the most freedom with your plans and with your Poodle, but you still need to prepare if you want the trip to be trouble-free. If you need to go from point A to point B in a short amount of time, traveling with a dog isn't much different than traveling with a child. In fact, it may be easier, because you don't need to play games with her, and your dog won't ask, "Are we there yet?"

Most dogs enjoy riding in the car, but if you take your dog for a ride only when it's time for a visit with the vet, she may be reluctant to get in the car. Can you blame her? You wouldn't look forward to a ride, either, if the trip always ended at the doctor's office. See Chapter 11 for info on getting your Poodle used to car rides.

On a car trip, heed the following advice:

- ✓ **For maximum safety of dogs and humans, dogs shouldn't ride loose in any vehicle.** A sturdy crate is the safest place for a dog in a vehicle. A crate keeps the dog from being thrown around in case of an accident, and it offers some protection if the car is seriously damaged. Emergency response workers can safely remove a dog in a crate from a wrecked vehicle, but they may be unwilling to handle a loose, injured, and frightened one.

  If your car doesn't have room for a crate, the next best protection is a harness specifically designed for canine car safety. Be sure that it's correctly sized for your Poodle and correctly and snugly fastened to the car's seat belt system. (See Chapter 5 for more about crates and harnesses.)

- ✓ **Never, ever leave your dog in a hot car unattended.** Even with the windows open, a car in the sun can easily reach an unsafe interior temperature for your dog, and dogs have a harder time keeping cool than people do. Even if you park in the shade, you must remember that the shade will move. A nice, cool spot at 10 a.m. can be in direct sun by noon, and even 75 degree weather can overheat your car.

- ✓ **You need to stop every three or four hours to let her stretch her legs and take a potty break.** A puppy may need more frequent stops, as may an older dog. Base the time between stops on your home schedule. If your old girl needs to go out every two hours, stop your car that often, too.

  If you have your dog in a crate with a water dish, replenish the water at these stops. If you have her riding on the seat in a harness, offer her a drink when you stop. Whether on the seat or in a crate, make sure she isn't receiving direct sunlight.

- ✓ **If you're visiting a state or national park, your dog may be allowed, but make sure you know the rules before taking your dog with you on your adventures.** Most parks insist that your dog remain on a lead, and you still need to pick up after your dog. And, although the idea of hiking with your dog seems appealing, make sure your dog is up to the hike. Dogs, like people, need to be in condition for long hikes. Carry water for both you and your pet, and pay attention to whether your dog is getting too warm or too tired; if your dog is panting heavily, slowing down, or wanting to sit or lie down, she has had enough. You should also check your dog's feet occasionally to make sure they aren't cut and bruised from the rocks. Use a flea-and-tick preventative, too; ticks are carriers of several serious diseases (see Chapter 15 for more information).

By air

If you're planning a trip that requires travel by plane, you need to make arrangements at least a month in advance if you want your dog to fly with you. If you have a Toy Poodle, most airlines allow you to take her in the cabin with you in a special carrier. You may even be able to take a Miniature in the cabin, but with the seating space getting smaller and smaller in airlines these days, that may not be possible. Have a Standard? Don't even think about it! Your Standard will have to ride in the baggage compartment.

The following sections outline the necessary preparations you need to make to carry your Poodle into the cabin with you or to trust the airliner to stow your precious cargo in baggage.

No matter where your Poodle rides, you can't just show up at the airport with your crate and a smile. Some airlines limit the number of animals allowed on a flight, and most airlines refuse to fly a dog in baggage if the temperature at any stop will be over 85 or under 45 degrees Fahrenheit. All airlines are different, and the rules change frequently, so make sure you get all the information you need well before your planned flight. Also, get a confirmed reservation for your Poodle and keep it with your own ticket while traveling.

Never tranquilize your Poodle before a flight. A tranquilizer can depress breathing. If the airline delays your flight and your dog gets overheated, she may not be able to pant properly to cool off.

Cabin traveling

You have less preparation if you can bring your Poodle into the cabin with you, but you still need to carry a small dish and a bottle of water, as well as a packet of food in case of delays. Also, you should carry a lead and collar for a quick walk before and after the flight and for the security clearance point. Security personnel will ask you to take your dog out of her carrier, and you want to make sure she's on a lead so she can't escape.

If you can find a grassy area for your walk, you're in luck. Otherwise, try to find a quiet corner, and, whether on grass or concrete, always pick up after your dog. Keep a few plastic bags in your pocket; a couple of paper towels and a bottle of water may also be helpful when cleaning up.

Ahoy! Enjoying the water safely with your Poodle

Poodles and water go together like, well, Poodles and water. The Poodle is a water dog, and that water-loving gene is still a part of today's Poodle. Just because your Poodle loves water, though, doesn't mean she can go without supervision and guidance to safely enjoy it. Introduce your Poodle to water in a safe environment. Start in a quiet, shallow body of water and have her swim back and forth between two people until she becomes comfortable. If you have a swimming pool with a shallow end, great. If not, stay in the water with your dog and gently support her until she starts to swim. Make sure she can get out of the pool on her own. If the pool has a shallow end with steps, show her where the steps are. If it has a ladder, find out if she can climb it. Some dogs can, but others can't. If your dog can't, install a ramp with a non-skid surface.

Here are some more tips and ways to avoid rocking the boat:

✓ Until your dog builds up some stamina, don't overdo the water play. Throw a stick for her to retrieve 6 or 7 times — not 20.

✓ If your water playground is the ocean, take the height of the waves into account when you play, and be aware of any areas where undertow may grab your dog.

✓ Don't let your Poodle drink salt water. The ocean may be a great place to play, but drinking salt water can make your dog violently ill.

✓ Never leave your Poodle unattended in the pool area, and make sure she can't get into the pool when you're not around. Even a water-loving dog who can swim can drown.

✓ Just as it is with children, the best pool protection for your Poodle is a sturdy fence. Even a good swimmer can get tired while searching for the way out of the pool and drown.

✓ If your Poodle joins you on board for boating fun, make sure she has her own life jacket. Retrieving sticks from the beach or taking a refreshing dip isn't the same as falling off a boat far from shore. Your dog can get tired and disoriented if she ends up in deep water with no landmarks, so make sure she has a life jacket, just like the rest of the family.

When your Poodle sits in the cabin with you, you need a special carrier that fits under your seat. Get your dog used to the carrier before the trip. A crate-trained dog should adjust quickly, but don't wait until the day of the flight to find out. Give your dog special treats in the carrier prior to the flight and praise her for being calm. You can also close her in the carrier and carry her so she's used to the feeling of being picked up and carried.

If you have that rare dog that barks at absolutely everything strange, even when she's in a carrier, you should consider another method of travel. Either check your dog as cargo, or make your trip by car.

Some airlines allow dogs only in the cargo section of the plane (never in the cabin), so before you purchase that special carrier, make sure that the airline you choose permits pets in the cabin.

Baggage traveling

If your Poodle has to travel in the baggage compartment (a common practice for Miniatures and Standards), your two main concerns are the crate you need to pack her in and the boarding process. You can control the crate, so start with that. Here are some things to consider when preparing your pooch for baggage travel:

✔ You need an airline-approved crate. Contact your airline's customer service to get the details. If your airline allows, you should consider a plastic or wooden crate because metal crates tend to hold more heat.

✔ Consider covering the bottom of the crate with absorbent materials. Stress and the unfamiliar can mean an accident for even the most well housetrained pet. Shredded newspaper topped with a piece of synthetic fleece is a good choice, or you can utilize the special pads used in housetraining (see Chapter 9 for details). Many brands have an absorbent core that helps to keep your Poodle clean and dry should she have an accident. However, if your dog tends to chew on bedding, especially when she's stressed, leave out the absorbent pad.

Don't feed your Poodle for at least 12 hours before the flight. This doesn't guarantee a clean crate at the end of the journey, but it helps.

✔ Tape your name, address, and phone number to the top of the crate. If you have a different number and address for your destination, include that information as well. Cover the label with clear tape to protect it from rain.

✔ Tape an envelope to the crate that contains your Poodle's health records, including a copy of her rabies certificate. Cover the envelope with clear tape.

✔ Freeze water in a bowl that you can fasten to the inside of the crate; this prevents the water from spilling when the airline workers load the crate into the plane, and it provides small amounts of water as the ice melts. You may also want to tape a bag of your dog's food to the crate.

✔ Fasten a bungee cord over the door to keep it closed in case the crate is dropped or bumped.

The second factor to consider for baggage travel is the board-ing process. Make sure you know ahead of time where to take your Poodle for boarding and where you'll pick her up at your destination.

If you don't see airline personnel loading your dog at the proper time, ask the gate agent to call the ramp and make sure the dog is on the plane. At your destination, if you don't get your dog in a rea-sonable amount of time, ask someone what's going on. Don't wait until your plane takes off again. You want your dog with you, not three states away!

Try to plan a nonstop flight to limit the chance that your dog will be lost en route.

Taking Care of Other Trip Details

Traveling with your dog is like traveling with another person when it comes to arrangements. You need to pack for your dog, check that she has the right identification, and make sure that she's wel-come wherever you're staying, as I explain in the following sections.

Packing it in

Whether you travel by air or by car, by land or by sea, your Poodle needs her own luggage. But what should you include? The follow-ing list gives you a rundown of materials to pack:

- ✔ **Make sure you have any medications your dog may need while you're away from home.** Also think about whether you'll need a flea-and-tick preventative at your destination. If you're flying, pack everything in your carry-on in case your luggage is lost or delayed.

- ✔ **Take a small first-aid kit.** It doesn't have to be elaborate — just some antibiotic cream, gauze pads, and baby aspirin. (See Chapter 16 for more details about first-aid kits.)

- ✔ **Pack enough food for the entire trip, even if you think your Poodle's brand of kibble should be available everywhere.** The food may be available, but stores discontinue items all the time, and you don't want to spend your vacation visiting supermarkets in search of your brand of dog food. Heck, even if a store has your brand, the packaging may be wrong. If you have a Toy Poodle, for example, and the only size bag a store carries is 40 pounds, you'll wish you'd packed your own.

✔ **Carry water for your Poodle.** A change in water may cause digestive upset, which isn't a wonderful addition to a vacation. If you're taking a short trip, you can carry all you need, but for a longer trip, you can try topping off the water jug at each stop, gradually replacing the water from home with "trip water." Another alternative is to buy and carry bottled water.

✔ **Pack a set of food and water dishes or a stack of paper plates.** You can put the dog's food on the plate and then throw it away, eliminating the need to wash dishes.

✔ **Take a spare blanket and some extra towels, as well as a roll of paper towels in case of an accident.**

✔ **Carry plastic bags for picking up at rest stops.** If you prefer a scoop, buy a plastic beach shovel. It's easy to pack and carry, and you can pop it into a plastic bag until you can clean it.

✔ **If your dog has a favorite toy, take it along.** Travel is stressful, and being able to curl up with a teddy bear can help the stress. This advice may not be a bad idea for the people on the trip as well!

✔ **Carry a crate.** If your dog is traveling in a crate, you're all set. If she rides in the car in a harness, consider a lightweight, folding crate for your motel room. The crate prevents damage to the room and keeps your dog from escaping if the room door is opened.

✔ **If you plan to stay in a motel room, carry a small piece of plastic sheeting to put under the crate and dishes to catch spills.** And, if you let your dog jump up on the bed (like me!), consider carrying a couple of sheets to cover the beds. Motels don't launder bedspreads after every guest's stay, and the plastic sheets keep the spreads clear of Poodle paw prints. If you don't want to carry your own sheet, ask housekeeping for one.

And if you need to wipe off muddy toes, use your own towels, not the motel's! Carry paper towels so you can throw them away; baby wipes also are a good way to clean Poodle paws.

Carrying the proper ID

Your Poodle may already have a tattoo to serve as identification or a microchip for tracking purposes, but you should consider a collar tag as well for travel. I'm a huge fan of microchips, but the contact number on file with your microchip registry is likely to be your home number, which won't help you when you're far away from home. Be sure to keep the microchip registry updated on all your contact information, and include your cell phone number as one of the alternate numbers. Take a copy of the microchip number and the registry's number with the dog's rabies certificate in case you should need them while traveling.

Consider making a special tag that features your name, your dog's name, and the phone number of your destination. You can also list your cell phone number on the tag. A cell phone listing means you'll always be available, no matter where you are geographically.

No matter what kind of a tag you choose, make sure you fasten it securely to a regular buckle collar that remains on your dog all the time. (Chapter 5 has more details on securing ID for your Poodle.)

Staying at a Poodle-friendly place

Traveling with a dog can be fun, but not every destination thinks that lodging a pet is fun. You need to accept the fact that not every place accepts dogs and plan where you'll stay each night. Some places charge a fee of anywhere from $5 to $50 for keeping a dog in the room, and it may or may not be refundable at checkout. Some places may not advertise that they take dogs, but they may be willing to accept crated dogs or dogs that have been obedience trained. When in doubt, ask! And ask ahead of time. In the pouring rain at midnight isn't when you want to have to find a motel that accepts dogs. Have the policy and fees confirmed in writing when you make your reservation, and carry the confirmation with you.

The AAA guide, *Traveling with Your Pet, 8th Edition,* lists thousands of places that do accept dogs, so that publication is a good place to start. The guide can't list every Poodle-friendly place, though, so if you don't see your favorite hotel, give the establishment a call to find out about its policy. Even if the guide lists the hotel, policies can change, so you should always call ahead.

No matter where you stay, pop your Poodle into a crate if you go out and leave her behind. Even the best-trained dog may decide to gnaw on a chair leg or eat a bit of bedspread if you leave her alone in a strange place. Turn the television or radio on low to help soothe your dog and to mask any strange noises that come from outside.

With your dog in a crate, you don't have to worry about her escaping if a housekeeper opens the door, and the housekeeper can work without worrying about your dog. Put a note on the door so the housekeeper knows that the dog is crated. If you think that the presence of a stranger may upset your dog, put the "do not disturb" sign on your door. You can make your own bed, and, if you want fresh towels, make arrangements to put your dirty towels outside the door in exchange for clean ones.

Leaving Your Poodle at Home

Sometimes, it just isn't convenient to take your dog with you when you travel. You may have to travel on business, go on your honeymoon, or visit someone who has no room for a dog. You may want to enjoy a vacation without the responsibility of caring for a dog.

In the following sections, I give you two options on what to do when you decide to leave your Poodle at home: boarding kennels and pet sitters. Choose what sounds best to you and best fits your situation, and enjoy a drink with an umbrella for me!

Boarding your Poodle

A boarding kennel isn't a jail. Yes, it has fences and locks, but these tools are there to keep your dog safe and out of trouble. You can think of a boarding kennel as summer camp for your dog. But, just so you feel better, I devote the following pages to preparing you and your Poodle for the boarding experience and to making your Poodle as comfortable as possible.

A good boarding kennel keeps your dog safe and secure. Kennel operators may know dogs better than a pet sitter, and they may be better able to tell whether your dog is under the weather. They may offer grooming services so your pal comes home smelling sweet and looking great. A kennel also is usually cheaper than a pet sitter, unless you're electing to have a deluxe suite for your dog.

The disadvantages of a kennel are that your dog won't get as much individual attention, and she'll be in a strange place. Most dogs adjust well to kennels, but some do seem to get homesick.

 If you leave your dog in a kennel, consider tagging your dog with the kennel phone number. Good boarding kennels are very safe and secure, but accidents can happen. Your home telephone number works well if your Poodle is staying at home with a pet sitter (see the later section "Picking a pet sitter" for more details).

Observing and selecting a kennel

The best way to find the right kennel for your poodle is to visit the boarding kennels in your area *before* you need one. The day you drop off your dog is not the time to discover dirty conditions or broken fences. A reputable kennel operator will welcome your visit. If you aren't allowed to inspect the kennel, don't board there.

All the fences and gates should be in good repair, with no jagged bits of wire or metal sticking out and no holes. The pens also should be clean. You may smell a doggy odor in the kennel, but it shouldn't smell like urine or feces. Each dog should have fresh water in clean buckets or bowls, and you should see no dirty food dishes.

If you live in a large urban area, your city may have kennels with individual rooms for the dogs, innerspring mattresses, and piped-in music. These amenities, of course, cost much more than the traditional kennel with cement-floored dog runs, but your Poodle will love them!

Here are a few important considerations as you select a kennel:

- ✔ Many kennels have large play areas for groups of dogs. Ask prospective kennels how they determine if the dogs are friendly and how they supervise the areas. If you don't want your dog to play with others, tell the operator before you leave your dog.

- ✔ If your Poodle is on medication, ask if the kennels are willing to treat her. Some kennels charge extra for this service.

- ✔ Find out what shots the kennels require. Most kennels require proof of rabies vaccination, as well as distemper, parvovirus, and bordetella (or "kennel cough" — an airborne virus that can travel rapidly through a kennel). If you don't vaccinate yearly but use a titer test (a blood test that shows the level of protection against a specific disease), ask whether this report is acceptable. See Chapter 14 for more about vaccinations.

- ✔ Most kennel operators ask for the name and number of your veterinarian. If they don't ask, make sure you give it to them. Find out how they treat medical emergencies and whether they have veterinarians they use, should yours be unavailable. If the veterinarian of the kennel you choose is closer than yours, you may want to give permission to use its veterinarian if time is a factor.

- ✔ Find out if the kennel has some kind of grooming facility. The kennel may be able to give your Poodle a bath before you pick her up. If the operator doesn't feel comfortable bathing and drying a Poodle, you may be able to request that a kennel operator take your Poodle to her own groomer just before pickup. It's also convenient to have the kennel take care of small tasks like nail clipping if you feel comfortable with this.

After you select a kennel, it's time to reserve a spot for your Poodle. The best time to make kennel reservations depends on the time of year you plan to board. Many kennels are booked for

Christmas by mid-November. Summer is always busy, and reservations will require a call three to four weeks ahead. But if you're boarding your dog in February, the day before is probably time enough!

Making your pooch's stay as comfortable as possible

The biggest mental hurdle associated with boarding kennels seems to be that people think their dogs will pine away without them. Yes, some dogs do get a bit depressed, but 99 percent of dogs do just fine. They adjust quickly and, if not as happy as at home, are able to settle in comfortably.

Try the following strategies to make your Poodle as comfortable as possible at the kennel:

✔ Even if you don't have a trip planned in the immediate future, consider boarding your dog for a night or two. The younger a dog is, the better she will adapt to boarding, and this will get her used to being away from home. Because you'll be picking her up soon, you let her know that when she's at the kennel, you haven't abandoned her. She also gets to know the kennel staff, so when she goes for a longer stay, she already has friends.

✔ You may want to have your Poodle's crate or bed put into the run. If you vote for a bed, use an old blanket or some towels. A dog who wouldn't think of tasting her bed at home may decide to shred it at the kennel.

Picking a pet sitter

Pet sitters are becoming more popular as alternatives to kennels — especially if your Poodle is anxious in strange places or is older and may need more individual attention than a kennel can give.

One advantage to hiring a pet sitter is that your Poodle stays in her own home and yard. She has nothing new to get used to, except the sitter. Having a pet sitter come to your home may also keep your home safer during your absence. There will be activity around the home, the lights will stay on, and the pet sitter may even bring in your mail and water your plants! Your Poodle also will get more individual attention during pet-sitter visits.

The downside of a pet sitter is the cost. A 30-minute visit runs between $15 and $20. A live-in sitter can cost $65 a day. The good news is that these fees cover multiple pets, but ask about the policy first.

Your sitter has a great responsibility, so you want to make sure the person is responsible (and affordable). But how can you find the good help you seek? One great place to find a pet sitter is on the Web. Check out these sites:

- Pet Sitters International (www.petsit.com)

- National Association of Professional Pet Sitters (www.petsitters.org)

- Pet Sitters Associates, LLC (www.petsitllc.com)

All three sites offer lists of member pet sitters in your area — a professional sitter will be bonded and have insurance. You may be able to find pet sitters listed in your phone book, or you may have a local friend who has used a pet sitter.

Ideally, the sitter you're interested in should come to your home once or twice to meet your dog. He or she should also visit at least once when you're not home but before you go on vacation. You can notice a difference between the ways a dog greets a stranger when you're present and how she greets that same person when you're absent. Make sure your dog and the sitter are comfortable with each other.

You may think that a neighbor is a good choice, but you shouldn't choose a neighbor just because of the "neighbor" status. The teenager next door may love dogs, but is she responsible? Can you trust her to remember your dog's needs? A neighbor may be cheaper, but cheaper isn't necessarily better. Consider your sitter's experience, and don't be afraid to ask for references.

And now that I've breached the cost issue, we can keep it going. The cost of a pet sitter varies, depending on what you expect. A sitter who drops by three times a day to let your dog out and feed her costs less than a sitter who stays to play or who has to administer medication.

Let your veterinarian know if you're hiring a pet sitter and that you authorize the caregiver to seek medical care if needed. Make arrangements to pay for any bills incurred so that no question arises over who pays the bill.

Chapter 13

Showing Off and Enjoying Your Poodle's Talents

*P*oodles are smart, active dogs. Any behavior you want to teach them, they can do, unlike kids, cats, and spouses. The only limitation may be size; you may be limited in what Toys and Miniatures can do physically. (Mentally, they can meet any challenge.) In this chapter, I explore some activities that you and your Poodle can do as a team. These activities provide great opportunities for exercise — for your Poodle's brain and his body.

No matter what event you're interested in, get a copy of the rules and regulations so you know what and what not to do. Order booklets about American Kennel Club (AKC) events at www.akc.org.

One more thing before you dive into the world of dog shows: You *can* successfully train your Poodle for competition by yourself. However, I suggest that you join a class. The environment adds distractions, and your Poodle will learn how to ignore other dogs in group exercises. See Chapter 10 for more about taking your Poodle to training classes and teaching a variety of commands.

Passing the Canine Good Citizen Test

Helping your Poodle to earn the Canine Good Citizen (CGC) award is a good place to start if you think you would enjoy obedience events (which I cover later in this chapter). The basic exercises are easy to teach your Poodle and make a solid foundation for advanced training. The CGC award is easy to earn, but that doesn't detract from its importance. When the initials CGC appear after your Poodle's name, everyone will know that he's well mannered around other dogs and people and an upstanding citizen of the canine world. In the following sections, I explain how to prepare your Poodle and what to expect during the test.

Preparing for the test

You can teach your Poodle all the things he needs to know to pass the CGC test on your own. However, you have help at your disposal to make the process go as smoothly as possible. Many kennel clubs offer classes aimed to prepare owners and dogs for the CGC test. A class provides a good learning environment and exposes your Poodle to other dog and people teams. (See Chapter 10 for general information on training classes.)

Besides teaching you and your Poodle how to take the CGC test, a kennel club class may make arrangements for you to take the final test. If so, you have one less thing to worry about.

When your Poodle is ready to take the CGC test, you'll discover that the AKC wants you to be a good citizen, too. Before the test, an administrator will ask you to sign a *Responsible Dog Owners Pledge,* which says you'll take care of your dog's health, needs, safety, exercise, training, and quality of life. You also agree to clean up after your dog in public places and to never let your dog infringe on the rights of others.

Taking the test

Are you prepared? Is your Poodle's tail wagging? The time has come to take the CGC test. The test consists of ten parts that test your Poodle's ability to obey and interact and your ability to handle, and it takes about ten minutes. Your dog must do the following:

1. Accept a friendly stranger without breaking his position or going to the tester

2. Sit quietly and allow the tester to pet him

3. Allow the tester to run a brush over him and handle his ears and feet

4. Walk on a loose lead and make several turns and stops

5. Walk through a crowd without straining on the lead or jumping on people

6. Be put in a sit position and then in a down position; left and then returned to

7. Come when called from a distance of ten feet

8. Show minimal reaction to other dogs and be polite

9. Recover quickly when presented with distractions, such as a thrown pair of crutches

10. Not show signs of separation anxiety while you're out of sight

If your Poodle growls at, snaps at, bites, or attacks a person or another dog at any time during the CGC test, he'll fail right then and there. But don't worry; your Poodle can retake the test.

Looking Good: Conformation Shows

You may contend that your Poodle isn't just another pretty face, but you'll still want to show off that side of your Poodle. A Poodle is a glamorous dog when properly trimmed and groomed (see Chapter 8), and many owners love to show off their companions so everyone can see how beautiful the dogs are. The conformation ring at a dog show is just the place to show off your gorgeous girl or boy.

Conformation judging considers more than just your Poodle's coat. Dog shows were originally staged to show off breeding stock, and that's still the main objective of a show. Your Poodle must fit the breed standard and must be in condition. A flabby Poodle that doesn't meet the standard won't win, no matter how lovely his coat looks. Chapter 2 has full details on breed standards.

In the following sections, I explain how you can prepare for an AKC conformation show, and I describe the inner workings of a show. (The United Kennel Club [UKC] also has conformation shows; see its Web site at www.ukcdogs.com and Chapter 2 for more information.)

How can you and your Poodle get ready for conformation shows?

When you purchased your Poodle, your breeder may have given her opinion as to whether your puppy is of show or pet quality (see Chapter 4 for more about getting a Poodle from a breeder). If the initial evaluation was that your Poodle is show quality, you should go back to your breeder for another opinion as your Poodle grows. If you know other owners who show their dogs, get their opinions as well (especially if you found your Poodle at a rescue group or shelter and you don't know a breeder). If everyone you speak with agrees that your Poodle fits the standard and has the personality to enjoy showing, you should give it a shot! At that point, you can start working on preparing your Poodle (and yourself) for a show.

Preparing your Poodle

Handling classes are a good place to start preparing, but you'll also want to work on your Poodle's coat. Showing in conformation requires special clips; the hair is kept much longer than you would ordinarily keep a pet's coat. Your pet may have longer nails than is appropriate for the show ring, and those teeth had better be snowy white.

You can show a Poodle in a puppy clip until he's a year old; after that point, he must have either an English saddle clip or a continental clip (see Chapter 8 for more information on the types of clips). The puppy clip of the show ring is very different from the puppy clip that you may be familiar with on a pet Poodle:

- ✔ The show coat is much longer in a puppy clip.
- ✔ The mane and topknot are already being developed.
- ✔ The flpas feature longer hair.
- ✔ The feet, face, throat, and the base of the tail are shaved clean.

Preparing yourself

You have the option of showing your Poodle yourself or hiring a professional handler. You'll have a great time and a rewarding experience if you show your Poodle yourself, but you may desire the help of a professional because of the intensive grooming required. If you love the idea of showing your own dog, you can still hire a professional to teach you the ins and outs of show grooming. You also may come across a bartering handler who can help you with grooming in exchange for your help feeding, exercising, or cleaning up after her dogs.

Ask your breeder or other dog people for handler recommendations. Go to shows and watch handlers in the ring. Do you like the way they treat their dogs? Do you like them?

If you plan to show your own dog, take handling classes, which many local kennel clubs offer, or find a handler willing to teach you what you need to know. Generally, this means going to shows and being unpaid kennel help as you learn.

How does a conformation show work?

At an AKC show, your Poodle needs a minimum of 15 points, includ-ing two majors, to earn the title of "Champion." The number of points is based on a scale that varies by geographical areas. The more dogs that your dog beats, the more points he wins. The maxi-mum number of points that a dog can earn at any one show is five. Three-, four-, and five-point wins are considered majors, and your Poodle needs at least two majors under two different judges to complete a championship. Theoretically, a dog could earn a five-point major at three consecutive shows and become a champion, but normally, it takes a lot longer.

You can enter six regular classes when you're showing your Poodle; each one has different requirements, such as age. In all classes, a judge reviews male dogs first and then moves on to bitches (females). Here's how the actual competition goes down after all the dogs separate into classes and gender:

1. **An official judges all the class males and calls the win-ners from each class to return to the ring, at which point she selects the *Winners Dog*.**

    This dog is the only dog to receive points toward a championship.

2. **The judge repeats the process with the bitch classes, and the Winners Bitch receives the points.**

3. **The Winners Dog and the Winners Bitch return to the ring with all the champions, or *specials,* who've been entered.**

4. **In this class, also known as the *Best of Breed class*, the judge chooses the Best of Breed, Best of Opposite Sex (to the Best of Breed), and Best of Winners.**

5. **The dog chosen as the Best of Breed goes on to compete in group judging.**

    Seven groups compete in group judging. If you have a Toy Poodle, you show him in the Toy group. If you have a Miniature or a Standard, you show him in the Non-Sporting group.

6. **The winners from each group advance to the *Best in Show* judging, where a judge chooses one dog as the Best in Show over all the other dogs entered.**

    Figure 13-1 is a visual depiction of all these categories.

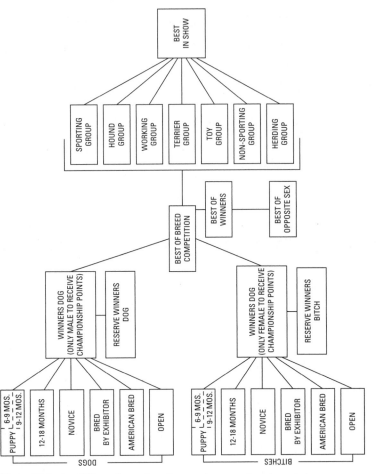

Figure 13-1: An AKC conformation show progresses from breed classes to Best in Show.

Testing Skills: Rally Events

If you and your Poodle enjoyed training for the CGC test (which I covered earlier in this chapter), you may want to continue training for competition with rally events. A rally event is less structured than an obedience event (I cover obedience in the next section), but it can still give you a feel for competition. Rally became an approved AKC event in 2005 and is really growing in popularity.

In rally, 10 to 20 stations make up the grid of the competition, depending on the rally level. When a judge starts you, you and your Poodle follow the designated station numbers and perform the exercises described on the cards at all the stations. A qualifying score is 70 points out of a possible 100. Your Poodle should be on your left during the rally and not be more than two feet from you, but a formal heel position isn't necessary. Your Poodle should sit when you stop moving.

Unlike in formal obedience competitions, you can give multiple commands and talk to (and encourage) your Poodle. You may not touch your Poodle, but you can slap your leg, clap, and/or use hand signals to complete each exercise at the stations.

The three levels in a rally event are as follows:

- **Rally novice:** The dog stays on lead for all the exercises, and you rally through 10 to 15 stations.

- **Rally advanced:** This level has between 12 and 17 stations, including at least one jump. Exercises are done off lead.

- **Rally excellent:** This level features between 15 and 20 stations and requires at least two jumps. Exercises are done off lead. At this level, the handler can give multiple commands but may not clap or pat her leg to encourage the dog.

Oh, Behave! Obedience Events

Many of the exercises in obedience competition are similar to the activities found in CGC tests and rally events (see the previous sections of this chapter), but the judging and rules are stricter in obedience competition.

AKC obedience events have four levels, each featuring a variety of exercises:

- Companion Dog (CD)
- Companion Dog Excellent (CDX)
- Utility Dog (UD)
- Utility Dog Excellent (UDX)

At each level, the exercises become more difficult. For instance, at the CD level, some exercises are done on lead. At the CDX level, all exercises are done off lead, and a jump and dumbbell retrieving are added, as well as a broad jump. At the UD level, your dog needs to master a scent discrimination exercise, in which he selects an article that you have handled and retrieves it. There is also a "directed retrieve" test; three gloves are dropped in a line, and your dog must retrieve the glove that you select.

At all levels of competition, your Poodle must earn a qualifying ribbon under three different judges. A qualifying score is 170 points out of a possible 200, which comes with the dog scoring at least half of the points assigned to each exercise.

After you've mastered these levels, you can work on your obedience championship (OTCH), which requires earning 100 points in specific classes.

You can see a Poodle in an obedience event in the color section. You also can check out the UKC's Web site at www.ukcdogs.com for more information about its obedience competitions.

The humble beginnings of obedience

Today, obedience is a popular activity for ambitious dog owners. Breeders now recommend basic obedience training for dogs in pet homes. However, it wasn't always this way. Two Poodle people are responsible for bringing obedience training to the attention of America's dog owners.

In 1931, Helene Whitehouse Walker imported three Standard Poodles from England, and she established Carillon Kennels. At the same time, she began reading about obedience tests that took place in England, and she became interested in bringing that practice to America.

In 1933, Mrs. Walker organized the first obedience test in America, which she held in Mount Kisco, NY. In 1934, three more tests were held: one at Mount Kisco and two at all-breed shows. That same year, Mrs. Walker spent six weeks in England to discover more about obedience training.

In December of 1935, Mrs. Walker submitted a pamphlet on obedience procedures to the AKC, and she requested recognition of the sport. The AKC approved of the new sport, and in April of 1936, the organization published "Regulations and Standards for Obedience Test Field Trials." The first AKC-licensed tests were held at North Westchester on June 13, 1936 and Orange Kennel Club on June 14, 1936.

With the AKC on board the obedience train, Mrs. Walker and her associate, Blanche Saunders (who wrote several books on obedience training), decided to spread the word about obedience across America.

In September of 1937, they began a 10,000-mile "trailer trek." They took three Standard Poodles on a trip to give demonstrations. They handed out pamphlets and lived in a 21-foot trailer, which they pulled with a Buick. They removed the backseat of the car, and the area became home to the three Poodles as they traveled!

Fast forward to 1976. The AKC created a new title, OTCH (Obedience Trial Champion), to recognize dogs who reach the highest levels of obedience. In an age when Golden Retrievers and Border Collies seem to dominate the obedience ring, you can take solace in the fact that a Miniature Poodle, Ch. Andechez Zachary Zee, UD, was the first breed champion of any variety to earn the OTCH honor.

Staying on Course: Agility Events

Poodles enjoy the challenges of learning obedience commands and taking obedience tests (see the previous sections in this chapter), but these tasks can become repetitive in a hurry. Poodles do get bored easily, so the repetition of obedience training may make them lose interest in the sport. If your dog requires variety in her exercise activities, agility may be just the sport for your active Poodle.

In the following sections, I describe an agility course, I outline the levels of agility competition, and I highlight special considerations in preparing Poodles for agility events. You can see a Poodle in an agility event in the color section.

Agility takes strength and stamina from both you and your Poodle. Depending on the organization holding an agility event, you may not be able to compete in agility until your Poodle is at least 12 or 18 months old. The age requirement gives your dog a chance to grow up and develop the muscles he needs for agility. You can take the time before your Poodle hits the required age to begin training.

Surveying an agility course

In an agility competition, your Poodle navigates through a set of obstacles, at your direction (or at the direction of a handler), in a set amount of time. The obstacles are fun, and you have many of them to consider, including a variety of jumps, an A-frame, a seesaw, a dog walk, a pause table, open and closed tunnels, and weave poles. The number of obstacles in an agility competition depends on the level of the competition (see the next section). The following list digs deeper into the different types of agility obstacles:

- ✔ Jumps may be simple bar jumps, tires suspended from chains, or bars in varying height combinations.

- ✔ *Contact obstacles* each have an area that the dog must touch as he gets on and off the obstacle. The contact zone helps protect dogs from injury; you don't want them leaping on or off an obstacle too far from the ground. The contact obstacles include the following:

  - • The A-frame is shaped like a giant "A," and your dog must go up one side and down the other.

  - • The seesaw is just like the one you remember from your childhood. Your dog must get on at the end that touches the ground and walk across it until the other side drops to the ground.

- The dog walk is a narrow plank that leads from the ground to another plank that is parallel to the ground. Another plank leading back to the ground is at the other end.

  A UKC agility course doesn't have a dog walk, but it offers a sway bridge and a swing plank (see Chapter 2 for more on this organization).

✔ At the pause table, your Poodle must sit or lie down, at the judge's discretion, for five seconds.

✔ An open tunnel is a long tunnel (pretty simple!); it can be straight or have bends in it. A closed tunnel consists of a rigid section where the dog enters and a "closed" section that's made of fabric. The dog must run through the collapsed fabric part to exit the tunnel.

✔ The weave poles are rows of poles through which your Poodle must navigate.

Looking at rules and levels

Both the AKC and the UKC offer agility competitions. The two other major agility organizations are the United States Dog Agility Association (USDAA) and the North American Dog Agility Council (NADAC). Each organization has its own set of rules and regulations, and these rules can change periodically. They apparently aren't worried about making it easy on you! You can find more information at www.usdaa.com and www.nadac.com.

Make sure you have a set of the most current regulations for the organization that's offering the trial. The regulations tell you about the specific heights of jumps and give you the rules for point deductions and nonqualifying scores.

Each organization that offers agility competitions has three levels of competition. You can go on to win agility championships within the levels of these organizations.

You can find other agility associations that offer events:

✔ Teacup Dogs Agility Association (www.dogagility.org) for dogs 17 inches and under

✔ Just for Fun (www.dogwoodagility.com/JustForFun.html) for dogs and owners who enjoy agility but not competition

If you have an older Poodle, you can try to find a veteran's class. The AKC offers a preferred class for seniors. In this class, jump heights are lowered by four inches, and your Poodle has five extra seconds to complete the course. (For more about senior Poodles, check out Chapter 17.)

On the Prowl: Hunt Tests

Poodles were bred to hunt decades and decades ago (see Chapter 2), but they've been so successful as companion dogs since they became popular that people have a hard time remembering their field origins. One event that lets your Poodle return to his roots and lets you see him in his natural environment is a hunt test. At a hunt test, a dog is judged on his ability to notice, or "mark," where a shot bird falls, and then on his ability to go to that spot when he's sent, retrieve the fallen bird, and carry it to the hunter.

Both the AKC and the UKC allow Standard Poodles to compete at hunt trials, but neither organization allows Miniatures or Toys to compete. The Poodle Club of America offers a hunting class for Standard and Miniature Poodles at its national specialty shows.

In the following sections, I explain how to train your Poodle for hunt tests, and I describe the different levels of hunting competition.

Equipping yourself and training

If hunting with your Poodle sounds like a great time for you, you should train for an event rather than run out the door with a shot-gun and your dog. To train and to eventually compete, you need

- ✔ **Guns:** For training, many people use blank or starter pistols. Otherwise, you'll need a shotgun.

- ✔ **Bumpers:** A *bumper* is a plastic or canvas cylinder that you can throw either on land or in the water, where it will float. The weight and size of a bumper simulate what your Poodle will experience when he retrieves a bird on a hunt. Many plastic bumpers, or *dummies,* have knobby surfaces to encourage a soft mouth on the bird. Bumpers come in various sizes, from 2 to 4 inches in diameter and from 9 to 15 inches in length. You can find them at sporting and gun shops, in dog supply catalogs, and online. They range in price from $10 to $20 each.

- ✔ **Birds:** Eventually, you'll need real birds to train your dog.

To train your Poodle, start by working with bumpers until your dog understands retrieving and is under control. At that point, you can mix birds with bumpers.

You should consider joining a retriever group for serious hunting training, because a club is more likely to have access to birds than individuals. And, even if you have access to birds, you know that each bird can cost $10 or more. To find a group, ask other dog people or your veterinarian, who may have clients to hunt. You also can search online for groups in your area.

Hunting at different levels

For the AKC tests, the levels are Junior Hunter, Senior Hunter, and Master Hunter. The following list outlines the AKC levels:

- ✔ A *Junior* dog is tested on four marks: two on land and two on water. A dog *marks,* or notices where a bird falls, before you can send him to retrieve it.

- ✔ For a *Senior* test, blind retrieves are added — both on land and on the water. A *blind retrieve* means that the dog can't see the bird. He still marks it, but he can't actually see the bird. On land, the bird may fall behind a bush; on water, the bird may be resting in reeds near the shore.

- ✔ At the *Master* level, your Poodle must deal with multiple marks and blind retrieves, as well as more distractions. Your dog also needs to honor another dog's retrieves; in other words, he must remain in the heel position next to you (or his handler) while another dog works, if called upon to do so.

Earning qualifying scores

Your Poodle competes for the hunting titles by earning scores from the two judges at each test. The following list outlines how your Poodle earns his titles:

- ✔ To earn the Junior Hunter (JH) title, your Poodle must receive qualifying scores at five AKC-licensed or member-club hunting tests.

- ✔ To earn the Senior Hunter (SH) title, your dog needs to qualify at five AKC-licensed tests. If your dog holds a JH title, however, he needs only four qualifying tests.

- ✔ To earn the Master Hunter title, your dog must qualify at six tests. If he already has the SH title, he needs only five qualifying tests.

To qualify, your Poodle must have an average overall score of 7, with each part of the test being scored from 0 to 10 by the two judges. Your dog also must have an average score of at least five in each part of the test.

The Nose Knows: Tracking Tests

Tracking is a test of a dog's sense of smell, and most Poodles are up to the challenge! Whether you have a Toy, a Miniature, or a Standard Poodle, you can compete in tracking.

A tracking competition involves a track that features a specified number of turns, depending on the difficulty of the test. Flags are used to mark the direction of the track. Along the track, a track-layer drops specific articles that the dog must find as he tracks. The dog, who wears a tracking harness and a lead between 20 and 40 feet long, tracks the scent of the tracklayer and indicates the dropped objects, which also have the tracklayer's scent. Each tracking test features two judges, and both must agree that your Poodle has passed a test in order for your dog to earn a title.

Your Poodle can earn three tracking titles in competition from the AKC:

- ✔ Tracking Dog (TD)
- ✔ Tracking Dog Excellent (TDX)
- ✔ Variable Surface Tracking (VST)

The difficulty of attaining each title is based on the length of the trail, the number of turns in the trail, and how the track has been "aged" — that is, how much time passes between when the track was laid and when a dog is allowed to run the track. A dog becomes a *Champion Tracker* (CT) when he earns all three of the tracking titles.

Sharing the Love: Therapy Poodles

Maybe, in spite of all the events you can participate in with your Poodle, you just don't have the competitive gene. Maybe you're more of a couch potato. Maybe, however, you're a noncompetitive couch potato with a very big heart. If so, helping your Poodle to become a registered therapy dog may be for you. With very little effort and no competition at all, you can share your Poodle's love with people who really need it. If you have the energy to complete a CGC test (which I cover earlier in this chapter), your Poodle can become a registered therapy dog.

How a therapy dog helps

Here are just a few of the things that a therapy dog does to help:

✔ Therapy dogs frequently visit healthcare facilities. A therapy dog can simply provide comfort, or he can take an active role in therapy sessions. For instance, a patient throwing a ball for a dog to retrieve can be a form of physical therapy.

✔ More schools bring in therapy dogs to be reading partners. Students like reading to dogs because dogs never criticize.

✔ Therapy dogs also can be of service during disasters. Not only can a therapy dog comfort the victims of a disaster but also rescue workers.

How to become certified (and other considerations)

Many people do informal therapy work, but if you want to have a certified therapy dog to feel more official, you can check out Therapy Dogs International, Inc. at www.tdi-dog.org or the Delta Society at www.deltasociety.org. These organizations register dogs who pass a test similar to the CGC test. After your Poodle is registered, you'll receive the following:

✔ An ID tag for his collar signifying his status

✔ A card for your wallet for showing proof of certification.

✔ Information on visiting hospitals or other healthcare facilities

✔ Depending on the registering agency, you may have insurance coverage for you and your dog in case of an accident

After your Poodle is certified, you can do as much or as little therapy work as you like. Contact local healthcare facilities; most welcome regular visits. If the idea of helping children appeals to you, talk to your local school system about visiting classrooms or starting a reading program.

Whether you want your Poodle to get certified or not, you need to make sure that he's comfortable around the people he's supposed to help. A dog who's afraid of children won't be of much use in a school. If you want to work in a healthcare facility, get your dog used to wheelchairs and walkers before you make your visits.

On your first visit to a therapy session, take a copy of your Poodle's vaccination records. Trim your Poodle's nails, and file the tips, if necessary. Older people have thin skin that can bruise and tear easily. And make sure your dog is clean! No one wants to pet a dirty dog, even if he doesn't shed.

Part IV

Maintaining Your Poodle's Health

"Janet, is this normal behavior for a Poodle?"

In this part . . .

I hope your Poodle enjoys a long, healthy life, but you can never be too prepared to address potential health issues. In this part, I start by giving you some tips for finding a good veterinarian, as well as information on alternative treatments (such as acupuncture). I explain everyday illnesses your Poodle may encounter, and I talk about certain health issues specific to Poodles. I include a chapter on first aid to help you cope with emergencies, and I finish with a chapter on senior Poodles so you know how to keep your aging Poodle happy and comfortable.

Chapter 14

Taking Basic Care of Your Poodle's Health

. . . .

In This Chapter

▶ Selecting and visiting a vet

▶ Organizing a regular checkup schedule

▶ Opting for alternative medicine

▶ Getting the facts on vaccinations

▶ Considering spaying or neutering your Poodle puppy

▶ Taking care of your Poodle's health at home

. . . .

*Y*ou've been a busy Poodle owner lately! You've found your perfect companion and readied your home for her arrival; you may have even drawn up a training schedule that you can't wait to start. However, one of the most important aspects of animal ownership awaits you: Securing medical care for your Poodle. You can start your Poodle on the path to a long and healthy life by finding a reputable veterinarian in your area and starting her a vaccination schedule.

In this chapter, I discuss options for selecting a good vet and making sound vaccine choices. I also cover alternative health options, spaying and neutering, and watching out for your Poodle's health at home.

Choosing the Right Veterinarian and Setting a Schedule

You can just go to the Yellow Pages and find a veterinarian, and this may work well for you, but you'll have better luck finding the best vet for your dog (and you) if take time to think about what you want in a veterinarian.

In the following sections, I let you know what to look for in a vet so you can make the right choice; I give you questions to ask a potential vet; and I explain the importance of scheduling regular check-ups with your vet.

Knowing what to look for in a vet

You can find a veterinarian before you get your Poodle, or you can wait until a Poodle has joined your family; either way, you should find a veterinarian *before* you need one. You don't want to waste time frantically flipping through the Yellow Pages when your Poodle is seriously ill or injured and needs immediate attention.

Getting a veterinarian before you get your Poodle means you can set up that important first visit right away. Most breeders give buyers a window of time for a medical exam. If a veterinarian finds a problem, the breeder will take the puppy back and refund the purchase price. When that window closes, most breeders will not refund money, although they may agree to replace the puppy with another.

Asking friends who have dogs for vet recommendations is a good place to start. Your breeder or rescue group may also be able to give you some tips. Keep the following points in mind as you go over your choices:

- ✔ **How far is the vet's office from your home?** You may have heard great things about a particular vet, but if his office is 20 miles away, he may not be the best choice for you. However, you shouldn't automatically use the vet next door. Distance should be a factor in choosing your vet, but it shouldn't be the *only* factor.

- ✔ **Do you prefer a hospital with more than one vet, or do you want the personal touch of a one-doctor practice?** At a small practice, the vet gets to know your Poodle personally and will have an understanding of her entire health history, but in an emergency, if you need to go to a different practice, your dog's records won't be on file. At a large practice, you may see a different doctor for each visit, but no matter who sees your dog, he has access to all her health records.

- ✔ **How does the vet handle emergency and off-hours visits?** At a large practice, the vets probably rotate being "on call," so a doctor is always available for an emergency. At a single-vet practice, you need to find out how it handles emergencies? Do you have an emergency veterinary clinic in your area? Does another practice cover for your vet during off-hours? Can you page the vet if you have an emergency?

In most larger cities, you can find at least one emergency veterinary clinic that handles after-hours cases. Ask your vet if he has a preferred ER clinic and where it is located and its hours of operation. If you have to use an emergency clinic, drive to it at least once, so you will know the way and not lose time finding it in an emergency.

✔ **Do you want a traditional veterinarian, a holistic vet, or a vet who combines the traditional Western approach with acupuncture and herbal treatments (which I cover later in this chapter)?** Don't expect your vet to change his ways to meet your needs. Find out what a practice offers before you make your choice.

✔ **Are the staff members at the vet's office helpful, courteous, and nice to the animals?** To get a good feel for the staff, you need to find an office before you're desperate for one. You can build a rapport with the staff if you check the office out before you get your Poodle. With one visit, you can get a general feel for whether the staff is friendly or all business.

✔ **Is the vet's office (and other work areas) clean?** The waiting room, as well as the individual examining rooms, should be clean.

✔ **Do you like the vet?** No matter how highly recommended a vet may be, if you don't get a good vibe from him and you aren't comfortable in his presence, you should find another vet. You and your vet are partners when it comes to your Poodle's health, so open communication is very important.

Asking a potential vet important questions

Sometimes, you just can't tell whether a potential vet is right for you and your Poodle without actually making an appointment and talking with him. A vet's office can be clean and close, and his staff can be friendly, but you need to get to know his views and principals to be comfortable with him as your vet. Be sure to cover the following topics during your interview — the answers should help you make your choice:

✔ **Vaccinations:** Which vaccinations does he routinely give? How often does he vaccinate? Some vets view certain vaccines as requirements, and others think they're optional. Many doctors no longer give boosters every year. In addition, does the vet consider *titer testing,* which evaluates an animal's level of immunity to a disease, instead of routinely revaccinating? (For more on vaccinations, see the later section "Taking a Shot at Good Health with Vaccinations".)

✔ **Second opinions and specialists:** Most vets don't hesitate to refer you to a specialist if you have questions and concerns about a diagnosis. If your area doesn't have a specific specialist, you can ask for a referral to a veterinarian college. Ask whether he has a problem with you seeking a second opinion or wanting a specialist to look at your dog. Ask whether he routinely consults with any specialists in the area.

✔ **Alternative healthcare:** You may be interested in combining traditional medicine with alternative forms of healthcare. Some vets combine traditional Western medicine with other treatments, such as acupuncture, herbal treatments, and chiropractic techniques. Other vets recommend that you see a specialist for these treatments if they don't offer the service themselves. Ask the vet which, if any, alternative forms of healthcare he practices. Ask whether he can refer you to practitioners. You may discover that a particular veterinarian won't treat your dog if you use alternative forms of medicine. You have to make the final decision on the type of care you want, because you won't change your vet's mind. (I cover alternative forms of healthcare later in this chapter.)

✔ **Experience with the health needs of Poodles:** Ask the vet about his familiarity with medical conditions that occur in Poodles, such as hip dysplasia in a Standard Poodle or patella luxation in Toys or Miniatures. A complete list is available at `www.poodleclubofamerica.org`.

Choosing a veterinarian is a personal choice. You need to weigh the pros and cons and decide what's important to you and your Poodle. Along with the vet's responses to the preceding topics, don't forget to take into consideration the office's distance from your home and whether single or multiple doctors are in the practice.

Setting up regular checkups

Along with the vaccination schedule you and your vet decide on (find out more about vaccinations later in this chapter), you need to book an annual exam schedule. Regular checkups give your vet a chance to check your Poodle's vital signs, ears, teeth, eyes, and weight. Your vet also may take blood tests to make sure nothing serious is going on. A regular checkup also gives you a good chance to ask your vet any questions you may have about your Poodle's health.

Typically, your veterinarian should see your Poodle at least once a year, and the recommendation now is twice a year. These wellness checks can help your veterinarian catch anything out of the ordinary before it develops into something harder to treat. No one time of year is better than any other.

Surveying Alternative Healthcare Choices

Veterinary medicine has come a long way since the "horse doctor" days, where a vet gave annual shots and smiled on your way out. Today, amazing medical advances have helped extend the quality and length of dogs' lives. Doctors and dog owners also are discovering that other treatments are available outside the realm of traditional veterinary medicine.

Holistic veterinary medicine, for example, deals with the whole animal — not just individual parts. Traditional medicine may treat varying symptoms, but holistic practitioners study everything in an animal's physical and social environment. Holistic treatment may include combinations of methods, including acupuncture, chiropractic treatment, massaging, herbal treatment, and Bach flowers. I cover these methods in the following sections so you can make informed decisions about your Poodle's health.

On pins and needles: Acupuncture

Acupuncturists have been treating humans for over 4,500 years and animals for about 2,000 years. These alternative medicine professionals use hair-fine needles to stimulate acupoints on the body. *Acupoints* are areas of skin that contain concentrated levels of nerve endings and blood vessels. Acupoints usually reside in small depressions on the body, detectable by trained acupuncturists.

Studies show that acupuncture has the following benefits for humans and animals:

- Increases blood flow, which speeds heeling
- Lowers heart rate
- Improve the function of the immune system
- Reduces the need for large amounts of pain medicine
- Encourages the release of neurotransmitters, such as endorphins (the body's natural painkillers) and cortisol (an anti-inflammatory steroid).

Specifically, veterinarians can use acupuncture to treat chronic conditions, such as arthritis, allergies, and skin conditions, along with the normal function of relieving pain. Acupuncture also may help with epilepsy and the side effects of cancer (for more information on addressing serious medical issues your Poodle may have, see Chapter 16).

Reiki, which is a Japanese technique, produces results similar to acupuncture but without the needles. It eases stress and promotes relaxation and healing by helping to increase and direct a person or animal's life force.

Many veterinarians use acupuncture as a complement to Western medicine. They make diagnoses based on traditional medicine and then use acupuncture to help ease pain and hasten healing. You can help your Poodle between acupuncture treatments by manipulating certain acupressure points. Ask a vet trained in acupuncture to show you how.

Another facet of acupuncture deals with *alarm points* on the dog's body. When stimulated, certain points on your Poodle's body may give an indication of when something is wrong. When a vet stimulates an alarm point, your Poodle may have no reaction at all, but if a problem exists with a specific organ in your Poodle's body, stimulating a certain alarm point may cause a reaction, at which point the vet can investigate.

A dog's reaction may be to bite when certain points are stimulated, so if you decide to stimulate alarm points in between vet visits to make sure all is good with your Poodle, use caution.

The frequency of acupuncture treatments depends on the reason for the treatments. Typically, there will be four to six weeks of one treatment a week, then a treatment every two or three weeks.

For as long as acupuncture has been around, people brought up on traditional Western thought have found it strange. There's just something about all those needles sticking into your pet. In reality, your Poodle feels no pain at all, and acupuncture can help your dog, especially with pain. Acupuncture does require more visits than if your veterinarian just prescribed some pills, but it has no side effects, as there can be with medicines. If you live in a larger metropolitan area, you'll have no trouble finding a veterinarian who practices acupuncture, but if you live in a smaller area, you may not be able to find an acupuncturist locally, which can be a downside to this healthcare alternative.

If your current vet (or a prospective vet) isn't familiar with acupuncture, ask him if he can refer you to acupuncturists in your area. If that route fails, you can search for veterinary acupuncturists by state at the International Veterinary Acupuncture Society Web site, www.ivas.org.

Back to basics: Chiropractic medicine

Chiropractic adjustments manipulate the spine and the connecting bones. The theory behind the practice is that if the bones around the spine are even slightly out of alignment, the situation irritates the surrounding nerves and causes discomfort. A chiropractor's job is to gently push the bones back into their correct alignment.

An active Poodle that performs in agility competitions (see Chapter 13) may misalign her spine during a jump or trick. The occasional chiropractic adjustment may be just what she needs to stay healthy and in tip-top shape. Even Poodles that exercise only by getting on and off the couch can benefit from chiropractic adjustments. They may land wrong as they jump off! You'll know that an adjustment may be necessary if your dog is lame or can't manage stairs easily, or if her back is *roached,* or hunched, indicating she's in pain. (However, Poodles as a breed are not known for having back problems.)

 If you suspect that your Poodle *is* having back issues, have your veterinarian examine your dog first to make sure she has no other causes for the soreness or lameness, such as a tumor. If your vet rules out serious illness, he may refer you to a veterinarian who specializes in chiropractic work. Some people take their dogs to chiropractors for humans if they can't find chiropractic veterinarians.

 To find out more about chiropractic adjustments for animals, visit the Web site for the American Veterinary Chiropractic Association, at www.animalchiropractic.org.

Doggie day spa: Massage treatment

A massage technically isn't a medical treatment, the likes of which only a vet can administer, but it can help to relax your Poodle and ease her stress and sore muscles. Symptoms of a problem that could use a massage include muscle soreness, a strained muscle from overactive play, or a wrong landing after a jump.

 Massaging isn't a substitute for veterinary care. If your Poodle is limping or in pain, you need to make an appointment with your veterinarian. If he gives you the go-ahead to massage along with administering any medications he provides, you've done your due diligence.

Linda Tellington-Jones developed what's possibly the best-known technique for massaging an animal. Her method, called *Tellington*

TTouch, uses repeated massage movements to generate specific brain-wave patterns that help ease anxiety — especially that anxiety that follows injury or surgery. The calming effect helps promote healing. Tellington TTouch is a very specific method of massage. In a highly populated area, you may be able to find Tellington TTouch practitioners. You can also visit the Web site, www.tteam-ttouch.com, for more information on how you can learn to use this method on your Poodle.

Much of massaging is just extended stroking, but you need to pay attention to how your Poodle reacts to a massage. If you seem to be hurting or annoying your dog, stop the massage. Not every dog loves every kind of massage, and the point of a massage is to soothe and relax your dog, not annoy her.

Massaging your Poodle also can help to strengthen the bond between the two of you. You can find out more about massaging your Poodle with the help of *Dog Massage* — a book by Maryjean Ballner (St. Martin's Griffin).

All-natural: Herbal treatments

In your search for a veterinarian that practices alternative medicine, you may notice the initials TCM attached to some practitioners. TCM stands for *Traditional Chinese Medicine,* which includes not only acupuncture but also herbal treatment. Many herbal compounds, when used correctly, are gentler than synthetic compounds used in traditional veterinary medicine to produce the same results.

Herbs are classified as pungent, sweet, sour, salty, or bitter:

- ✔ **Pungent herbs** help with circulation problems.

- ✔ **Sweet herbs** relieve pain and slow the progression of diseases.

- ✔ **Sour herbs** solidify. If your Poodle has diarrhea, a veterinarian trained in the proper use of herbs would prescribe a sour herb.

- ✔ **Salty herbs** have the opposite effect of sour herbs. Vets use them to relieve constipation and to treat muscle spasms and enlarged lymph glands.

- ✔ **Bitter herbs** treat kidney-related diseases.

Just because herbs are "natural" doesn't mean that you can give them to your Poodle indiscriminately. Don't be tempted to diagnose a condition and treat it on your own. You can make your dog sicker, or even kill her. Consult with a veterinarian who's trained in the use of herbs, or get a referral from your veterinarian.

Many people who are concerned about additives, preservatives, and the overuse of chemical for themselves extend this concern to their pets. Herbs may be gentler and have fewer side effects than mass-produced pills. This type of treatment can be more expensive and again, depending on where you live, you may not be able to find someone trained in the use of herbs for dogs.

Buying the (state) farm:
Pet insurance for your Poodle

Veterinary costs continue to rise as technology improves and as animal medicine continues to follow human techniques. Dogs can get MRIs, X-rays, and hip replacements. Procedures for dogs that were unheard of ten years ago are now commonplace. Medicine is giving our dogs longer lives and a higher quality of life.

But these benefits come at a cost to your wallet. Your Poodle may never ask for a pair of designer jeans or special jogging shoes, but she may require expensive medical attention in the future. During a time of crisis, you'll want pet insurance to come to your rescue.

An insurance policy for your Poodle can cost between $10 and $70 a month as of press time, although some companies offer discounts for carrying multiple pets on a policy. Like insurance for humans, pet insurance policies cover different situations. Some policies cover accidents, injuries, and illnesses, but not regular check-ups. Other policies cover annual visits but not hereditary diseases or visits to specialists. You may be able to add options to the basic policy you purchase, depending on the type of coverage you want. Generally, you choose your own vet, pay the bill, and then send in your claim for reimbursement.

If you want to pursue alternative therapies for your Poodle's condition, such as acupuncture, shop around for a policy that covers this type of care. As an alternative, many dog owners open savings accounts for veterinary care. They deposit monthly sums to prepare for situations when their dogs will need something more than a booster shot.

If you register your dog with the American Kennel Club (AKC), you can sign up for the AKC Pet Healthcare Plan. You can also find several insurance companies online:

✔ www.petcareinsurance.com

✔ www.petinsurance.com

✔ www.petshealthplan.com

Before deciding on an insurance policy for your Poodle, request a complete list of what's covered, especially exclusions of genetic conditions that can occur in Poodles.

Many holistic vets recommend Rescue Remedy for your dog's first-aid kit. This mixture contains five of the single Bach essences, named for Edward Bach, an English doctor who studied the healing properties of plants and identified 38 flowers and trees with specific healing powers. You use Rescue Remedy in cases of shock, collapse, or trauma. Many health-food stores carry Rescue Remedy. (See Chapter 16 for more info on stocking your Poodle's first-aid kit.)

Homeopathy

Homeopathy is based on the theory that "like heals like." A substance, frequently a plant, is diluted in stages so that it's harmless, and free from side effects, but can still heal. Homeopathic remedies come in liquid form, in tablets, in powders, and in ointments.

The concept may be hard to grasp, but one homeopathic practitioner explained it to me as being similar to a vaccine that is made from a weakened, or killed, virus. These weakened or dead germs, in vaccine form, prevent the disease that they would normally cause, were they at full strength. To discover more about homeopathy as an alternative form of healthcare for your Poodle, check out the Academy of Veterinary Homeopathy's Web site, www.theavh.org.

Taking a Shot at Good Health with Vaccinations

In the following sections, I give you the basics on setting up a vaccination schedule for your Poodle, and I present the types of vaccinations available to Poodles.

Checking out available vaccines

As veterinary medicine continues to advance, along with medical advances in all fields, more and more vaccines are becoming available. The vaccines you choose for your Poodle depend on where you live and may also depend on how much you travel with your dog. The following sections list the vaccination options you're most likely to encounter. Your veterinarian will help you to decide what your dog will need.

Your area of the world may have regional diseases, so ask your vet if your Poodle needs any special vaccines, based on where you live.

Core vaccines

Core vaccines are vaccines that a veterinarian will always give a dog. Core vaccines protect against deadly diseases. As recently as five years ago, there were more core vaccines than there are today. In fact, it was common to give every vaccine available. Today, veterinarians realize that this isn't always a good idea. Dogs can have severe reactions to too many vaccines. Today, the core vaccines are rabies, distemper, and parvovirus:

✔ **Rabies:** A *rabies shot* is the one vaccine your Poodle absolutely must have, according to state law. The shot is the only protection your Poodle has against rabies. Currently, no cure exists for rabies, which attacks a dog's central nervous system. The animal either becomes paralyzed or enraged — the "mad dog" response with snapping, snarling, and biting randomly. The disease spreads through the saliva of bats, foxes, raccoons, and skunks. The disease is fatal after the symptoms appear.

✔ **Distemper:** Distemper is a highly contagious, deadly virus with a very low recovery rate. The virus is spread by airborne and droplets from the respiratory system of infected dogs. The threat of distemper is greatest for dogs under 6 months and over 6 years of age. The symptoms include coughing, vomiting, and fever. Add a distemper shot to your list of "must haves."

✔ **Parvovirus:** This virus is potentially fatal, and puppies are highly susceptible to it. An adult Poodle with a mild case may recover, but puppies generally die. Symptoms include fever, lethargy, and depression. If your Poodle also starts vomiting and having bloody diarrhea along with the other symptoms, she may die no matter her age. Parvovirus is spread through the feces of infected animals. If your dog sniffs, tastes, or eats contaminated feces, she may contract parvovirus.

Noncore vaccines

Noncore vaccines protect against many diseases, but your Poodle may not need all available vaccines. It can depend on where you live and what diseases are likely to threaten your dog. Talk to your vet about what vaccines may be necessary where you live. Here's a sampling of some available noncore vaccines:

✔ **Bordetella:** This highly contagious airborne disease, known as *kennel cough,* is caused by a virus. Its symptoms include a dry, hacking cough. In severe cases, the dog may have a persistent, low-grade fever. If your Poodle has been around other dogs and exhibits the symptoms, she may have bordetella. Check with your veterinarian.

Most boarding kennels require that dogs have a bordetella vaccination before they can gain acceptance. Although you shouldn't take any disease lightly, you can treat kennel cough with antibiotics, and it isn't usually serious. If you're traveling with your Poodle or showing her (see Chapter 13), you may want to vaccinate against bordetella. Remember, though, that over 100 varieties of bordetella exist, and a vaccine only protects your Poodle against a few of them. Your dog may still get kennel cough even if you vaccinate.

✔ **Hepatitis:** The hepatitis virus spreads through the feces and urine of dogs. Its symptoms include fever and lethargy. Your Poodle may be reluctant to move. Her abdomen may be tender, and her mucus membranes may be pale. In severe cases, she may begin to vomit, have diarrhea, and cough. A dog usually can recover from a mild to moderate case of hepatitis in about a week; however, in severe cases, a dog can die.

✔ **Leptospirosis:** These bacteria are generally transmitted through the urine of rats and mice. This condition can be fatal. Symptoms of leptospirosis include vomiting, fever, and a reluctance to move. Leptospirosis also can cause renal failure. Your Poodle may urinate more frequently as her kidneys begin to work harder and with less efficiently, or she may stop urinating altogether. If you think your Poodle will be exposed to rat and mice urine, you should have her vaccinated against leptospirosis; otherwise, this may be one of the shots you can skip.

Having a leptospirosis vaccine in a combination shot seems to increase the risk of your Poodle having a reaction to the shot. However, a newer leptospirosis vaccine is hitting the market; it causes less reaction and can be given as a separate shot. Talk to your veterinarian about this option.

✔ **Lyme disease:** This disease causes lethargy, lameness, and loss of appetite in dogs. Deer ticks, which are more prevalent in the eastern part of the United States, spread Lyme disease. If you live in this part of the United States or you plan on traveling there, talk to your veterinarian about having your Poodle vaccinated. You need to understand all the benefits and risks of Lyme vaccination. You can also treat the disease with antibiotics or through a topical tick preventative.

Scheduling shots

In the "good old days," you took your newly acquired puppy to the veterinarian's office, where the vet gave your dog a vaccine for every condition there was a vaccine for. Generally, a vet gave five or six vaccines in one shot, and he followed that combination shot with a rabies shot, all during the same visit.

Today, vets are moving away from the practice of loading your Poodle with shots in one visit. Instead of giving a shot that includes vaccines for distemper, hepatitis, leptospirosis, parainfluenza, and parvovirus, many vets now vaccinate for distemper and parvovirus during one visit, along with a rabies shot, leaving the other shots for another visit. Some vets even schedule distemper and parvovirus for different visits.

After you get your Poodle puppy and find the right vet for you (see the previous sections in this chapter), you should contact your vet to set up a vaccination schedule. Your Poodle probably came to you with a record of shots that her breeder had already started. Many vets give puppies their first shots at 8 weeks, 12 weeks, 16 weeks, and then annually. (Breeders may let their puppies go anywhere between 8 and 12 weeks, although it could be longer. A breeder will wait as long as necessary to place a puppy in the right home.) Some vets recommend shots at 18 to 20 weeks as well and then annually following that period. Make sure your breeder gives you the shot record for your puppy, and share the record with your vet.

When setting up your schedule, ask your veterinarian about how and when he inoculates. He may recommend yearly vaccinations for young Poodles or Poodles that travel frequently. If you adopt an older, stay-at-home Poodle, your vet may suggest vaccinations every three years.

REMEMBER The exception is the rabies shot. Every state requires a rabies shot by law. Some states require that dogs have the shot every year, and some extend the period to every three years. Ask your vet about the law in your state.

WARNING! When your Poodle gets her first shots, don't head for home right away. Hang around the waiting room for a bit to see whether she has a reaction to the shots. A mild reaction may be some swelling at the site of the injections. If the reaction is more serious, your Poodle could itch or have hives, her face could swell, or she may vomit or have diarrhea. If you leave the office and any of these symptoms occur, call your vet immediately.

Nip and Tuck: The Basics of Spaying and Neutering

Neutering and spaying can help keep your dog healthier and will definitely prevent unwanted litters. A neutered male will be less apt to wander, and neutering may eliminate annoying marking. In the following sections, I explain both processes, and I let you know when you should have one of them performed on your Poodle.

What happens during spaying and neutering?

Unless you want to show or breed your Poodle and have an entire litter scurrying through your house, spaying or neutering should be on your Poodle's upcoming agenda. *Spaying* is the removal of a female's reproductive organs. *Neutering* is the removal of a male's testicles.

Technically, you can apply the term *neutering* to both males and females. Spaying may be the removal of a female's reproductive organs, and castrating the removal of a male's testicles, but common usage refers to castration as neutering, so I do, too.

To neuter your Poodle, the veterinarian makes a cut at the base of his scrotum, removes his testicles, and then stitches up the cut. Frequently, vets use dissolving stitches. If not, your vet will have you and your Poodle return about ten days after the procedure so he can remove the sutures. Usually, dogs go home the same day.

If you prefer a "natural look" for your male Poodle, ask your vet about a vasectomy or implanting artificial testicles (called *neuticles*). Both of these alternatives cost more than just plain neutering, however and with a vasectomy, your dog will still produce testosterone and still be able to mate (without reproducing). A vasectomy won't eliminate or reduce marking or dominance behaviors.

Spaying involves abdominal surgery for a female Poodle. The veterinarian cuts through the abdominal muscles to remove both the ovaries and the uterus and then stitches up the wound. After about ten days, you'll go back so he can remove the sutures, unless he has used dissolving stitches. If you can see the stitches, they need to come out. If you can't see them, they will dissolve.

Neutering is the less invasive of the two procedures, and problems are rare (but possible) in a healthy, young Poodle.

Keep an eye on the surgery site in the days after your Poodle's procedure — especially with a spay. If the area becomes red or puffy, seems warm to the touch, and/or is oozing puss, go back to your vet's office, because the site may be infected. To minimize the chance of infection, keep the area clean. This time isn't good for your Poodle to roll in the dirt.

When should you spay or neuter your Poodle?

Ideally, you should neuter or spay your Poodle before he or she reaches sexual maturity and has the opportunity to meet your neighborhood Barbie or Beefcake. The following sections describe the right times for neutering or spaying males and females.

I don't know of any shelter or rescue group that doesn't spay or neuter an adult dog before sending her or him to a new home. However, if your adult Poodle is the exception to this rule, remember that it's never too late to spay or neuter.

Males

With male Poodles, sexual maturation usually happens sometime between the ages of 6 to 18 months, so you need to be on the lookout as that time nears. Look for the following signs:

- ✔ **Your Poodle will start to lift his leg to urinate.** He wants to mark his territory to let other males know that the neighborhood is his turf. Your walks, if you let them, will become a series of bush-sniffing and leg-lifting exercises. Your male also may decide to mark his indoor territory, choosing table legs and sofa fronts as his targets.

- ✔ **Your Poodle may become less tolerant of other males.** Generally, Poodles are good-natured with other dogs.

- ✔ **Your Poodle will definitely take an interest in girl dogs.** When a male dog smells a female dog who's in season (see the following section for the definition of *in season*), his brain turns to mush. If he gets loose, he'll follow her seductive scent wherever it leads. Obeying your calls for him to come will be far down on his to-do list.

Neutering before maturation behavior starts prevents it from ever happening. Talk to your veterinarian about neutering at one of your first appointments with your puppy. Neutering also can prevent prostate problems in males, so you're doing your Poodle's health a favor.

Females

Females reach sexual maturity sometime between the ages of 6 and 18 months. This period is marked by the female coming in "season" or "heat." Females come into heat about every six months, and this cycle is marked by a bloody discharge. A heat cycle lasts 21 days, but your dog is only receptive to a male for three to five of those days. If you have both a male and a female, consider boarding the female while she's in heat. A male in love can be pretty persistent, as well as vocal, and three weeks of whining and crying can be a long time.

Ask your breeder when her females typically come in season for the first time. If you can't get this information, Toys and Miniatures should be spayed between 6 and 10 months, and Standards between 9 and 14 months. I'd go with the lower age in both cases.

If you have a fenced-in yard and plan to let your female out unattended, make sure you can't find any holes or gaps in the fence. The fence also should be high enough to keep out any wandering neighborhood males. When walking your Poodle, keep a firm grip on her lead and keep a sharp lookout for any amorous males.

Spaying your female Poodle before she comes into season for the first time can help reduce the possibility of her developing mammary tumors. After her third heat cycle, you see no difference in the frequency of tumors. Removing the uterus also eliminates the possibility of your female getting *pyometra,* which is an infection of the uterus.

Keeping an Eye on Your Poodle's Health at Home

In the following sections, I explain how to exercise your Poodle, how to check her regularly to make sure she's in good health, and how to give her necessary medicines.

Exercising your Poodle

I've seen a sign in a gift shop that says, "If your dog is fat, you're not getting enough exercise." I certainly can't judge whether you're getting enough exercise, but I know that if your Poodle is fat, she isn't. In the following sections, I explain why and how a Poodle should stay fit.

The benefits of exercise

Extra weight on a dog is as bad as extra weight on a human. Extra weight causes stress on your Poodle's joints and makes her heart and lungs work harder.

Certain health-related issues, such as thyroid irregularities, can cause your Poodle to gain weight. If you believe your Poodle is overweight by no fault of your own, go see your vet.

Your Poodle doesn't have to be overweight to benefit from exercise. Along with the health benefits, you get the fatigue benefits. A tired dog is a good dog. If you give your Poodle some exercise before you leave for work, she'll be more content to snooze away the hours until you return.

Another benefit of exercise is that many physical activities exercise your Poodle's brain. Involvement in a competitive event requires that your Poodle learn commands and think about what she's supposed to be doing. Games like hide-and-seek make her use her nose and her brain. Even a walk around the block presents all kinds of sights and scents beyond what your Poodle experiences in your backyard.

 An adult Standard Poodle should weigh between 40 and 55 pounds. A Mini should weigh in the range of 10 to 15 pounds, and a Toy somewhere between 4 to 7 pounds. Besides getting your Poodle weighed, you can run your hands along her sides. If you can't feel her ribs, she could stand to lose a few pounds! Remember: Males generally weigh more than females.

Effective methods for trimming down

Exercise and fewer treats can make all the difference between an overweight, sluggish dog and a trim, healthy one. Why not try the following options for adding exercise to your Poodle's day?

- ✔ If your daily exercise consists of walking three times around the block, make it four. Add another shorter walk to your regimen. The length of the walk depends on the size of your Poodle and her overall health. Build up gradually. Don't go from once around the block to a five-mile jog.

- ✔ Go out in the yard and play a game of fetch or tag.

- ✔ Consider joining an agility class. Even if you don't have an interest in participating in competitions with your Poodle, an agility class can be good exercise for you both. (See Chapter 13 for more about agility events.)

 If your Poodle is extremely overweight due to very little exercise and too much food, start out slow. Begin with brisk walks around the block and work up to the mile jog that you may set as a goal. You don't want to cause injury by putting too much stress on your Poodle's body too quickly.

 Cutting back on treats is another way to keep your Poodle fit. Through your training (see Chapter 9), your Poodle may become used to receiving treats at certain times, but you can make the treats smaller. Break dog biscuits in half, or buy a smaller size. If your veterinarian recommends cutting back on food, add some canned pumpkin or green beans to your dog's smaller portions to make her feel fuller. (See Chapter 7 for more details on feeding your Poodle.)

Checking your Poodle regularly

One advantage of the need to groom your Poodle frequently (see Chapter 8) is that you have your hands on her three or four times a week. You can take advantage of those grooming sessions by keeping an eye on your Poodle's health. Follow these tips for maximum benefits:

✔ Run your hands over your Poodle's body and legs. Feel for any lumps or bumps that you don't think should be there. Look for cuts and scrapes. As you're doing this, watch her reaction. Does she flinch as your run your hand over a leg? Does she pull away or snap when you touch a certain spot?

✔ When you trim your Poodle's nails, check the pads of her feet and in between her toes for any objects that may have gotten stuck.

✔ Check inside your Poodle's ears for any redness, swelling, or discharge.

✔ Look at your Poodle's eyes. Are they clear, or are they running?

If you notice any problems during your checks, place a call to your vet. Scanning your Poodle as you groom only takes a minute, and the earlier you find a problem, the easier and faster you can fix it. Check out Chapter 8 for the full details on grooming.

Giving medications

Trust me, even the healthiest Poodle needs some kind of medicine during the course of her life. And unless Poodles make some amazing evolutionary strides in the near future, you'll be the one to give your Poodle her meds. In the following sections, I show you how to administer pills, drops, and salve to heal your Poodle's aches and pains.

Pills

Giving your Poodle pills is a fairly easy task. You can just hide the pill in a tasty treat and let your dog eat away. The tasty treat can be anything that will cling to the pill. Try burying a pill in the following foods:

✔ In canned food

✔ In the center of a piece of hot dog

✔ In a dab of cream cheese or peanut butter

If your Poodle has breathing problems, don't use peanut butter to hide pills. Peanut butter can stick to the inside of her mouth and make breathing even harder for her as she struggles to get the substance off her mouth surfaces.

✔ In a small spoonful of ice cream

✔ In some butter

If the pill you must administer is an antibiotic, put it in a large spoonful of live-culture yogurt. Antibiotics kill all the "bad stuff" that they target, but an antibiotic isn't selective. It also kills the "good stuff" that your Poodle needs — the organisms that live in your dog's intestines. The yogurt helps to renew those organisms.

Some Poodles are just too "clever" to eat treats that contain pills. If your Poodle is a pill detective, you may have to give pills the old-fashioned way. Follow these steps:

1. **Grasp your Poodle's upper muzzle from the top.**

2. **Push in on her upper lips.**

3. **When she opens her mouth, put the pill as far back on the tongue as possible, close her jaws, and, while holding her muzzle up, stroke her throat until she swallows.**

4. **Give her a treat for being a good girl!**

Using a soft treat, such as a tiny spoonful of yogurt or vanilla ice cream or a small amount of milk will help soothe her throat and allow the pill to go all the way down the hatch. You also may find that it helps to straddle your Standard Poodle when giving her any kind of medicine so you can keep her in place.

Drops and salve

Someday, your Poodle may need some eye drops, salve (a medical ointment that you can use to treat eye issues), or ear drops to combat certain medical conditions, such as tearing and infection.

Use the following technique for applying eye drops:

1. **Straddle your Standard Poodle and turn your feet in, under the dog.**

Your legs help hold the dog steady and your feet prevent her from backing out of your leg hold.

Note: For Toy and Miniature Poodles, have the dog sit in front of you, facing to the side. Put the dog on a chair or table, so the dog is closer to eye level and also less able to get away from you. Then, you can go on to complete Step 2 and Step 3.

2. **Use one hand to hold your Poodle's head and open her eye.**

3. **Squirt the drops into the inner corner of the eye, and then hold the eye shut for a moment to help spread the drops around.**

You use the same technique for applying salve, except that you try to start in the outer corner of the eye. You still hold the eye closed, but in this case you want to melt the salve. However, the inner- and outer-corner advice is the ideal. Sometimes, I consider it a victory to hit the eye at all!

Poodles are susceptible to ear infections. If your poodle does get an ear infection, request that the vet do a culture and sensitivity test to determine the specific causative agent and the antibiotic that will eliminate it. Using the "shotgun" method of prescribing a general antibiotic often results in the dog developing an antibiotic resistant strain of bacteria or fungus in the ears, which can be extremely difficult to treat. Follow the vet's instructions for this medication exactly and don't stop until it is entirely used up. After the infection is clear, be sure to use regular hygiene to prevent a recurrence.

Prevention of ear infections is far better than treating them. Ear cleaning should be a part of your Poodle's regular grooming routine. You should start young, so that your Poodle accepts this necessary hygiene. The following are two schools of thought on this issue:

✔ Many Poodle breeders use a medicated powder to dry the ear canal, and then remove the hair from the ear canal, using blunt tweezers or an instrument called a *hemostat,* which can be obtained from your vet or many dog-supply catalogs. This cleaning should be done monthly. If you have your poodle professionally groomed, be sure the groomer does this.

✔ The other prevention method uses a weekly cleaning with a mixture of half vinegar and half water, or you can use rubbing alcohol to clean and dry the ear, but leaving the hair in place. Pour in the cleaning mixture, rub the ear to distribute it, and then wipe the ear clean with a cotton swab.

Chapter 15

Considering Common Poodle Conditions

*N*o dog is perfect — health wise, that is. Unfortunately, you may have to deal with a sick Poodle once in a while. This chapter discusses common Poodle health issues with and how you can fight back. I also address everyday Poodle illnesses and injuries.

Generally, any minor but still uncomfortable health problem that lasts for more than 24 hours calls for a trip to the veterinarian. Any problem that worsens over several hours, such as fever, weakness, or lack of appetite, needs veterinary attention immediately. When you get a Poodle, put your vet's phone number on speed dial, memorize it, and post it next to your home phone (see Chapter 14 for tips on finding the right vet for you).

Ouch! Treating Everyday Illnesses and Injuries

In the following sections, I describe a variety of ordinary illnesses and injuries that may afflict your Poodle.

Cuts and scrapes

Your Poodle can acquire cuts and scrapes in many ways, just like kids. You can treat surface scrapes and shallow cuts on a Poodle the same way you treat your own cuts or scrapes. Wash the area with soap and water, and apply a bit of antibiotic cream. Watch the area in the hours that follow; if it gets red or puffy or feels warm to the touch, go to your vet's office. If the wound is deep, get to your vet.

Lumps and bumps

Lumps and bumps can go undetected under your Poodle's coat, which is why you should run your hands all over your Poodle at least once a week (see Chapter 14 for details on checking your Poodle regularly). A lump or bump may be the result of a fall or bumping into something, or it may just be a fatty deposit. You have no way of knowing what a lump or bump is without seeing your vet. Any lump or bump should be aspirated.

Skin problems

All kinds of things can irritate the skin: allergies to bug bites to serious diseases, like sebaceous adenitis. I cover many common skin problems and how you can treat them in the following sections.

Allergies

Just like people, dogs can have allergies. If your Poodle is scratching and biting at his skin, he may have fleas (see the later section "External parasites" for more about getting rid of these pests). If he's chewing and licking his feet, he may have a food allergy. Dogs also can be allergic to airborne substances, such as pollens and molds. Some dogs can even be allergic to people dander.

Make an appointment with your veterinarian if your Poodle is biting, licking, and scratching. This is a common symptom of food allergies. If she suspects a food allergy, she'll put your Poodle on a single-food diet and add other ingredients gradually to try to determine what's causing the problem. If an allergy is airborne, your vet may recommend frequent baths or prescribe a medication. If she determines that the problem is fleas, she'll suggest a flea preventative, and she may also give you medicated shampoo for bath time (see Chapter 8 for more on bathing your Poodle).

Hot spots

Hot spots are raw, oozy sores that your Poodle creates when he bites and chews at an itchy spot, caused by an irritation (like flea bites). The spots form quickly if they happen to be covered with hair, because hair holds in the moisture and further irritates the spots.

I treat hot spots with a dab of triple antibiotic cream, which you can find at any drug store. If you don't trust the drugstore, your vet can supply something to help. Listerine can also help dry up a hot spot. If a hot spot you treat doesn't clear up in a couple days, visit your vet, who may prescribe an oral antibiotic.

Sebaceous adenitis

Sebaceous adenitis (SA) is an inflammatory disease of the sebaceous glands and may be inherited, metabolic, or immune-mediated in Standard Poodles. Because SA is hereditary, buyers should only buy puppies from parents who have had an annual skin punch biopsy to prove that they aren't currently affected with this disorder. Currently, you can't find a DNA test for the SA gene, and unfortunately, SA has no cure.

The condition is hard to diagnose, because it may look like an allergy or hypothyroidism (which I cover later in this chapter). Your dog may lose hair, have dry, brittle hair, or develop white scales and skin lesions.

Any Standard Poodle who develops an unresponsive skin ailment should have a skin punch biopsy to test for SA. You can download forms, instructions, and a list of qualified diagnostic laboratories from the Orthopedic Foundation for Animals Web site (www. offa.org). Medicated shampoos can help; soaking scaly areas with baby oil and then shampooing removes scales. Your vet may also prescribe medications to guard against infection.

Tummy aches

Many dogs have sensitive stomachs. If you happen to change your Poodle's diet for a day, for instance, or if your little guy gets into something he shouldn't have, be prepared to clean up some messes later. You can probably suppress a simple tummy ache with a day of fasting and then a day of feeding well-cooked lean ground meat or chicken with rice to your Poodle (make sure meat is drained of fat). Make sure your Poodle drinks plenty of water while fasting. Offer ice cubes if that helps. If your Poodle is vomiting or has diarrhea for more than 24 hours, however, you need to make a trip to the vet.

Ear issues

Poodles have floppy ears, which prevent air from circulating — a situation that can lead to infection. You may notice a smelly discharge or the ear may be red and painful. Pulling hair from your Poodle's ears and using ear cleaner once a week can help prevent ear infections. If your Poodle still winds up with an infection, you'll probably have to give him drops prescribed by your vet.

Internal parasites

Internal parasites that invade dogs include tapeworm, roundworm, hookworm, whipworm, and heartworm. With the exception of heartworm, which migrates to the dog's heart, these parasites find your dog's intestines to be the perfect home. And all, without exception, require aggressive treatment. For some parasites, you can give your dog preventative medicine. Some heartworm pills now also contain medication to prevent hookworms and roundworms.

Tapeworm

Tapeworm is the least harmful of all the worms. Your Poodle can get tapeworm from eating a flea, which is another good reason to keep your dog flea-free (see the next section for details). Another way to get tapeworm is to eat birds or small mammals. Tapeworms rob your Poodle of his nutrients, so get rid of the worms fast.

Tapeworm segments look like grains of rice in your dog's stool. If you see them, or if your Poodle starts scooting his rear across the floor, contact your vet for a checkup and the proper medication.

Roundworms

Roundworms, which frequently show up in puppies, can cause abdominal distension, colic, coughing, and poor appetite. These worms are life threatening in puppies. The good news is that vets routinely worm most puppies. Roundworms can produce the same symptoms in adults, but the worms aren't as threatening. Twice-yearly fecal tests should let your vet know whether your Poodle has any type of worm, and your vet will then prescribe the appropriate medication to kill the worms.

Whipworms

Whipworms cause large-bowel inflammation, resulting in diarrhea that often contains mucus and fresh blood. Whipworms can be difficult to diagnose on fecal exams, and false negatives aren't uncommon, but the classic symptom is the three-part stool. The dog passes stool that starts out normal, then becomes soft, and the last part is runny, often with mucus or even blood.

Whipworm eggs form in soil, and they can stay viable in soil for years. It's very easy for a dog to ingest the eggs from grass or twigs, or almost anything a dog may put into his mouth (the eggs can get on paws and fur and be licked off as well). Therefore, after your dog receives a whipworm diagnosis, you need to test regularly for a recurrence of the worm, and your vet will prescribe the appropriate medication. You can't get rid of the worms in the soil, unless you pave your yard!

Hookworms

Hookworms are bloodsuckers that can leave bite sites that continually seep blood. Blood loss can leave your Poodle with pale mucus membranes; he may have dark, tarry stools; and he could experience either diarrhea or constipation. Other symptoms include a cough or a poor appetite. Hookworms get picked up in the environment, either from the dog ingesting the eggs, or from the larvae penetrating the skin of the dog. If you suspect hookworms are sucking the life out of your Poodle, a fecal exam can diagnose the problem, and your vet will prescribe medicine.

Heartworms

Mosquitoes transmit heartworms when they bite your dog. Your Poodle's blood carries the microfilaria to the heart. In the heart, the worms mature into adult worms and gradually clog the chambers of the heart. Fortunately, you can administer a preventative medicine for heartworm. After your vet uses a blood test to determine that your Poodle doesn't have heartworm, he'll put your dog on a monthly pill or chewable. If your dog goes off the medication for any amount of time, for instance, during winter months, your vet will test annually. If your dog stays on the medication year-round, your vet may test every three years or so as a precaution.

It is very important never for your Poodle to never miss a dose of his heartworm preventative medicine. A missed dose will allow the worms to become adults in the heart.

If your dog is diagnosed with heartworm, a cure exists. But the medication that kills the worms is harsh, and dead worms can cause a problem as they travel to the lungs, possibly blocking blood vessels, so your dog's activity must be limited for four to six weeks. Some dogs show no signs of the disease, however, so keep your Poodle safe. Get the blood test and put your dog on a preventative.

External parasites

Fleas and ticks are the most common external parasites that attack dogs. I cover both of these bugs in the following sections.

Fleas

Fleas are nasty little critters that bite dogs and suck their blood. One flea can bite your Poodle as many as 400 times in just one day. Fleas bring the danger of anemia from a large infestation. Many dogs also are allergic to flea saliva; they'll bite and chew themselves because the saliva makes them itch. They may also scratch. This biting, chewing and scratching can lead, in turn, to raw sores, or hot spots (see previous section on this topic).

Fleas seem to be everywhere. Wild animals, besides dogs and cats, can have fleas, and the flea eggs are hardy. Any grassy area can harbor fleas. If you think your Poodle is harboring some of these nasty freeloaders, roll him over and check his tummy, where his hair is thinner — especially near his hind legs. If you don't see a flea at all, you may notice little black flecks of "flea dirt." Gather a few of these flecks and put them on a paper towel or piece of white paper and dampen the surface. If the black flecks turn red, you've got yourself some flea dirt. The war has begun!

If your Poodle is scratching and biting, but you can't find any evidence of fleas, have your vet look at your dog to make sure she can't find some other kind of skin problem.

To launch a full-scale attack in your war with fleas, perform the following tasks:

- ✔ Give him a bath in flea shampoo. Remember that flea shampoo will kill many fleas, but will not further prevent infestations.

- ✔ Vacuum regularly to keep the flea numbers down in your house. Before you vacuum, cut up a flea collar and put it in the bag or canister. Empty your vacuum cleaner frequently so it doesn't turn into a breeding colony for fleas.

- ✔ Wash your Poodle's bedding. The fleas have been laying their eggs there, as well as everywhere else in your house.

- ✔ You can set off a flea bomb. Bombs do work, but you have to make sure there's no food out, and you need to wash down all food preparation surfaces. You can't leave any living thing in the house when you bomb it. I've had good luck with other methods and would rather avoid poisoning my entire house.

After you win the first stage of the war against fleas, or before if you're a pacifist and want to avoid the war altogether, consider putting your Poodle on one of the following flea preventatives:

- ✔ *Program* acts as birth control for the prevention of flea births. Fleas absorb the medicine with their blood meals, and it prevents cocoons from forming so the flea larvae never develop. You can use Program with other products, too.

- ✔ *Frontline,* a topical flea preventative, fights ticks for a month.

- ✔ *Advantage* is a monthly topical product.

Different people have different preferences and needs when it comes to these preventatives. If you're unsure whether to put your Poodle on a preventative or when to do it, be sure to consult with your vet to find the best option for you and your Poodle.

Ticks

If you and your Poodle take long walks in tall grass or shrubs, you're more likely to pick up an unwanted hitchhiker than if your Poodle is always in a nicely mown lawn, although that doesn't mean your Poodle can't still pick up a tick. Besides making your dog an unwilling blood donor, ticks can transmit Rocky Mountain Spotted Fever, Lyme disease, and tick paralysis. Talk to your vet about what ticks may be in your area.

Because ticks carry many serious diseases, effective prevention of tick bites is very important. Spot-on products labeled for ticks are more effective than tick collars.

Ticks can be hard to see, but you may be able to feel them as you run your hands over your Poodle. Push your dog's hair aside and check his skin. If you find a tick, use tweezers to remove it. Grasp firmly where the tick is attached to your dog and pull gently and slowly. You want to make sure you don't leave the tick's head imbedded in your dog, so don't crush or squeeze the tick. Placing alcohol on the tick may make it back out on its own.

Don't handle the tick, and if you do touch it, wash your hands immediately. After the tick is off your dog, flush it down the toilet, or drop it in a container of alcohol. Wash the area where it was imbedded in your dog, and then apply a topical antiseptic. Keep a close eye on the area of the tick bite for several weeks afterward. If you see a rash, or if the dog develops any illness symptoms, see a vet immediately, and be sure to tell her exactly when the tick bit your Poodle. This info will help the vet determine whether your pet has possibly contracted a tick-borne disease.

Never use a cigarette, or anything else that will burn, to remove a tick. No doubt holding a lit cigarette to a tick will get the tick's attention, but you might also burn your dog.

If you can't remove a tick yourself, or you're afraid to try, get your dog to your veterinarian. Never leave ticks on your dog.

Limping

Limping can be caused by something serious or by something as simple as slipping while chasing a squirrel. If you know what caused the problem — you watch your dog fall or see another dog bump him during play — then wait a day or two and see if it resolves itself. A baby aspirin or two can help ease the soreness.

If your dog is limping and you don't know why, check his paws. He may have cut a pad or picked up a burr or a thorn. If it's winter, ice balls may be between the pads. If everything looks fine, but he's still limping, call your vet. Some large dogs experience lameness because of rapid growth, but you won't know without an exam.

Surveying Other Common Poodle Health Issues

Hopefully your Poodle will never show signs of any of the serious problems I present in this section, but I discuss them here because these health issues do affect Poodles. If you notice any of the symptoms I mention (or if your dog is just not acting right), don't hesitate to contact your veterinarian with your concerns right away.

Bloat

Bloat, or Gastric Dilatation-Volvulus (GDV), is more common in larger dogs, but any dog can have the condition. This means your Standard Poodle is more apt to have the problem than a Toy or a Miniature. If a dog has bloat, his stomach fills with gas and bloats, or stretches, which causes abdominal pain. After some time, the stomach flips over, which cuts off any chance for the gas to escape. The flipping also cuts off the blood supply, and the dog will die unless a vet performs surgery as soon as possible. The dog shows signs of discomfort, and the abdomen may be distended. The dog may pace and cry or try to vomit but won't be able to because the stomach is closed off.

You can help prevent bloat in a few different ways:

- ✔ By feeding your Poodle two or more smaller meals a day rather than one large meal once a day

- ✔ By waiting at least an hour after meals to exercise your Poodle

- ✔ By waiting an hour after strenuous exercise before feeding your Poodle

See Chapter 7 for general info on properly feeding your Poodle.

Epilepsy

Epilepsy can occur in all three Poodle varieties (see Chapter 2 for more on variety distinctions). *Idiopathic epilepsy* is an inherited condition that can cause mild or severe seizures, which is the only recognizable sign. We have no cure for it, but certain medicines can help stop or lessen the seizures. Other factors can cause seizures, too, so you need to see your veterinarian if your Poodle has a seizure so you can determine the cause.

Current research indicates that it is best to put a dog that has a seizure on medication to prevent seizures right away, in order to prevent the development of a seizure pattern in the brain. A number of effective medications are available.

Some dogs may bite during seizures. Don't try to handle or restrain your Poodle during a seizure.

Hormonal problems

Sometimes, the hormones in your Poodle can become unbalanced. Your Poodle may have an autoimmune reaction that upsets the normal production of a hormone. When that happens, the health problems in the following sections can occur.

Addison's disease

Addison's disease, or *hypoadrenocorticism,* is a lack of sufficient adrenal hormones produced by the adrenal glands. *Cortin* is a complex of hormones that help regulate weight, mineral balance, the structure of connective tissue, some white-blood-cell production, and skin health. Addison's may be caused by an immune problem, or it may be triggered by a condition like pituitary cancer, which interrupts the production of hormones that trigger the adrenal glands. You also may trigger Addison's when you suddenly stop giving your Poodle a cortisone drug that he's been taking regularly.

Symptoms of Addison's, although they can be vague and similar to renal failure, include vomiting, lethargy, and poor appetite. If a dog has high stress levels, and his potassium levels rise, his heart may be involved and he could die.

The only way to diagnose Addison's is with an ACTH response test. ACTH is adrenocorticotropic hormone from the pituitary gland. The test should stimulate the production of cortin. If it doesn't, the dog has Addison's. Your vet may give fludrocortisone acetate, suggest salting your Poodle's food, or prescribe corticosteroids like prednisone.

Cushings

Cushings, or *hyperadrenocorticism,* is the opposite of Addison's. With Cushings, the adrenal glands produce too much cortin. A tumor on the adrenal glands or on the pituitary gland can cause Cushings. A dog with Cushings may have the following symptoms:

✔ Increased appetite

✔ The need to drink and urinate more

✔ High blood pressure

✔ Hair loss

✔ Muscle weakness

✔ Bulging, sagging abdomens

A vet diagnoses Cushings with a blood test. You can treat cases caused by a tumor on the pituitary gland with drugs, but you can't cure them. The drugs can ease the symptoms and improve the quality of life for your Poodle. If the cause of Cushings is a tumor of the adrenal glands, it may be possible to remove the tumor.

Hypothyroidism

Hypothyroidism is the inadequate production of thyroid hormone. The production of thyroid may be affected by an autoimmune problem, which causes the condition. If you notice the following symptoms, your Poodle may have a thyroid problem:

✔ Skin problems

✔ Persistent hunger

✔ A coarse coat

✔ Inability to stay warm

✔ Weight gain

✔ Lethargy

A blood test can tell your veterinarian if the problem lies in your Poodle's thyroid. If your Poodle gets a hypothyroidism diagnosis, your vet will prescribe daily medication to correct the problem.

Orthopedic issues

Poodles, like people, can deal with the aches and pains of orthopedic issues. Here I describe three common orthopedic issues that can appear in Poodles, including hip dysplasia, Legg-Calve-Perthes disease, and patellar luxation.

Hip dysplasia

Hip dysplasia is a malformation of the hip joint. The socket of the joint wears on the head of the femur, which doesn't fit properly into the joint. Sometimes, the femur comes out of the joint altogether, causing pain and damage to surrounding ligaments. A dog also may develop arthritis in the joint.

Larger dogs, like Standard Poodles, are more prone to hip dysplasia, although any size dog can have it. Larger dogs also are more apt to show signs of a problem than smaller dogs. If your dog is limping or shows a reluctance to sit, it may be a sign of hip dysplasia.

You can treat mild cases of hip dysplasia with proper exercise and diet. Severe cases require corrective surgery. Consult your vet for a proper diagnosis.

Legg-Calvé-Perthes

In a Poodle with *Legg-Calvé-Perthes Disease* (LCPD), the head of the femur bone dies and then reforms, causing an irregular fit in the hip socket. The condition causes stiffness and pain, similar to hip dysplasia (see the previous section). The disease appears to be genetic, but no precise cause is known.

If you notice that your dog is limping, have the vet check him out. X-rays will determine if the problem is Legg-Calvé-Perthes. The disease is common in small dogs, and Toy Poodles come from a breed with a high incidence rate.

The Orthopedic Foundation for Animals offers a database for LCPD similar to its database for hip dysplasia evaluations.

Patellar luxation

Patellar luxation is the dislocation of the patella, or kneecap. The condition is common in Miniature and Toy Poodles. : Like hip dysplasia, patella luxation is a polygenetic hereditary trait. Toy and miniature Poodles used for breeding should be certified by the Orthopedic Foundation for Animals as being clear of this disorder.

Your Poodle may have patellar luxation if he

- ✔ Has trouble straightening his stifle
- ✔ Is limping
- ✔ Has a hock that points outward while his toes point inward

Each case of patellar luxation has a different grade of severity, and the problem can progress from not-too-bad to very serious, so you should treat it early. Surgery can correct the problem.

Vision conditions

If your Poodle shows signs of limited vision, or appears to be blind, the cause could be one of the three conditions listed in this section.

Optic nerve hypoplasia

In *optic nerve hypoplasia,* the optic nerve fails to develop normally, causing a dog to have visual impairment from birth. The condition eventually causes total blindness.

One or both eyes may be affected by the condition, and no cure exists. The disease is hereditary in Miniature Poodles and is also seen in Toy Poodles. Breeding stock should be tested for this problem, and affected dogs shouldn't be bred.

Progressive retinal atrophy

Progressive retinal atrophy (PRA) is an inherited disease that affects the retina and eventually leads to blindness. The condition is seen in many breeds, including Toy and Miniature Poodles.

In Toys and Minis, *progressive rod-cone degeneration* (prcd) is the PRA form you see most often. The rod cells in the retina lose function, and then the cone cells follow. Initially, a Poodle exhibits diminished vision; finally, he'll succumb to total blindness. There is no known cure for PRA.

According to the Poodle Club of America's Web site (www. poodleclubofamerica.org), OptiGen (www.optigen.com) offers a genetic test that can identify whether a Toy or Miniature Poodle has, or is a carrier of, prcd-PRA. This test isn't available for Standards because the prcd form of PRA isn't common in them.

Breeders should test their breeding stock for PRA. The Canine Eye Registration Foundation (CERF) maintains a registry, similar to the databases of the OFA and PennHip for hip dysplasia (which I cover earlier in this chapter).

Von Willebrand's Disease

Von Willebrand's Disease (vWD) is an inherited bleeding disorder in which a clotting agent, the *von Willebrand factor* (vWF), is in short supply. After the dog uses up the short supply of clotting ingredient, he bleeds more. This condition can be a big problem during situations like surgery. We have no cure for the condition, but thyroid supplementation may increase the vWF in hypothyroid dogs (see the section "Hormonal problems" for more).

Responsible breeders test for von Willebrand's Disease and won't breed affected dogs. A DNA test is now available, and breeding stock should be tested prior to breeding. Be sure not to buy a Poodle from a breeder who doesn't test her stock.

Chapter 16

Staying Prepared with First-Aid Basics

In This Chapter

▶ Keeping important items in a canine first-aid kit

▶ Trying your hand at basic first-aid techniques

▶ Knowing what to do in emergency situations

*H*opefully you'll never have to deal with a canine health emergency, but, as is the essence of an emergency, you can't predict when or if one will happen. Emergencies are unexpected situations that call for quick action. Your best course of action is to follow the Scout motto and "be prepared" to act if your Poodle needs your help. In this chapter, I describe the must-haves for your Poodle's first-aid kit; I show you how to perform basic first-aid techniques; and I explain what you can do in specific emergencies to rescue your beloved pet.

 The most important thing to do in all circumstances is to get your Poodle to a veterinarian as soon as possible. First aid is just a way to control a situation until you can get professional help. Don't spend more time on first aid than is absolutely necessary.

Stocking the Essentials in Your Canine First-Aid Kit

You have a first-aid kit for your family or yourself (I hope!), stocked with everything from bandages to antibacterial cream. And, because your Poodle is part of your family, you should have one for her as well. You can buy an official canine first-aid kit from a catalog or at a pet-supply store, or you can stock some basic supplies that you buy individually to create your own; in the following sections, I give you lists of traditional and holistic products to include.

In your residence, designate one shelf in a cabinet for your Poodle's first-aid supplies, or store them in a small box that can travel throughout your home. If you travel with your Poodle, you should keep a small first-aid kit in your vehicle. A tube of antibiotic ointment, some gauze pads, and some aspirin may suffice for your portable kit.

Traditional medicines

The following list presents the traditional items you can include in your Poodle's first-aid kit (a pre-made kit should contain most of these items). You use many of these products for human emergencies, too, so don't let the length of the list scare you.

- **Vet wrap and adhesive tape:** Vet wrap holds bandages or splints in place, and it won't stick to your Poodle's hair. If you keep the hair on your Poodle's flaps long (see Chapter 8 for more on grooming), you may already have vet wrap with your grooming supplies. If not, you can find the wrap in pet-supply catalogs and stores. Put a roll with your first-aid supplies as well. Adhesive tape can hold bandages in place, too, but it can make a mess of your Poodle's coat and could pull hair and hurt your dog when you remove it.

- **Antibiotic ointments:** For use on scrapes and shallow cuts. I use a triple antibiotic cream, which is available at drug stores.

- **Artificial tears:** Apply to your Poodle's irritated eyes.

- **Benadryl:** For allergic reactions (such as those that often come with insect stings). Give one milligram per pound of body weight.

- **Betadine:** You can readily find this antiseptic in the pharmaceutical department of grocery stores or in drug stores. You use it to treat minor cuts, and doctors use it to prepare the skin prior to surgery. It contains 10 percent povidone-iodine.

- **Children's aspirin:** For fever or pain, adult-strength aspirin is fine for a Standard Poodle; most vets recommend buffered aspirin. You also can cut an adult tablet in half or in quarters if you don't have any children's aspirin for Toy or Miniature Poodles. Give one tablet for every 10 to 15 pounds of body weight.

Don't ever give your Poodle ibuprofen, naproxen sodium, or acetaminophen. It can be fatal.

- **Cotton balls:** Good for applying salves or for the external application of liquid medicines. In a pinch, a cotton ball can replace a gauze pad.

✔ **Gauze:** A roll of gauze can secure dressings on wounds your Poodle may have. You can purchase various sizes of gauze pads; the size you get depends on the wound and the size of your Poodle.

✔ **Hemostats and/or tweezers:** You use these tools to remove slivers, or large bits of debris that may be stuck in a wound. You may already have hemostats in your grooming kit for removing flap hair (see Chapter 8 for more about grooming).

✔ **Hydrocortisone ointment:** For use on bug bites or rashes.

✔ **Hydrogen peroxide:** A product used to clean and disinfect wounds. You also can use hydrogen peroxide to induce vomiting, if your dog has ingested something poisonous and you know what the substance is. If you already have a large bottle of hydrogen peroxide, you can cross syrup of ipecac off your supply list.

Hydrogen peroxide loses strength in storage. You should replace it yearly if not opened and more often if opened.

If you suspect your dog has ingested a cleaning product, *do not* induce vomiting. The caustic chemicals will burn your dog's esophagus and mouth.

✔ **Kaopectate:** Helps control diarrhea. Give one teaspoon for every five pounds of body weight, at a clip of every four hours.

✔ **Petroleum jelly:** Can sooth minor scrapes or burns.

✔ **Rubber gloves:** Can make dealing with assorted bodily fluids much nicer.

✔ **Scissors:** For cutting gauze or vet wrap.

✔ **Syringes:** You should stock 3-, 6-, and 12-centimeter syringes for administering liquid medications. They can make it easier to get your dog to swallow hydrogen peroxide or Kaopectate, for instance.

✔ **Syrup of ipecac:** Give by mouth to induce vomiting if your Poodle ingests a poison. You can find the syrup at your pharmacy.

✔ **Thermometer:** For taking your Poodle's temperature. Normal temperature for a dog is between 100 and 102 degrees Fahrenheit.

✔ **Veterinarian's phone number:** Keep an index card inscribed with your veterinarian's phone number and the number of your local emergency clinic on your Poodle's medical supplies shelf or in her first-aid kit.

✔ **Veterinary first-aid manual:** Most pet-supply stores and many book stores sell canine first-aid manuals.

Holistic medicines

You may prefer holistic choices for your Poodle's first-aid kit. Some people consider more natural products better than products that contain synthetic chemicals, and some holistic products may have fewer side effects. Many health-food stores and some larger pet-supply stores may have holistic choices. The following are good holistic items you can add to the kit:

- ✔ **Aloe vera:** A product that helps to relieve pain and itching in and around hot spots, insect bites, and other skin irritations. Along with being nontoxic, Aloe vera has a bitter taste, so it may discourage your Poodle from licking and biting at problem areas.

- ✔ **Arnica gel:** For use on sprains and bruises to reduce pain and swelling.

- ✔ **Calendula gel:** Apply this gel to scrapes and wounds to promote healing. It has antiseptic properties and can help reduce swelling.

- ✔ **Cayenne pepper:** You can sprinkle this pepper on a wound to stop the bleeding.

- ✔ **Comfrey ointment:** Good for minor scrapes and wounds. Comfrey contains allantoin, which speeds up the natural replacement of cells and promotes healing.

- ✔ **Rescue remedy:** A mixture of five of the single Bach essences (see Chapter 14 for more details). You use the remedy to treat shock, collapse, or trauma.

Performing Basic First-Aid Techniques on Your Poodle

Having a sound knowledge of canine first-aid techniques makes it easier to be calm and collected during times of injury or crisis. During an emergency, you may feel the need to panic, but you need to stay calm in order to help your Poodle. Your instincts will tell you to hurry, but resist the temptation to act without thinking first. Improper handling can further injure your dog. I once took a class in animal first aid, and the vet teaching the class advised that the first step in treating an emergency is to take a deep breath. Sound breathing coupled with knowledge can pave the way to good health!

Taking an animal first-aid class is a good way to prepare yourself for emergency situations. Having some basic knowledge allows you to help your Poodle until you can get to your vet's office, and it helps you to remain calm. Many Red Cross branches offer animal first-aid classes.

The following sections present some basic first-aid techniques that you should know in case your Poodle ever needs medical assistance.

Taking your Poodle's temperature and pulse

Knowing how to take your Poodle's temperature gives you a method for gauging how sick or injured your pet may be. A Poodle's normal temperature should be between 100 and 102 degrees. Anything below 100 or over 102 means that your Poodle needs treatment; call your vet right away.

A rectal thermometer is the way to go for taking your Poodle's temperature. You can ask for guidance on the technique during a regular visit to your vet's office for a checkup. Practice taking your dog's temperature before an emergency arises.

You also should prepare for an emergency by finding out how to take your Poodle's pulse. Trying to find your pet's pulse for the first time during an emergency probably won't work. To take your Poodle's pulse, use the femoral artery on the upper portion of her rear leg, near where the leg joins the body on the inside. Find the top bone of your dog's leg, the femur, and then move your fingers forward until you feel the artery. (See Chapter 2 for an illustration of the parts of a Poodle.)

Ask your vet during a routine visit to show you how to find the pulse if you have trouble on your own. Make a note of your Poodle's normal pulse rate. A normal rate for a dog is between 80 and 140 beats per minute. The smaller the dog, the higher the number.

Muzzling your Poodle

If your Poodle is severely injured, you should muzzle her before giving her treatment. Even the most loving dog may snap when she's frightened or hurt. You can buy a muzzle from a pet-supply catalog or a pet-supply shop. Keep it with your first-aid kit so you can find it in a pinch (see the earlier section on this topic). If you don't have one on hand for an emergency, you can try to make a muzzle with a scarf, panty hose, or a length of rope.

Don't put a muzzle on your Poodle if she's having trouble breathing. Use a blanket, a magazine, or newspaper to wrap around your dog's head, with the material extending beyond her muzzle. You can hold the material in place with gauze, adhesive tape, or vet wrap. A blanket or newspaper will protect you from your Poodle's snapping jaws, but it won't hinder your Poodle's breathing.

To muzzle your Poodle with a scarf, a nylon stocking, or man's tie, follow these steps:

1. **Stand behind your Poodle or straddle her to avoid her attempts at bites while you apply the muzzle.**

2. **Bring the material up from under her jaw and tie a half-knot on top of her muzzle.**

3. **Bring the ends of the material down and tie another half knot on the underside of your dog's muzzle.**

4. **Tie the ends behind your Poodle's head. Use an easy-release knot such as a half hitch, or tie the ends in a bow.**

Moving your Poodle safely

If your Poodle has severe injuries, you need to take her to your vet's office for emergency care. For the trip, you should consider transporting her on a blanket or a board — especially if you suspect she has spinal cord damage. You want to move her around as little as possible, and a board helps this cause.

Try to shift your dog onto the board or blanket all at once. If you have a Toy or Miniature Poodle, gently scoop the dog up, using both hands to keep her as still as possible. With a Standard Poodle, slip your hands under her body at the shoulders and hips and ease her onto a board or blanket. If you have help, all the better.

Be sure to put your Poodle in a secure position in the car, where she won't slide off a seat if the car suddenly stops.

Giving artificial respiration

During a medical emergency, your Poodle may stop breathing. Advanced heatstroke, poisoning, electrocution, a car accident, or a dogfight: All these emergencies can cause injuries that lead to your Poodle no longer being able to breathe on her own (see the following section for treatment advice for some of these emergencies). You need to start artificial respiration until your dog can breathe on her own or until you reach medical help. Follow these steps to start artificial respiration:

1. **Extend your Poodle's neck by gently grasping her jaw and pulling forward.**

2. **Clear any mucus or debris from her mouth.**

3. **Pull her tongue forward.**

4. **Breathe into her nose, closing your mouth tightly over her nose holes, for three seconds.**

5. **Rest for two seconds.**

6. **Continue Steps 4 and 5 until your Poodle can breathe on her own or until you reach your vet's office.**

If you don't want to put your mouth around your Poodle's nose for respiration, you can use the top of a water bottle. Find a bottle appropriate for the size of your Poodle, and cut off the top below the narrow mouth. (To be prepared, you can keep a bottle at the ready with your first-aid equipment.) The bottle won't form as effective a seal as your mouth, but it will work.

Another method of artificial respiration is the *compression method,* although if you suspect that your Poodle has internal injuries, this method may cause more damage. To perform the compression method on a Poodle without internal injury, follow these steps:

1. **Place both of your hands on your Poodle's side, near her last ribs.**

2. **Press down and release quickly.**

3. **Try to complete 12 compressions per minute, or about one every five seconds.**

   If you have another person with you, he or she can drive you to the veterinarian's office while you continue with the compressions.

The compression method isn't CPR. The compressions are to the lungs, not the heart, and are in place of breathing into the dog's nose.

Treating shock

A dog, like a human, can go into shock after experiencing any traumatic injury. Shock can result from being in a car accident, from being electrocuted, from getting poisoned, or from a near-drowning experience. Shock manifests itself as a circulation problem; its symptoms may include the following:

✔ Shallow, rapid breathing

✔ A rapid pulse rate (see the earlier section "Taking your Poodle's temperature and pulse")

✔ Pale mucus membranes

✔ Cool skin and legs

✔ Staring eyes

A dog in shock also can be unconscious. Follow these steps to treat your Poodle if she goes into shock:

1. **Make sure your Poodle is breathing by feeling her chest and putting your hand by her nose.**

   Clear her airway and start artificial respiration if necessary (see the previous section for details).

2. **Wrap her in blankets, towels, or even newspapers — any material that will conserve heat.**

   Never use heating pads or lamps to keep your dog warm. If they get too hot, your Poodle won't be able to move away, and she may suffer burns.

3. **Try to keep your Poodle quiet.**

   Don't let her struggle or move around, even if she appears to be feeling better. Keep her quiet and warm.

4. **Get your Poodle to the vet immediately.**

   Remember that first aid is just a means of stabilizing your dog until she can get proper medical attention.

In the event of a serious injury, treat your Poodle for shock before you see any symptoms. Don't wait! Try to stop any serious bleeding and keep her warm and quiet until you can get medical attention.

Coming to Your Poodle's Rescue in Specific Emergencies

Although any emergency involving an injury to your Poodle can be life-threatening, emergencies come with degrees of danger. Head wounds, for example, bleed profusely and seem dire, but they may not be as life-threatening as internal damage caused by poisoning. A broken bone is serious, but if properly treated, it may not be as bad as a puncture wound that collapses your Poodle's lung.

Chances are, you'll never have to splint a leg, cover a chest wound, or protect an injured eye. Your Poodle probably won't chew on an electric cord or get into poison. But, just in case, you should know how to rescue your Poodle if she does have a major accident. The following sections show you how to deal with your Poodle during serious emergencies until you can get her to your veterinarian's office.

If your Poodle sustains a serious injury, call your vet immediately, give him a brief description of your Poodle's situation, and tell him that you're on the way. You may not think you have time to make the call, but that information can help save time at the vet's office. The call gives the vet's staff time to prepare for your dog's arrival and lets them know what kind of problem they'll soon be facing.

Lacerations and bleeding

Surface cuts and scrapes on your Poodle's skin may bleed, but they're not necessarily life-threatening. You should wash a minor cut thoroughly, which may be all the attention it needs. You can add some antibiotic ointment to prevent infection (see the section "Traditional medicines" earlier in this chapter). This method works for all minor cuts except those on the head; head wounds bleed heavily, even if they aren't serious.

If your Poodle has a wound with heavy bleeding that doesn't show signs of stopping, apply pressure with a bandage, and get to your vet's immediately. If you don't have a bandage handy, use a sanitary napkin or a towel. If all you have is your hand, use it. Bottom line: You need to curtail the bleeding as much as possible, as sanitarily as possible, until you can get professional help.

Use a tourniquet only as a last resort — in other words, if you're certain that your dog will die without it. A tourniquet stops the blood flow completely, and because of this, the tissue below the tourniquet starts to die. If you must use a tourniquet, tighten it only enough to stop the bleeding, and get to your vet as fast as possible.

Different types of wounds

Wounds that your Poodle could sustain vary in seriousness. I explain how to handle different wounds in the sections that follow.

Puncture wounds

Puncture wounds are small, deep wounds created when a sharp object penetrates deep into your Poodle's skin. If your Poodle gets in a fight with another dog, she can receive puncture wounds from teeth. Your dog also may step on a nail, tack, or sharp stick.

If your Poodle gets a puncture wound, clean it with hydrogen peroxide and leave it open to the air. After you clean it, talk to your veterinarian about applying an antibiotic, and keep an eye on the wound to make sure it doesn't become infected.

In a car accident — or if your dog impales herself on a larger object — a puncture wound could penetrate your Poodle's chest cavity. If that happens, try to make the wound as airtight as possible to facilitate breathing. You can use kitchen plastic wrap or even a plastic bag to seal the area if you have one handy. If not, do the best you can.

If the object that created the wound is still in place, don't remove it. Pulling out the object could cause more damage and heavier bleeding. Leave it in place and let your veterinarian remove it.

Eye injuries

Eye injuries to Poodles aren't common, but they can happen. If you notice a cut or laceration in one of your Poodle's eyes, or if one of her eyelids is bleeding, put a gauze pad gently over the eye. Just remember the word *gently*, because too much pressure can damage the eye further. If you see blood inside the eyeball, get to your vet's office immediately.

Internal injuries

You may not be able to see some of your Poodle's worst wounds. If your dog gets hit by a car or gets in a fight with another dog, she may suffer some internal damage. She may look just fine, but she could have severe bruising, muscle injury, or organ damage. Your dog may go into shock (I show you how to treat shock earlier in this chapter), or her injured tissue may break down and overwhelm her kidneys. If your Poodle goes through a dangerous, traumatic situation, get her to the vet's office for a checkup, even if she acts fine.

Broken bones

Your Poodle can receive broken bones in many different ways. You could have a car accident, or your dog could slip and fall down some steps. If you have a Toy Poodle, you need to watch where you step, because you could be the cause of a broken bone.

I focus on broken ribs and legs in this section because you can't bandage or splint other bones, such as the pelvis, back, or shoulder. In these cases, just get to the vet's office as soon as possible.

If you suspect that your Poodle has broken or cracked ribs, gently wrap a bandage around the ribs to help hold them in place until you can get to the vet's office. Don't wrap the bandage too tightly, though; you don't want to restrict your dog's breathing.

If one of your Poodle's legs is broken, you need to splint the leg and head for the vet's office immediately. Follow these steps to fashion a splint:

1. **Protect the leg with padding.**

   Use any kind of soft cloth or gauze pads if you have some handy.

2. **Grab a stick or a piece of wood to use as a splint. Place the splint above and below the joints on either side of the break.**

You also can roll a newspaper or magazine around the broken leg. Make sure the splint extends beyond the joints on either side of the break.

3. Tie the splint in place with strips of gauze, vet wrap, nylon, or a knee-high sock.

On the way to the vet's office, do the best you can to keep your dog immobile. If you can find a helper to come along, great.

If the broken bone is protruding from the skin, don't try to push it back into place. Cover the protrusion with gauze, stabilize the area as well as you can, and get immediate medical attention.

Heatstroke

Poodles have long muzzles, which prevents heatstroke in most cases, but it can still happen. *Heatstroke* occurs when a dog can no longer cool her body. If you leave your Poodle in a hot car or in a yard with no shade or water, heatstroke can result. High humidity also can contribute. Symptoms of heatstroke include the following:

- Drooling
- Foaming at the mouth
- Vomiting
- Diarrhea
- A temperature over 106 degrees
- Collapsing
- Hot and dry skin
- Pale lips

If your Poodle is unconscious due to heatstroke, get to your vet's office immediately. On the way, wrap your dog in damp towels and, if you have it, turn your air conditioning up. If your Poodle is conscious and you suspect that she's suffering from heatstroke, follow these steps:

1. Move her into the shade.

2. Soak her with cold water.

3. Rinse her mouth with cold water, and offer her small amounts to drink.

4. Move her legs gently to increase circulation.

5. Get to your veterinarian's office as soon as possible.

Waiting to see whether your Poodle's temperature will come down could result in permanent brain damage if her temperature doesn't drop.

Frostbite

If a dog stays outside for too long in stormy, windy, cold weather, she may suffer frostbite on exposed skin. Sensitive areas include the pads of the feet, the scrotum for males, and, depending on how you clip your Poodle (see Chapter 8), the edges of the flaps.

If you see a pale patch of skin on your Poodle and she seems to be in pain, she may have a localized case of frostbite. Warm the affected area gradually with lukewarm water or a blanket. Don't use a heating pad or a hair dryer. Also, don't overheat the area, and never rub it to get it warm; you don't want to further injure the damaged tissue. After the area has thawed, apply a bit of petroleum jelly or antibiotic cream to aid in healing.

After an area of skin or a pad has been damaged by frostbite, the area is even more susceptible in the future. You need to take great pains to make sure you protect that area from the cold when your Poodle is outside from that point on.

Providing a sweater for winter walks may protect exposed skin (depending on how you clip your Poodle). A coating of petroleum jelly on the pads helps protect against cold and irritation from salt, or you can buy special booties for your Poodle at a pet-supply store.

Choking

Dogs will put anything and everything into their mouths, and sometimes an "anything" gets stuck in a dog's throat. If your Poodle is gagging, coughing, or pawing at her mouth, she could be choking.

You need to open her mouth and have a look in her throat, although she won't want you to. Therefore, try to enlist help if you can, and follow these steps to rescue your Poodle:

1. **Place the handle of a screwdriver between your Poodle's back teeth to prevent her from chomping on your hand as you check her mouth and throat.**

2. **If you can see the object that's blocking the airway, try to use your fingers or a pair of needle-nosed pliers to remove it.**

3. **If you can't reach or see the blockage, lift your Poodle by her hind legs and shake her.**

4. **If that doesn't dislodge the object, perform the Heimlich maneuver.**

   Make a fist and apply sudden, forceful pressure to her abdomen at the edge of her breastbone. Temper this action to the size of your Poodle; a Standard needs a bit more force than a Toy or Miniature.

If none of your efforts have any effect, get to your veterinarian's office immediately.

After you remove the object, you have to deal with an aching Poodle. Her throat may be sore for a day or two, so switch to soft food or soak her kibble until she recovers.

Poisoning (including insect bites and stings)

You have dozens of products in and around your home that can poison your Poodle. Beautiful plants in the yard can be deadly if your Poodle decides to snack on them, and household cleaners are grave threats. If your Poodle has access to the garage, she may try to ingest antifreeze, gasoline, or kerosene. You need to dog-proof your residence just as you need to toddler-proof it if you have children. Don't leave poisonous items where your Poodle can reach them, and make sure that your cupboard doors are securely shut so she can't taste-test the cleaning supplies. (See Chapter 5 for more details on safely Poodle-proofing your home.)

Despite your best efforts, however, your Poodle may ingest something harmful. If you suspect that your dog has been poisoned, get her to your vet's office immediately. Symptoms of poisoning may include any of the following:

- ✔ Abdominal pain
- ✔ Diarrhea
- ✔ Excessive drool
- ✔ Slow breathing
- ✔ Vomiting
- ✔ Weakness

Keep in mind that insect bites and stings, as well as reptile bites, are types of poison. If you notice a lump on your Poodle that seems tender or looks like a bite, and your Poodle seems ill, head for your vet's office. If your Poodle's breathing is labored, give her an antihistamine, such as Benadryl. You also can apply hydrocortisone to a bite or sting.

If you know what your dog has ingested, take a sample with you to the vet's office. If you don't know, but she has vomited, take a sample of the vomit.

If you know that your Poodle ate a plant or a certain food, such as chocolate, give her hydrogen peroxide to make her vomit. Give one or two teaspoons every five minutes until she vomits, and then get to the vet's office

Never encourage vomiting if you don't know what your Poodle ingested. Many cleaning products contain caustic ingredients that can do additional damage when vomited up. If you suspect that your Poodle has ingested a household cleaner, give her milk or vegetable oil to drink before you head to the vet's office. These products dilute the caustic substance and coat and protect your Poodle's digestive tract.

If you suspect that your Poodle has ingested a poisonous chemical or substance, and you can't reach your vet, find help over the phone:

- ✔ Call the Pet Poison Helpline at 800-213-6680. The charge per case is $35.

- ✔ Call the ASPCA's (The American Society for the Prevention of Cruelty to Animals) Animal Poison Control Center at 888-426-4435. You must pay a $55 consultation fee, so have your credit card ready.

Electrocution

Electrocution poses the biggest threat when your Poodle is a curious puppy, eager to put everything she finds into her mouth and chew away. The danger comes when she decides to chew on an electrical cord. A downed wire also can put a Poodle of any age at risk.

If your Poodle chews through or comes in contact with a live wire, your first reaction is to grab your dog. Don't! You risk being electrocuted along with her.

So, what should you do instead? Follow these steps:

1. **Turn off the power to the electrical source, if possible.**

2. **Use a wooden stick or a broom/mop handle to move your Poodle away from the wire.**

3. **Get your Poodle to the vet immediately.**

Chapter 17

Easing Your Senior Poodle into the Golden Years

*J*ust like an older person, a senior Poodle can be active and happy. However, just like an older person, your Poodle may need some adjustments to his lifestyle. In this chapter, I explain how to feed and exercise a senior Poodle, how to handle a variety of health issues, and how you can part with your beloved pet when the unfortunate time comes. (For more information, check out *Senior Dogs For Dummies* by Susan McCullough [Wiley].)

Your Poodle may still act like a puppy, but by the time he reaches 7 years old or so, you may notice some changes. He may not want to play as long or as hard. He may be a bit stiff after a nap. Whether you notice any outward signs, seven is a good age to ask your veterinarian to do a geriatric profile, which includes a complete physical and a blood workup. Ordering an annual blood workup gives your vet a chance to detect and stop any problems before they progress too far beyond help.

Instituting a Sensible Senior Diet

Around age seven or so, your Poodle may show signs of aging in many areas, including appetite. Even if he still seems as active and as hungry as ever, his metabolism could be changing. Schedule an appointment to talk to your veterinarian about your Poodle's diet. She may run blood tests and, depending on the results, suggest a senior food fit for your Poodle. Senior foods have many benefits for your dog, including the following:

✔ Senior foods typically have less protein and fat.

✔ They may include supplements such as glucosamine and chondroitin.

✔ Many senior foods have omega-3 fatty acids to help control arthritis.

✔ They also may have omega-6 fatty acids for healthy skin and coat.

Even if your vet doesn't recommend that you give your senior Poodle a different food, you should keep watching to see if your dog starts adding a few pounds. You may not want to cut back on his normal food, but you can cut back on or change the snacks and treats you've been giving him. Try the following tactics:

✔ Buy smaller dog biscuits or break the larger biscuits in half.

✔ Find low-calorie treats. Keep a bag of carrot sticks in your refrigerator to give to your Poodle instead of cookies.

✔ Replace rawhide chewies with nylon bones.

Exercising Your Senior Poodle

Exercise goes hand in hand with watching your Poodle's diet — a statement that holds true from the time your Poodle is a puppy to when he hits senior territory. For your senior Poodle, a touch of arthritis may make it harder for him to enjoy the long walks he's used to. He may no longer be able to compete in performance events or fetch a ball endlessly. In his golden years, you need to be creative and find ways to exercise your Poodle without putting him at risk for injury. Exercise for a senior Poodle is as important as exercise for a senior human. Dogs, like people, need to keep active to maintain muscle tone and to help fight weight gain. Exercise also helps with mental awareness. The following list has a few ideas:

✔ If you and your Poodle have always exercised by taking long walks, consider going on more frequent and shorter walks. If you've always taken a long walk in the morning and one in the evening, try to shorten those walks and work in a walk during mid-afternoon. With this schedule, the distance you travel can be the same, but you put less stress on your Poodle. You can use the same tactic for sessions of fetch. Instead of playing for 20 minutes, try holding two 10-minute sessions.

✔ Poodles who have competed in performance events (see Chapter 13) still enjoy the events in their golden years, even if they can't run as fast or turn as quickly now. Many older agility dogs are able to compete in the preferred agility division, which has lower jumps and allows more time to finish the course.

✔ Show dogs often enjoy trips to shows, even after they retire. A long weekend may be too much for your Poodle, but if a show is taking place close to home, take him along. Your Poodle will like the outing, and you'll appreciate all the people who fuss over your senior.

No matter how much or how little exercise you provide for your senior Poodle, try to include him in as many family activities as possible. Don't isolate him just because he can't keep up with everyone in the family anymore. He still needs your love and companionship.

Handling Senior Health Issues

Many Poodles are healthy and active far into their senior years. Occasionally, however, problems start cropping up as the gray hairs increase and the playtime winds down. A proper diet, plenty of exercise, and regularly scheduled visits with your veterinarian go a long way toward keeping your Poodle healthy, but old age may bring some health issues that you can't foresee or prevent. I discuss some health issues your Poodle may face in the following sections.

Potty problems

Your older Poodle may need to go out for bathroom breaks more often as he gets on in years. During the day, increase the number of times you take your Poodle out. (Of course, if you have a Toy or Miniature who uses a litter box or a papered area, he already has access to the appropriate area all the time.) A schedule that was perfect for your dog when he was younger may not be enough now that he's a senior. Taking your Poodle for breaks every four hours can make him more comfortable and prevent accidents indoors.

Incontinence, or the inability to restrain a natural discharge from the body, is a common problem with older dogs and one of the main motivators for euthanasia. If you've noticed that your Poodle has this potty problem, schedule an appointment with your vet to make sure that the leaking isn't a symptom of an issue more serious than weakening muscles. For example, your Poodle may have a bladder infection. When the vet rules out other causes, she can prescribe medication to stop or lessen the problem.

Arthritis

Arthritis is a common problem that comes with old age (in dogs and in people). Your Poodle may have arthritis if he's stiff and slow moving after naps or if he limps. Take your dog to your vet for diagnosis. For a mild case of arthritis, a daily aspirin may be all it takes to keep your Poodle comfortable; talk to your vet about dosage and about using buffered or coated aspirin so it's gentler on your Poodle's stomach. If aspirin doesn't do the job, talk to your veterinarian about giving your Poodle glucosamine and chondroitin supplements, or treating him with acupuncture (see Chapter 14 for details). Rimadyl also may be an option for severe cases.

Rimadyl is a drug veterinarians frequently prescribe for arthritis. It can free your Poodle from back pain, but it also has its drawbacks. If your Poodle has any liver problems, Rimadyl may not be appropriate to deal with arthritis. If your vet doesn't bring up this topic, mention it to her so she can have blood tests done to confirm that your Poodle has no existing liver problems. Afterward, you should have tests done every six months to make sure that the Rimadyl isn't affecting your Poodle's liver.

Besides giving medication, you can do the following to help your arthritic Poodle:

- ✔ **Make sure your Poodle doesn't overexert himself.** Stop games before he has the chance to get sore or injured. Exercise is important, but you need to give it in smaller doses. (I cover exercise for senior Poodles earlier in this chapter.)

- ✔ **Make sure his bed is in a draft-free area.** He may have enjoyed sleeping in a cool corner when he was younger, but if your Poodle has arthritis, a warmer space may make him feel more comfortable.

- ✔ **Invest in a thick, plush bed.** His bed doesn't have to be expensive; you can make your own plush bed with two or three layers of egg-crate foam, depending on the size of your Poodle. (Chapter 5 has more details on buying bedding.)

- ✔ **Be wary of stairs.** Your senior Poodle may manage on the level quite well, but stairs may be a real challenge for him. Consider purchasing or building a ramp for small flights of stairs. Otherwise, you may need to take on the responsibility of carrying your Poodle up and down stairs. If you live in a building with an elevator, but you've always taken the stairs for exercise, try using the elevator to make life easier for your Poodle.

Hearing problems

You may fondly recall many occasions when your Poodle pretended not to hear you, but as a senior dog, your Poodle may really be having trouble hearing. If he doesn't come when called or doesn't respond to noises that would otherwise alert him (like the refrigerator door opening), take your dog to your vet to get his hearing checked. Hearing loss is progressive, so you may not notice your Poodle's condition until it progresses to the point where it's obvious.

Some common causes of hearing problems include the following:

✔ Your Poodle may be suffering from age-related hearing loss or *presbycusis.*

✔ If you've hunted with your Poodle, the noise from numerous gunshots may have damaged his ears.

✔ Ear infections can cause temporary or permanent deafness. If there's a discharge from or nasty smell in the ear, if you notice pus, or if your dog is shaking his head or scratching his ear, head for your vet.

You and your Poodle can adjust to his hearing troubles and continue with your lives if you follow these suggestions:

✔ **Let your Poodle know you're coming.** Stamp on the floor as you approach so you can alert him with vibrations.

✔ **Use hand signals.** If you haven't taught your Poodle hand signals before, he'll quickly learn that he needs to look at you for direction. Decide on an appropriate signal, be consistent, and retrain. For instance, for the "come" command, have your dog on a long line, get his attention, give your hand signal, and then gently reel him in. Praise and treat. This is one way you can teach an old dog some new tricks. You'll be surprised at how fast your dog learns the signals.

✔ **Use a small flashlight rather than a clicker when teaching new behaviors (see Chapter 10 for more about training).** Go for a flashlight with a push button; switch flashlights are too slow for training.

✔ **Replace your Poodle's regular collar with a vibrator collar.** A vibration can mean that your Poodle has done something right, or you can vibrate to get your dog's attention so that he knows "someone wants me." You can even combine the collar with hand signals and treats. Use the collar all the time if the vibration means "someone wants me."

✔ **Keep your Poodle on his lead when he isn't indoors or in a fenced area.** He may not be able to hear approaching cars or other dangers. The job of keeping him safe falls on you.

Fading eyesight

Your Poodle's eyesight may start to fade with age, due to the following canine (and often human) conditions:

- ✓ **Cataracts:** A clouding of the eye's lens, which gives the eye a murky, whitish-blue look. Your dog's eyes may start to look bluish simply due to age, which doesn't affect his vision. Check with your vet if you notice a difference in your Poodle's eyes.

- ✓ **Corneal ulcers:** These can happen at any age if your Poodle experiences irritation in or an injury to an eye. Left untreated, a corneal ulcer can lead to blindness. If your Poodle is squinting or has redness, discharge, or discoloration in his eyes, schedule an examination with your vet right away.

- ✓ **Glaucoma:** A condition that produces elevated pressure in the eye; the amount of pressure determines how quickly a dog goes blind. If your dog's eye is red or painful, or if it looks cloudy or enlarged, it may be glaucoma. If you catch the condition early, you can give medication to lower the pressure temporarily. Surgery may help, but it doesn't always work. More than 40 percent of all dogs who get glaucoma go blind, no matter what's done to treat the problem.

- ✓ **Progressive retinal atrophy (PRA) or sudden acquired retinal degeneration (SARD):** Your Toy or Miniature Poodle may inherit the former condition, but the latter is a noninherited form. Both of these diseases cause blindness, generally affecting dogs between the ages of six and eight years. With PRA, the dog's night vision goes first, and eventually he becomes totally blind. With SARD, the dog is suddenly and totally blind. If you think your dog has trouble seeing, make a vet appointment.

Blindness or limited eyesight certainly limits your Poodle, but maybe not as much as you expect. If he still has his hearing and his sense of smell, these senses allow him to navigate quite well in familiar surroundings. In other words, if your Poodle goes blind, don't rearrange the furniture! Try the following guidelines instead to make life as simple as possible for your pal:

- ✓ When you walk your Poodle, keep your eyes peeled for anything in his path, like a child's toy or a fallen branch. Steer him clear of any obstacles.

- ✓ Always talk to your Poodle as you approach him, and remind others to do the same. Any dog may snap when touched unexpectedly.

- ✓ Keep his food, water bowls, and bed in the same places.

✔ Don't wash his plush toys unless they become absolutely filthy. The scent on the toys enables him to find them.

✔ Give him squeaky toys or balls with bells so he can locate his toys without much trouble.

✔ Keep the basement door shut so your Poodle doesn't accidentally tumble down the stairs. If your residence has two stories, put baby gates at the top and bottom of the stairs.

✔ Add textures to your floors. A throw rug near a set of stairs can act like a warning track on a baseball field. A rough mat by the outside door can serve the same purpose.

Saying Goodbye to Your Beloved Poodle

No matter how long your Poodle lives, his life won't be long enough. Toys and Miniatures can live to be 18 years old, and a Standard may live to be 14. However, none of those ages are long enough. The unfortunate truth is that in most cases, the day will come when you have to say goodbye to your most cherished companion.

It would be nice to think that when the time comes, your Poodle will just pass on quietly in his sleep, but that's rarely the case with dogs. Most of the time the owners must make the decision to euthanize.

Euthanasia is the painless process of putting a dog to death, and the process is carried out by your veterinarian. Most vets use an overdose of the anesthetic pentobarbital. Some vets agree to sedate the dogs first. No matter your vet's method, you can be sure that the procedure is fast and painless.

Letting go of an adored pet isn't easy, but you can take some comfort in knowing that when your Poodle's quality of life is poor, and he's constantly in pain, the compassionate thing to do is to release him. In the following sections, I walk you through the stages of saying goodbye to your Poodle.

Knowing when the time has come

Many people say that your dog will "tell" you when the time to say goodbye has come — that you'll just know deep down. I'm not convinced that this is the case. All owners want their dogs to stay with them as long as possible, so sometimes owners deny that their dogs have serious problems. I've seen blind and deaf dogs that could hardly move; their quality of life was poor, yet their owners couldn't make the final decision to euthanize.

Making arrangements in case your Poodle outlives you

A dog's life is so much shorter than a human's, which makes it easy to forget that your dog may outlive you. You may believe that family members and friends will step in and care for your pets, but that may not be the case. My mother, for example, is always willing to pet sit, but she has no room, or desire, frankly, to care for two dogs permanently. My brother knows that my dogs are a part of my family, but caring for two dogs fits neither his lifestyle nor his desire.

Include care of your dog in your will. At the very least, leave a letter with your lawyer about your desires for your Poodle's care. Remember to keep your desires updated, because situations can change. Years ago, I had a casual arrangement in place with two other women. We agreed that if anything happened to one of us, the other two would step in and care for that person's dogs, by keeping them ourselves or finding good homes for them. One summer, we were all in the same car, and we had an accident. It was minor, but it made me realize that I needed another plan.

Whatever arrangement you make, be sure that your will also makes provisions for the cost of dog care. A friend or relative may be happy to take your Poodle, but that person may not have the resources to care for a Poodle — especially a senior dog, a pet that can require more money for care. Also, consider how well your dog may adapt to his new home. If my breeder isn't available to care for my old male, and no friend or relative of mine can give him a home, I'd rather have him put down than sent to a shelter. I don't want my dog's last days to be spent in a shelter.

Another possibility is to make arrangements with a Poodle rescue program to care for and find good homes for your Poodle. Every Poodle Club of America local affiliate club has a rescue chairperson, so you can contact a Poodle club in your area to get information. Go to www.poodleclubofamerica.org to locate an affiliate club near you.

Very rarely will a vet tell an owner what to do in this case, but your vet can advise you in matters of your senior Poodle and help you make an educated decision about when you should say goodbye. The following list gives you some questions to ask yourself:

- Does your Poodle have a terminal disease?
- Is he in constant pain?
- Can he eat and drink normally?
- Can he urinate and defecate on his own and without pain?
- Does he still enjoy walks and playing games, even if the activities don't last as long?

Pain is a huge determining factor for many owners, but the decision to euthanize must be yours. Don't be swayed by others. Always do what's best for your Poodle.

Deciding whether to be with your Poodle at the end

After you make the decision to have your Poodle euthanized, your vet will ask if you want to be with your pal at the end. This decision is a personal one, based on your state of mind and preference. Don't feel guilty if you can't be with your Poodle.

If you have children, be honest with them. Tell them what's happening with clear language. Don't tell a child that the dog will be "put to sleep"; the child may develop a fear of falling asleep. Tell your children ahead of time so they can say goodbye.

Memorializing your Poodle

You need to talk to your veterinarian ahead of time about how you want to deal with your Poodle's remains. You have some options: traditional options, such as those in the following list, or unique memorials (which you can couple with the traditional options):

- ✔ You can bury your Poodle in a pet cemetery, if your area has one, or you can opt to bury him under his favorite tree in the backyard. If you want to bury him on your property, make sure that option is legal in your area. And on a practical note, make sure that the grave you dig is deep enough. A local ordinance may specify the required depth.

- ✔ Many vets offer individual or separated cremations. In individual cremation, which is the more expensive process, only your dog is cremated. In separated cremations, multiple dogs are cremated, but each one is in a separate tray. Your vet returns your Poodle's ashes to you in an urn or a box.

A memorial to your Poodle can be a comforting reminder of your wonderful life spent together. A memorial can be as simple as a stone in your yard with your pal's name on it, or it can be as elaborate as a framed photo collage.

Many people find comfort in specific graves, memorial stones, or urns. You shouldn't feel guilty or "funny" about the way you choose to handle the loss of your beloved pet. Whether you choose to have a grave in your backyard or to put a photo memorial on your mantle, do whatever is best for you.

Dealing with your grief

Grieving is a natural process; it isn't something you should be ashamed of. Stay away from people who say, "It was only a dog," and spend time with the people who understand your loss and sympathize with you. Going to activities like a dog show or a training class may help with your loss. Many communities offer grief counseling for pet loss. Check with your local YMCA or YWCA or talk to a member of the clergy or a counselor.

Another option to aid in your grieving is to write a letter to your deceased dog. It can be as short or as long as you need it to be. You can express your love for your dog, or you can explain to him what it was like during his final illness. What you write can help you deal with your loss.

The following is an excerpt from a piece by Ben Hur Lampman in *The Oregonian* in 1925; it sums up the way I feel about remembering all the wonderful times I had with each of my dogs:

> " . . . For if the dog be well remembered, if sometimes she leaps through your dreams actual as in life, eyes kindling, laughing, begging, it matters not where that dog sleeps. On a hill where the wind is unrebuked and the trees are roaring, or beside a stream she knew in puppyhood, or somewhere in the flatness of a pastureland where most exhilarating cattle graze. It is one to a dog, and all one to you, and nothing is gained and nothing lost — if memory lives. But there is one best place to bury a dog.
>
> If you bury her in this spot, she will come to you when you call — come to you over the grim, dim frontiers of death, and down the well-remembered path and to your side again. And though you may call a dozen living dogs to heel, they shall not growl at her nor resent her coming, for she belongs there.
>
> People may scoff at you, who see no lightest blade of grass bend by her footfall, who hear no whimper, people who have never really had a dog. Smile at them, for you shall know something that is hidden from them.
>
> The one best place to bury a good dog is in the heart of her master . . ."

Part V
The Part of Tens

The 5th Wave   By Rich Tennant

CHASING STICK

GOOD DOG   BAD DOG

BOWL DRINKING

"Okay, let's get into something a little more theoretical."

In this part . . .

What's in the Part of Tens? You find all sorts of fun odds and ends and bits and bobs. I start off with a bunch of great Poodle resources you can turn to in times of need, and be sure to check out the chapter on what to do for your Poodle if disaster strikes. I enjoy Parts of Tens in *For Dummies* books, and I hope you do, too.

Chapter 18

Ten (or So) Great Sets of Poodle Resources

*I*n this chapter, I provide easy-to-reference Web sites, books, and other resources to help you with travel, health, grooming, training, performance events, and more. Keep in mind that I can't include every dog resource in this chapter. I may not mention your favorite training book, and you may know of a wonderful Web site for travel that I've omitted. I give you these resources only as a starting point. Explore. Enjoy. And start your own notebook of Poodle resources.

Kennel and Poodle Clubs

If you're interested in showing your Poodle or competing in performance events, you need to register with a kennel club. The following major kennel clubs (which I introduce in Chapter 2) pack their Web sites with information and resources:

✔ **The American Kennel Club (AKC)** is the registry most dog owners know about. The Web site gives you information on all AKC events, as well as event rules and regulations. The site even includes an online store. For registration information, contact one of the following:

Phone: (919) 233-9767

www.akc.org (e-mail info@akc.org with questions)

AKC
5580 Centerview Dr.
Raleigh, NC 27606

✔ **The United Kennel Club (UKC)** is the second largest all-breed dog registry in the United States after the UKC. For information on UKC events, and to find out how to register your Poodle with the UKC, contact one of the following:

Phone: (269) 343-9020

Fax: (269) 343-7037

www.ukcdogs.com

United Kennel Club
100 E. Kilgore Rd.
Kalamazoo, MI 49002

If you want specific information on Poodles, the first place to look (well, other than here) is the Poodle Club of America at www.poodleclubofamerica.org. You can find breed information, breeder referrals, affiliate clubs, and rescue and health information.

Rescue Groups

Some folks buy their Poodles from a breeder, but you may be a gracious soul who chooses to rescue a Poodle instead (see Chapter 4 for more information on both options). To find some information on Poodle rescue, see the Poodle Club of America site at www.poodleclubofamerica.org, or you can e-mail Poodle Rescue at PoodleRescue@poodlerescue.org.

Grooming

Grooming is a vital part of Poodle ownership. I cover grooming in Chapter 8, but you can check out the following resources as well:

✔ *Dog Grooming For Dummies* by Margaret H. Bonham (Wiley)

✔ *Poodle Clipping & Grooming: The International Reference* by Shirlee Kalstone (Howell)

Training

A well-behaved Poodle is a happy Poodle (which makes for a happy Poodle owner!). I cover housetraining in Chapter 9 and basic training commands in Chapter 10, but try the following resources if you want more information:

✔ *Dog Training For Dummies* by Jack and Wendy Volhard (Wiley)

✔ Any book by Carol Benjamin; my favorites include *Mother Knows Best: The Natural Way to Train Your Dog* (Howell) and

> *Surviving Your Dog's Adolescence: A Positive Training Program* (Howell)

✔ *How to Raise a Puppy You Can Live With* by Clarice Rutherford and David H. Neil (Alpine Publications)

✔ *How to Be Your Dog's Best Friend* by The Monks of New Skete (Little, Brown and Company)

Travel

The following list gives you some great travel resources:

✔ *Traveling With Your Pet*

This book published by AAA lists more than 12,000 pet-friendly hotels, motels, and campgrounds. The book also includes phone numbers, directions, and prices.

✔ www.petsonthego.com

✔ www.tripswithpets.com

✔ www.petswelcome.com

✔ www.pettravel.com

Performance Events and Other Fun Activities

Many Poodle owners have great fun by allowing their dogs to participate in performance events. For sanctioned kennel club events — such as conformation, rally, and obedience events — visit www.akc.org or www.ukcdogs.com (I cover these clubs earlier in this chapter).

Therapy Dogs

You can take your well-mannered Poodle to nursing homes, although some health facilities require dogs to be registered therapy dogs (see Chapter 13 for registry tips). For more information on how to train and register your dog for therapy purposes, you can contact the following organizations:

✔ The Delta Society (www.deltasociety.org)

✔ Therapy Dogs International, Inc. (www.tdi-dog.org)

✔ Therapy Dogs Inc. (www.therapydogs.com)

Healthcare

The resources in this section can help you find a specialist, prepare home-cooked meals, give medication, and deal with your
Poodle's health issues. For information on specific problems relat-
ing to your Poodle, you should talk to your veterinarian. (Part IV
has full details on Poodle health issues.) The following list presents
resources that deal with healthcare for your Poodle:

- **The American Veterinary Medical Association,** at `www.
  avma.org,` provides articles on various health conditions.

- **The American College of Veterinary Ophthalmologists**
  allows you to search for an ophthalmologist in your area
  (`www.acvo.org/locate.htm`).

- **The International Veterinary Acupuncture Society's** Web site
  lists certified veterinary acupuncturists by state (`www.
  ivas.org`).

- **The American Veterinary Chiropractic Association** can give
  you information about your Poodle's chiropractic issues
  (`www.animalchiropractic.org`).

- **The Academy of Veterinary Homeopathy** has a Web site,
  `www.theavh.org,` if you're interested in homeopathy for
  your Poodle.

- If your Poodle has a health problem that requires a special
  diet, you can find special homemade diets for dogs with heart
  or kidney problems, diabetes, or allergies at `www.2ndchance.
  info/homemadediets.htm`.

Memorials

When your Poodle is gone, you can remember her in many different ways (see Chapter 17 for more information about saying goodbye to your Poodle). The following list gives you some resources
you can use to honor your Poodle's memory:

- The Senior Dogs Project (`www.srdogs.com/Pages/loss.html`)

- Valley Monuments, Inc. (`www.valleymonuments.com`)

- My Crystal Companion (`www.mycrystalcompanion.com`)

- SoulBursts (`www.soulbursts.com`)

- Gray Parrot Glass Memorials (`www.grayparrotglass
  memorials.com`)

- Comfort Pets (`www.comfortpets.com/index.asp`)

Chapter 19

Ten Ways to Help Your Poodle if Disaster Strikes

*I*n the United States, a disaster often is the result of a natural force like a hurricane, tornado, flood, fire, ice storm, or mudslide. And even if you don't live in an area of the country where natural disasters occur, you can experience smaller, personal disasters, like a house fire.

Sometimes, you receive warning of an impending disaster. Depending on the type of disaster, you may have a few days, a few hours, or a few minutes to prepare. Play Boy Scout and be prepared for the unforeseen by following the tips in this chapter.

Stock and Store Necessary Supplies

In an emergency, it's easy to panic and forget the essentials in the following sections. If you can't stockpile these items, keep a list of what you need. Relying on a list isn't ideal, but it's better than nothing. Chapter 5 has full details on the supplies you need for your Poodle.

A crate

Keep a crate assembled and ready for your dog to use as shelter. A broken-down crate stored in the basement won't help in an emergency. You may already have a crate in your car for rides, but if not, keep a crate in an easily accessible location — in your garage or carport, for example.

Depending on what size crate you own, you can use it to store other handy items, like blankets, old towels, and a first-aid kit.

Food and water

Have at least three days' worth of dog food ready to go. If your dog eats canned food, keep a can opener with the food. Rotate the stock so it doesn't spoil. Also, you should keep two or three gallon-size jugs of water handy. If you have room in your Poodle's crate for these supplies, great. Otherwise, store them in rodent-proof containers or areas in the garage or house; a preferable location would be in a cupboard near the door.

Medications and vaccination records

If your dog is on medication, make sure you take it with you during an emergency. Keep a week's supply in an envelope or bag, and rotate it just as you do the dry food (see the previous section). Store the meds near the emergency supply of food.

Make a copy of your dog's vaccination records as well — especially his rabies certificate. Keep the copy in your car's glove box.

Identification

Make sure your Poodle has the proper identification on his collar and/or is microchipped.

Keep in mind that your home phone number is worthless when an emergency forces you out of your home. A better option is to include both your home phone number and your cell phone number on your Poodle's ID. If you don't have a cell phone, list the number of a friend or relative outside your area. Your veterinarian's phone number also may help.

An extra lead

Keep an extra lead in your car, or attach one to your Poodle's travel crate. I, for one, frequently call my dogs to get in the car unleashed. If you need to get out of dodge fast and you forget your Poodle's lead by the door, you'll be glad you have a spare.

Make a List of What You Need

If you don't have the room to store all your disaster supplies in one convenient place, you should make a list of what your dog needs. During an emergency, when you may not be thinking clearly, a list can help you organize the necessities quickly. Keep the list in a convenient place, such as the following:

- ✔ In an envelope pinned to a corkboard
- ✔ With the travel crate
- ✔ In your car's glove box
- ✔ In an envelope taped to the side of a storage bin that contains food and other supplies

Consider Places Where You Can Go

While you have your wits about you and things are calm, you should think about where you can go in an emergency. Do you know of a safe motel out of harm's way? Does it allow dogs? Do you have friends or relatives who are clear of the danger you're in? Do they have room to accommodate you and your dog(s)? If you live in an area threatened by hurricanes, those friends or that motel may need to be in another state. Ask friends or relatives now whether staying with them would be possible. If you find a suitable motel, add the motel's phone number to your emergency supply list, program it into your cell phone, or keep it on a scrap of paper in your wallet. Find a backup motel, too; you won't be the only one searching for shelter.

If you can weather the threat in your own basement or storm cellar, you still need all the supplies listed in the earlier sections. Add newspapers to act as a potty area; you won't be able to walk your Poodle in the middle of a storm. Purchase plenty of paper towels and plastic bags to hold waste, and have a flashlight or battery-operated lantern handy, as well as a battery-operated radio (so you'll know when you and your Poodle are safe).

Examine Your Transportation Options

Do you have a vehicle big enough to hold all your dogs? If you have one or two Toy or Miniature Poodles, you shouldn't have a problem.

If you have multiple Standard Poodles, it may be time to buy a van. You should think *now* about how you can get all your dogs to safety. For instance: Do you know other dog people who would have room in their vehicles?

Plan to Leave Your Poodle with Other Folks if Necessary

You may run into a situation where you can't take your dog with you to safety. Since Hurricane Katrina ravaged the Gulf Coast in August of 2005, many pet owners and animal organizations in many areas have worked together to get policies changed to allow crated pets to stay with owners at shelters, either in the same areas or in special pet areas that many shelters are creating. Of course, owners must bring their own crates, food, water, and other pet supplies. However, shelters in your area may not be on board with this movement. What do you do with your dog when you can't take him along and no shelters will accommodate him?

- ✔ Consider friends or relatives who may be able to care for your Poodle(s).

- ✔ Look for a boarding kennel out of harm's way that you can reach and that will accept your Poodle.

- ✔ Find out if your breeder can care for your Poodle.

- ✔ Locate an animal shelter that isn't threatened by the disaster. Keep in mind, though, that they fill up fast with lost or abandoned animals.

Find out ahead of time whether any of these options are possible. The day of a storm isn't the time to start making phone calls.

Succumb to Your Last Resort: Turn Your Poodle Loose

If you don't have room in your car, you're running out of time, and you can't find anyone to care for your Poodle, you may have to leave him. Don't shut him in the house, with no way to escape. Turn him loose and give him a fighting chance. However, you should plan ahead so this drastic measure is never necessary.

Index

• D •

BUSINESS, CAREERS & PERSONAL FINANCE

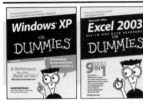

0-7645-5307-0   0-7645-5331-3 *†

Also available:

- Accounting For Dummies †
  0-7645-5314-3
- Business Plans Kit For Dummies †
  0-7645-5365-8
- Cover Letters For Dummies
  0-7645-5224-4
- Frugal Living For Dummies
  0-7645-5403-4
- Leadership For Dummies
  0-7645-5176-0
- Managing For Dummies
  0-7645-1771-6

- Marketing For Dummies
  0-7645-5600-2
- Personal Finance For Dummies *
  0-7645-2590-5
- Project Management
  For Dummies
  0-7645-5283-X
- Resumes For Dummies †
  0-7645-5471-9
- Selling For Dummies
  0-7645-5363-1
- Small Business Kit For Dummies *†
  0-7645-5093-4

HOME & BUSINESS COMPUTER BASICS

0-7645-4074-2   0-7645-3758-X

Also available:

- ACT! 6 For Dummies
  0-7645-2645-6
- iLife '04 All-in-One Desk Reference
  For Dummies
  0-7645-7347-0
- iPAQ For Dummies
  0-7645-6769-1
- Mac OS X Panther Timesaving
  Techniques For Dummies
  0-7645-5812-9
- Macs For Dummies
  0-7645-5656-8
- Microsoft Money 2004 For Dummies
  0-7645-4195-1

- Office 2003 All-in-One Desk
  Reference For Dummies
  0-7645-3883-7
- Outlook 2003 For Dummies
  0-7645-3759-8
- PCs For Dummies
  0-7645-4074-2
- TiVo For Dummies
  0-7645-6923-6
- Upgrading and Fixing PCs
  For Dummies
  0-7645-1665-5
- Windows XP Timesaving
  Techniques For Dummies
  0-7645-3748-2

FOOD, HOME, GARDEN, HOBBIES, MUSIC & PETS

0-7645-5295-3   0-7645-5232-5

Also available:

- Bass Guitar For Dummies
  0-7645-2487-9
- Diabetes Cookbook For Dummies
  0-7645-5230-9
- Gardening For Dummies *
  0-7645-5130-2
- Guitar For Dummies
  0-7645-5106-X
- Holiday Decorating For Dummies
  0-7645-2570-0
- Home Improvement All-in-One
  For Dummies
  0-7645-5680-0

- Knitting For Dummies
  0-7645-5395-X
- Piano For Dummies
  0-7645-5105-1
- Puppies For Dummies
  0-7645-5255-4
- Scrapbooking For Dummies
  0-7645-7208-3
- Senior Dogs For Dummies
  0-7645-5818-8
- Singing For Dummies
  0-7645-2475-5
- 30-Minute Meals For Dummies
  0-7645-2589-1

INTERNET & DIGITAL MEDIA

0-7645-1664-7   0-7645-6924-4

Also available:

- 2005 Online Shopping Directory
  For Dummies
  0-7645-7495-7
- CD & DVD Recording For Dummies
  0-7645-5956-7
- eBay For Dummies
  0-7645-5654-1
- Fighting Spam For Dummies
  0-7645-5965-6
- Genealogy Online For Dummies
  0-7645-5964-8
- Google For Dummies
  0-7645-4420-9

- Home Recording For Musicians
  For Dummies
  0-7645-1634-5
- The Internet For Dummies
  0-7645-4173-0
- iPod & iTunes For Dummies
  0-7645-7772-7
- Preventing Identity Theft
  For Dummies
  0-7645-7336-5
- Pro Tools All-in-One Desk
  Reference For Dummies
  0-7645-5714-9
- Roxio Easy Media Creator
  For Dummies
  0-7645-7131-1

* Separate Canadian edition also available
† Separate U.K. edition also available

Available wherever books are sold. For more information or to order direct: U.S. customers
visit www.dummies.com or call 1-877-762-2974.
U.K. customers visit www.wileyeurope.com or call 0800 243407. Canadian customers visit
www.wiley.ca or call 1-800-567-4797.

SPORTS, FITNESS, PARENTING, RELIGION & SPIRITUALITY

0-7645-5146-9   0-7645-5418-2

Also available:

Adoption For Dummies
0-7645-5488-3

Basketball For Dummies
0-7645-5248-1

The Bible For Dummies
0-7645-5296-1

Buddhism For Dummies
0-7645-5359-3

Catholicism For Dummies
0-7645-5391-7

Hockey For Dummies
0-7645-5228-7

Judaism For Dummies
0-7645-5299-6

Martial Arts For Dummies
0-7645-5358-5

Pilates For Dummies
0-7645-5397-6

Religion For Dummies
0-7645-5264-3

Teaching Kids to Read
For Dummies
0-7645-4043-2

Weight Training For Dummies
0-7645-5168-X

Yoga For Dummies
0-7645-5117-5

TRAVEL

0-7645-5438-7   0-7645-5453-0

Also available:

Alaska For Dummies
0-7645-1761-9

Arizona For Dummies
0-7645-6938-4

Cancún and the Yucatán
For Dummies
0-7645-2437-2

Cruise Vacations For Dummies
0-7645-6941-4

Europe For Dummies
0-7645-5456-5

Ireland For Dummies
0-7645-5455-7

Las Vegas For Dummies
0-7645-5448-4

London For Dummies
0-7645-4277-X

New York City For Dummies
0-7645-6945-7

Paris For Dummies
0-7645-5494-8

RV Vacations For Dummies
0-7645-5443-3

Walt Disney World & Orlando
For Dummies
0-7645-6943-0

GRAPHICS, DESIGN & WEB DEVELOPMENT

0-7645-4345-8   0-7645-5589-8

Also available:

Adobe Acrobat 6 PDF
For Dummies
0-7645-3760-1

Building a Web Site For Dummies
0-7645-7144-3

Dreamweaver MX 2004
For Dummies
0-7645-4342-3

FrontPage 2003 For Dummies
0-7645-3882-9

HTML 4 For Dummies
0-7645-1995-6

Illustrator CS For Dummies
0-7645-4084-X

Macromedia Flash MX 2004
For Dummies
0-7645-4358-X

Photoshop 7 All-in-One Desk
Reference For Dummies
0-7645-1667-1

Photoshop CS Timesaving
Techniques For Dummies
0-7645-6782-9

PHP 5 For Dummies
0-7645-4166-8

PowerPoint 2003 For Dummies
0-7645-3908-6

QuarkXPress 6 For Dummies
0-7645-2593-X

NETWORKING, SECURITY, PROGRAMMING & DATABASES

0-7645-6852-3   0-7645-5784-X

Also available:

A+ Certification For Dummies
0-7645-4187-0

Access 2003 All-in-One Desk
Reference For Dummies
0-7645-3988-4

Beginning Programming
For Dummies
0-7645-4997-9

C For Dummies
0-7645-7068-4

Firewalls For Dummies
0-7645-4048-3

Home Networking For Dummies
0-7645-42796

Network Security For Dummies
0-7645-1679-5

Networking For Dummies
0-7645-1677-9

TCP/IP For Dummies
0-7645-1760-0

VBA For Dummies
0-7645-3989-2

Wireless All In-One Desk Reference
For Dummies
0-7645-7496-5

Wireless Home Networking
For Dummies
0-7645-3910-8